I HEARD MY COUNTRY CALLING

I HEARD MY COUNTRY CALLING

Elaine Madden,
Unsung Heroine
of the SOE

Sue Elliott

First published 2015

The History Press
The Mill, Brimscombe Port
Stroud, Gloucestershire, GL5 2QG
www.thehistorypress.co.uk

British Library Cataloguing in Publication Data.
A catalogue record for this book is available from the British Library.

ISBN 978 0 7509 6125 7

Typesetting and origination by The History Press
Printed in Great Britain by TJ International Ltd. Padstow

CONTENTS

I heard my country calling, away across the sea,
Across the waste of waters she calls and calls to me.
Her sword is girded by her side, her helmet on her head,
And round her feet are lying the dying and the dead.
I hear the noise of battle, the thunder of her guns,
I haste to thee my mother, a son among thy sons.

ᘒ

The little-known middle verse of the popular patriotic hymn,
'I Vow to Thee, My Country', lyrics by Cecil Spring-Rice, music
by Gustav Holst (taken from *Jupiter* from *The Planets Suite*).

INTRODUCTION

Many accounts of exceptional bravery start with a claim: 'This is a true story.' Some are truer than others. The reader is entitled to know what kind of truth the author is after. A true-to-the-facts catalogue of who, what, when, where and how? A cracking tale 'based on real-life events' where drama takes precedence over factual fidelity? Or perhaps a dramatised reconstruction, the literary form of the television drama-documentary, with some imagined scenes and invented characters that nevertheless aims to uncover a greater truth?

I first learned about Elaine Madden in 2008 while researching a book and BBC documentary about the children of the British Memorial School in Ypres and their bravery in the 1939–45 war. Hers was just one among many accounts of courage but even then it stood out as deserving more than a bit-part, albeit a striking one, in a much wider-ranging history. There was never any doubt that her story was exceptional; my challenge five years on was to find the fullest and most truthful way to tell it, given that in the intervening period my subject had died and there was no scope for further interrogation or elucidation.

On some periods of her life I had a great deal of detail, on others I had virtually none. Research took me only part of the way; to fill some gaps I had to imagine what might have happened, what might have been said, given the available information. The assurance that I can give is that every significant event, conversation and detail in this book can be substantiated by Elaine's own testimony over extensive interviews with me and with others, and by documentary evidence including Special Operations Executive files, military records, family letters and photographs. Where conjecture was necessary to maintain the narrative, for example where characters exchange dialogue, I aimed to stay true to the available evidence. Quotes in italics are taken from surviving documents and interview transcripts.

Elaine's recall was remarkably good; she made few 'errors of memory'. Where, rarely, she couldn't remember (or didn't mention) a name I have had to invent one. Her first fiancé, 'Luc', existed but I never knew his real name. Some incidental characters are also inventions, although every principal actor in Elaine's unfolding story existed, their characters and motivations based on what she told me and what I have independently discovered from contemporary documents and other sources.

By the time I met her in 2008 Elaine was recounting, late in life, her childhood and wartime experiences in detail for the first time. This brought her joyful reunions with childhood friends but also painful memories of long-suppressed horrors. Even in old age she was a striking character: elegant, straightforward, absolutely credible, with more than the occasional glimpse of the attractive and committed young woman who did extraordinary things in dangerous times. It was a privilege to have known her, and now to be able to tell her story in full for the first time.

Sue Elliott
London, 2015

ONE

PONT ST ESPRIT

2010

There's something not right about this town. More than just quiet or unfriendly, there's a darkness, a corruption here. Even in the penetrating Provençal sunshine when the wide Rhône sparkles and the ancient bridge brings tourists on their way south to the coast, nothing lightens its atmosphere or exposes its secrets to daylight.

The old woman is confined to a place apparently in the shadow of a curse, infamous in this part of France for the mystery of *le pain maudit*. Medieval in character and impact, this visitation of evil seemed to have come from another century entirely, but happened less than sixty years ago, not long after the war. For a nightmarish week a kind of madness seized the town: mass hysteria in the streets, screaming, sleepless nights, hellish visions of ravenous beasts and all-consuming flames. After days of unexplained chaos and horror, seven people were dead, dozens held in straitjackets or chained to their hospital beds. Wild theories as to the cause abounded – and continue to surface from time to time – but most people subscribe to the hypothesis that bread from one of the town's main bakeries had been infected by a grain fungus with powerfully hallucinogenic effects, but whether put there by malice or Mother Nature, no one could be sure.

She wondered whether perhaps the cursed bread was just a symptom of the town's malady rather than its source. Whatever the origin of the darkness, it is not a comfortable place. She has been here for fifteen years but never felt at home. Her daughter lives close by, and wanted her near, to keep an eye on her now she is older. Not quite infirm yet, thank God, but at eighty-seven some frailties are to be expected. So here she is in this small first-floor apartment in a side street near to where the bridge joins the town to the outside world.

It is early in the morning, the shutters are back and the windows are wide open, but it feels oppressive in the August heat. The buildings on the other side of the street crowd in too close. There's no view, no air, no room to breathe. A small oxygen cylinder stands sentry by the bed, a comfort and a necessity these days.

'Before you go, be a dear. Pass my cigarettes, would you?'

Her voice, deeper and more breathless these days but still confident, has an accent that marks her out from her neighbours. When she first arrived they would say to her, with their suspicious looks, 'You're from the North then?'

'Yes', she'd reply, laughing. 'I'm English.'

The carer takes the unopened packet from the *buffet* where, among the family photos, stands a portrait of a glamorous young woman in the uniform of an elite wartime regiment. With a gesture of disapproval, she throws the packet to the small figure in a dressing gown sitting on the bed. The old woman catches it and looks back at her, like a child unjustly reproved.

'What? You think they might kill me? Good luck to them.'

She has smoked for more than seventy years and she's not dead yet. Her doctors have given up telling her to stop. They say smoking kills you, but it takes a hell of a long time. That's just the trouble. She hates this business of being old, dependent on others.

There are still a few pleasures left: her grandchildren, English novels, a drop of whisky. Some old friends – the oldest – stay in touch. And there was that late, energising interest from the press. That charming man from the *Radio Times* who arrived in his sports car. He spoke such immaculate French. And the television crew from England who missed their plane, got themselves lost and turned up six hours late. They kept asking their questions and filming her till two in the morning. She'd kept going on adrenaline, whisky and memories. She smiles at the thought. Great fun. Like the old days. The carer breaks her reverie.

'See you tomorrow then, Elaine. Go easy on the smoking.'

The apartment door shuts and footsteps echo on the stone stairs and out into the street. A car passes. She settles back against the pillows, cigarette and ashtray balanced expertly in one manicured hand. She is alone again, but from habit blows her cigarette smoke upwards. It drifts through the open window, a blue wraith.

The old days. She'd never spoken about them till recently. Did she ever sign the Official Secrets Act, or was her silence some kind of self-denying ordinance? More likely that it never seemed the right time, or no one was particularly interested, or it wasn't important enough to mention, or it was no one else's damn business. All of these things, at one time or another. There were more pressing reasons too: possible hurt to those still living; memories she'd much rather leave well buried.

But now? There's no one left to hurt, and though some memories still trouble her, the nightmares have long since passed. What could be worse than the fear of death itself? She's not afraid of that, not now or ever.

No, it's the waiting she finds intolerable. Her life is so *small* these days, her routine so predictable. Up at eight, an appointment with her oxygen inhaler, shower, daytime television. Midday, to her daughter for lunch, back by a quarter to two for her television serial, sleep for an hour, then knitting, reading, more television. Some frozen stuff into the microwave, then the late film and to bed at midnight. Some nights she is so lonely she thinks, wouldn't it be wonderful if I went to sleep and didn't wake up again? But when she gets depressed she'll pick up the phone and talk to someone in England, and laugh. Then things are better.

She looks around the high-ceilinged room. Comfortable enough, but getting shabby now. The small renovations she managed to get done when she first moved in were skimped and now it shows. Nothing works properly any more. It makes her cross. She likes nice things, small comforts – she deserves them at her age – but her pension doesn't stretch much further than her immediate needs, the essentials: weekly visits to the hairdresser, cigarettes.

And this damned petty small town. What *is* she doing here? It isn't as if she didn't try to make friends, infiltrate herself into this tight little community. When she arrived she invited people in for a drink but they told her they don't go in foreigners' houses. She couldn't find a bridge partner for love nor money, and at the pensioners' club the women all ignored her. The French are so unfriendly. Damn them then. If they won't make the effort, why should she?

She goes to her daughter's every day of course, for lunch, which is just as well because otherwise she'd probably starve. She never was much of a cook. There's little conversation there though, a bit of nagging, occasional shouting. They are too much alike. She'd probably been a poor sort of mother. And after she'd promised herself she'd be a good one, making a proper home and family.

'The thing is …' She speaks her thoughts aloud these days and in English; it helps break the unbearable quiet. '… I never had a proper home myself. Still don't.'

But 'home' has never been a place, rather a state of mind. She has lived in many places, felt at home in none, but in her heart and soul she still feels British – a fierce pride instilled from childhood. She thinks back to her time in London, five years lived in the midst of danger and chaos. Young and fearless, she embraced it, revelled in it.

'How I lived! I was someone. I did something.'

And she recalls another August, in another country all that time ago. Innocent then of the worst horrors and cruelties of the world, she floated in the warm night air under a full moon. So light, so unencumbered by care, she hardly touched the ground. That was her enchanted time.

She stubs out the half-smoked cigarette. So what if life has treated her more roughly than most? That she's made mistakes, God forgive her? She's had luck and blessings too. They say you have to be ready, to be in a state of grace before you can move on to the next life. She's not convinced there is one, but that doesn't matter. She is glad of the life she's had, ready for whatever may come next.

TWO

FLANDERS

1920

L arry Madden relit his half-smoked Woodbine and lay back in his cot. The second Armistice Day was fast approaching. Back in London the new stone Cenotaph was about to be unveiled in Whitehall. But he was still here clearing up the bloody mess.

In the oil-lit fug of the Nissen hut, semi-clothed men lazed, scratched, groaned, uttered quiet profanities, wrote home or sipped from battered hip flasks. The rest slept, exhausted by their ghastly labours. The blankets were rough and the company rougher, his countrymen the worst of a rum bunch. There'd been a near mutiny among the Australian gangs only last month. It wasn't comfortable but it was familiar. The sprawling encampment of tents and huts that made up the war graves depot at Rémy Sidings just outside Poperinghe was much like his old Anzac camp in Weymouth. No cleansing salt breezes here though. Here, in the flatlands just behind the old battle lines of the Ypres Salient, the October evening lay heavy as usual with the odour of death.

When he started the work he couldn't decide what was worse, the sweet stench of rotting cadavers in the summer heat, or the reeking disinfectant he had to soak the canvas body bags in. They both clung to him. No Woodbines or whisky or woman's scent could mask the taint of corruption or the images they conjured. The smell would fade but the images would linger as long as memory itself. Perhaps beyond.

There were polite Pommie names for this hellish work and the men who did it. He was a 'field assistant', engaged on 'concentration' work: disinterring and reinterring the dead. Bodysnatchers more like, going out into the Flanders fields to harvest the men left behind in the rutted mud of the battlefields: the overlooked, the hastily buried between bombardments, the poor blighters entombed in collapsed trenches and those left behind in temporary graves.

There were hundreds of these clustered round the railhead at Rémy where the casualty clearing stations had been sited just out of shelling range. From here trains would take the badly wounded to the coast for evacuation to Blighty. He'd been one of them after the Somme. Those they could patch up were sent back to the trenches *tout suite*. The others remained in the shallow earth, awaiting eternal rest in one of the vast new cemeteries now starting to dot the dun-coloured landscape with white.

The Imperial War Graves Commission camp at Rémy Sidings served what would be one of the biggest. Lijssenthoek – Listen Hook to Anglophone ears – already held ranks of pristine Portland stone but was still mostly a jumble of different wooden crosses. Headstones to replace them were starting to come in by train, hundreds, all the same, shining white and stacked up in rows like Doomsday. It would be some kind of wonderful place when it was done, he'd heard, what with the flowerbeds and trees and all. Clean, ordered, peaceful. A nice rebuke to the bloody madness they'd just been through.

But first there was more clearing up to do. Identification was the thing he hated most. He'd be rootling among the rotting remains, looking for identity discs, fragments of letters, rings, regimental badges, buttons, anything that meant the poor soul who had originally owned them would have a name on his grave, so that his mother, sister or sweetheart could find him.

They weren't 'bodies'; there was nothing whole about them. With the effects of time and the attention of rodents, most were nothing but gnawed bones. Early on he would see some that looked perfectly sound, until he touched them and they disintegrated into rancid jelly in his hands. Even now they'd come across the odd one where Nature's due process had been arrested and some semblance of corporeal flesh remained. More often than not all that was left were random bits and pieces. They did their best, but sometimes it was doubtful whether the name on the grave matched all – or any – of the bits and pieces in it.

Perhaps it didn't matter: for the relatives, recording the name in stone was the important thing. That was what would remain. So he grieved for all those without a name to their grave. There would, he guessed, be thousands of 'Known Unto God' graves by the time they'd finished. Worse, there would be untold numbers left behind in the fields for the rats to pick clean and the plough to churn up over decades yet to come. He tried not to think about the lads he'd missed, still waiting among the poppies.

He was no longer being shot at or bombarded in a trench but it was hell in so many other ways. They got by on booze and gallows humour. He was twenty-one but on bad days he felt sixty. Melbourne could be wet but it was nothing to the oppressive damp of a Flanders winter: those endless flat grey skies with little but desecration beneath them. His third winter here was fast approaching and he doubted it would be his last.

Thank God for 'Pop': Poperinghe, the nearest thing to civilisation in those blast-blown parts. A small place but it offered everything a man's heart could desire. Busier now than during the war – certainly than before it – what with the cemeteries being built and the wholesale reconstruction going on in Ypres just a few miles away. The graves boys, the peacetime army of builder-labourers, military types waiting for demob, they all piled in of an evening looking for distraction, comfort or oblivion.

Larry's preferred off-duty spot was the bar of the Palace Hotel, a 'proper' establishment with pretentions to sophistication in a town full of bars and brothels. There were cheaper places, but the Palace offered a singular attraction. Their beer was alright, but their barmaid was something special: a very classy kind of barmaid, all he'd managed to get out of her so far was her name. Caroline Duponselle – even her name spoke of mystery and delicacy – was young, sixteen perhaps, but she had poise, a commanding stillness about her as she wove through the mass of khaki with her laden tray.

Larry was giddy about the girl, but he'd have to go carefully. He had few advantages as a suitor. He wasn't tall, particularly good-looking or well off. Lifting and shifting corpses all day wasn't an attractive occupation. Worse, he was a foreigner and an uncouth Australian at that. His family were Irish and he'd been brought up Catholic, but these Belgian Catholics were more devout than anything he'd known, and they kept a tight rein on their daughters. He saw how her big brother Charles watched her from behind the bar as he wiped glasses with a deliberation that bordered on menace.

But Larry Madden, the blue-eyed larrikin, could charm and twinkle with the best of them. He'd play the long game. Time and money spent at the Palace Hotel was a fine investment. He was thinking of the future, that wonderful peacetime future he dreamed of as he dug spent lads from the Flanders clay.

He stubbed out the last smoke of the day on his tobacco tin.

'I'll bide my time to catch my Caroline', he vowed in a low prayer to the assembled congregation of snoring men. 'But catch her I will.'

THREE

YPRES AND POPERINGHE

1933–39

The earth was round Mr Allen said and the classroom globe confirmed it. So why was everything so flat where they lived? Elaine pondered this today, as she so often did on her early evening walks with her father. They always took the same route: from their café, the Prince Albert, opposite the station along the top of the Ramparts to the old Lille Gate, with the town on one side, the countryside on the other.

The ancient walls, one of Ypres' few monuments left still more or less intact by 1918, afforded the best view of the town. From here on the left she could see beyond the roofs of the rebuilt houses to the Cloth Hall belfry still cocooned in its wooden scaffolding, and close by the soaring new spire of St Martin's Cathedral. On her right, the moat, with hop fields and scattered farms stretching across miles of flatness unbroken by hills or woods. Green in summer, grey in winter, this placid vista held no magic for Elaine, unlike the images of foreign places on her classroom walls filled with colour and the promise of adventure: women in bright saris picking tea, big dark-skinned men working jungle rubber plantations, Delhi durbars and the bustle of Piccadilly Circus by night. This was the British Empire to which she belonged.

The low evening sun gave her a long shadow: a slight little girl with a mass of dark hair and a serious face, the pleats of her gymslip splaying out as she skipped ahead on the hoggin path. It would be her tenth birthday soon and Maman had promised to take her to buy a new dress. Time alone with her mother was so rare that this was a special treat, but there was one thing she wanted more than anything in the world and that was a party.

Her friends Rene and Dorothy had parties, and she was invited to lots of them in other people's houses, but she'd never had one of her own. Perhaps it was because she didn't live in a house like everyone else, didn't have home lives like them.

'Daddy?'

He looked back at her, distracted from gazing into the distant, flat countryside and took the cigarette from his mouth.

'What, love?'

'Can I have a party for my birthday? Everyone else does. *Please* can I?'

'Maybe. You'll have to ask your mother.'

It was always the same. He had a way of dodging every important question, as if he didn't want to be bothered with it. Or her. Why he insisted on her coming with him on this nightly ritual she didn't know. It was a penance for them both: he didn't seem to enjoy her company and she would rather be reading or out playing with her friends. She turned back to the path, head down, burning quietly with disappointment. She already knew what Maman's answer would be.

Just before the Lille Gate, they came to the tiny cemetery on the outward side of the Ramparts. Elaine lifted the latch and entered the small enclosure. This was part of their routine in the summer months if there was a little time to spare before the finale of every walk, the part she liked least. But she loved this place. Its calm atmosphere at once soothed her hurt. Sheltered from the world, it sloped gently down to a wide moat of water fringed with young willows now bursting with leaf. A perfect, small universe of its own contained by a low stone wall, the only sounds hooting coots and the blackbird's evening song.

She trod the soft turf among the headstones, reading the inscriptions. *A Soldier of the Great War, Known Unto God* she mouthed to herself. Her father broke the quiet.

'You know Winston Churchill called the whole of Ypres "Holy Ground"? And you know why?'

She knew. He'd told her often enough. It was because the place was blasted to smithereens in the war and lots of men had died. He was in the war and he never stopped telling her about it, how it was so terrible and mustn't ever happen again. That was why they went on these walks most evenings. In late summer he'd point out to the fields flecked with red and say: 'See all those poppies? For every one, a man died.' For a long time, she thought that must mean the fields were full of bodies, one where every poppy grew. And perhaps that's what he wanted her to think. Now she understood that they were here and in the other cemeteries scattered around the town and beneath the spreading acres of white headstones at Lijssenthoek and Tyne Cot.

He took her to these places often. That was his job, working on the war graves. Many of her school friends' fathers did the same. Sometimes they all met up and played together in the cemeteries. Not raucous games, and well away from people visiting graves, but wheelbarrow rides, playing in the mounds of grass cuttings, seeing how many flowers and birds they could identify. But Daddy hadn't taken her on his cemetery rounds for ages. He didn't seem to go to work at all these days, and Maman was even crosser with him than usual.

When they were in the cemeteries, he'd tell her about the regiments from their insignias on the headstones, and how proud he was to have been part of the Australian Imperial Force and to have fought somewhere called Pozières on the Somme. He'd tell her how, when the fighting was all over, he helped build these great cities of the dead. Just as often though he was away in his own world, as if she wasn't there at all.

But *this* was her world, among the war graves. She'd grown up in a place where the dead were more important than the living, the past more significant than the present or the future. As they played in the old trenches, picked blackberries on Hill 60 or joined the pilgrims as they flooded into the town at Eastertide and around Armistice Day they didn't feel special or different from other children. They knew no other.

There was a right answer to her father's question.

'It's because so many soldiers from Britain and the Empire were killed here, defending Ypres from the bastard Boche.'

'That's my girl', he laughed, 'but don't say that in your mother's hearing.'

She was his girl, but sometimes wished she wasn't. She knew about the war and the dead and everything, but wasn't sure what it had to do with her, and why she had to go through this boring ritual every night with him when there were so many other interesting and more cheerful things to do.

She felt sorry for all the poor people who had died, but she didn't want to be reminded of them quite so often. The reminders were everywhere around her already. Even her school just across from the cathedral was a memorial to the war dead. It was a very special place, different from all the other schools in Ypres, and it was a great privilege to be one of its pupils. She'd started there as soon as it opened in 1929, built with subscriptions from the relatives of the 342 Etonians who had died on the Ypres Salient. Etonians, they were told, were men who'd gone to the most prestigious school in England called Eton College that produced prime ministers and leaders of men. The names of the ones who'd died defending Ypres were all on a board in her classroom. Generals and bishops and ladies in big hats came to tell them how lucky they were to be British and how proud they should be to belong to the British Memorial School. She didn't need to be told. She loved her school and everything about it: Mr Allen and the teachers, pounds shillings and pence and English literature, 'I Vow to Thee, My Country' and Empire Day.

A distant church bell chimed the three-quarter hour. Time to go. They shut the heavy wooden gate behind them and headed north round the walls' path towards the colonnaded brick and stone monument rising proud above the roofline ahead. It caught the last of the evening light in an ethereal way that reminded Elaine of the strange painting her father was so fond of. It was called *The Menin Gate at Midnight* and it hung in the bar at the Prince Albert, showing the monument glowing white, towering over ranks of skeletal figures – the ghosts of Australian soldiers he said – among the stooks of corn in the unearthly light. Every time they came here she was haunted by the image of those ghosts.

Just before eight o'clock, they climbed down from the walls to street level on the town side and joined the crowd going through its vast stone portals. Old soldiers, pilgrims, grieving parents, the people of Ypres – Belgian and British – were coming together to perform what had become a solemn daily rite in the five or so years since the memorial was opened in 1928.

Her father acknowledged workmates, customers and drinking pals with a nod as the last echoes of conversation bounced from the high white walls, the names of The Missing rolling up in great lists, forty, fifty feet to the roof. The fire brigade buglers took their places at the Menin Road entrance.

Elaine's fidgeting was stilled by a nudge and a finger to the lips. She stood to attention. She'd have to stay like this for ten whole minutes in this draughty mausoleum while the buglers played their sharp, sad tunes and everyone was upright, silent and solemn when she wanted to be noisy and happy. As the opening notes of the last post echoed round the vaulted roof of the monument, she clenched her fists, closed her eyes, forced the ghostly soldiers from her mind and conjured instead her mother, laughing, and a pretty dark-haired girl in a party frock playing blind man's buff with her friends.

⌒⌒

'So. What are you doing about it?'

The warning tone of her mother's heavily accented English drew Elaine to the half-closed door. It was late and she shouldn't be out of bed. The Prince Albert café was quiet at last.

'I'll find something. Stop fretting.'

'But it's been almost a year since the Commission laid you off. You know there's no other work round here and your French is bad. Your prospects aren't good. You could do more to help me here – instead of drinking the profits away every night with your friends.'

'Jesus, Caroline, don't nag. We'll be alright. Egide and Marie won't see us starve.'

'We can't keep running to Papa. We've relied on them too much already. They bought us the Majestic and look what happened, it nearly killed me. Perhaps if you'd helped me more then we'd still have a decent hotel in town instead of a station bar. Don't look at me like that. I mean it, Larry.'

If there was a reply, she didn't wait to hear it. Back in her attic room, Elaine drew the bedclothes close and shut her eyes.

'Dear God. Keep Maman and Daddy safe but please stop them being so cross with each other all the time, and make Daddy help more so that Maman can be happy again. Amen.'

She readied for sleep, but then remembered something else.

'And, God, if You're still listening, I have tried to be very good, so could You please let me have a party, because …'

Her mother's voice, in French now, outside the door:

'Who are you talking to, *chérie*? You should be asleep.'

Caroline came in and sat on the bed, an intimacy so rare that Elaine made no pretence of being asleep and sat up, wide awake. Her mother looked beautiful in the half-light, so different from the flat Flemish faces of the local women or the dowdy British wives. She wasn't glamorous like film stars in magazines; it was a quiet kind of beauty that drew you to her. She was so proud of her mother, and it hurt to see her lined with work and worry.

'It's late. What's the matter? Did you have a bad dream?'

'When will we go to choose my new dress?'

'We'll go on Saturday morning to the department store in the market-place. Then we'll go to Poperinghe to visit Mémère and Pépère. Would you like that?'

'Mm. And Maman …'

This was her one chance.

'… please may I have a birthday party?'

'But *chérie*, where would we have it? How would we have it? We don't have the space.'

'But you said that when we were at the Majestic and that was *much* bigger than here.'

'Yes, it was bigger and there were more customers around. Our business is serving our customers and they have to come first, whether we're in a big place or not.'

'We could hire a hall or something. Other people do.'

As soon as she said it, she knew what the reply would be.

'We're not other people. We can't have a party, but we'll have a lovely time together on Saturday and I'll take you for tea at Dunn's. You can ask Rene and Dorothy if they'd like to come too. How's that?'

Rene and Dorothy were her best friends at school, even though they were two years older. They had brothers and sisters and mums and dads and pets and parties, and they lived in proper houses with sitting rooms and cosy kitchens where they cooked food only for themselves and never had customers to look after. How she loved going to Rene's home in Elverdinghe Street after school where Mrs Fletcher would make them Marmite sandwiches for tea.

So the English teashop with her friends would have to be good enough. She accepted her mother's goodnight kiss.

'*Bon nuit, ma petite fille chérie.*'

ᘒ

Belgian cathedrals were usually gloomy and thick with dust, but St Martin's in Ypres was clean and bright inside, its Gothic architraves and stained glass undimmed by centuries of benign neglect. This was because it was brand new, rebuilt after the war in the image of its medieval self, its gold-leafed saints glowing in the watery February light, its chequerboard marble floor a shining path to the high altar.

None of this pristine splendour was apparent to Elaine as she stood with her grandparents, aunts and uncles by the entrance. She might just as well have been in gloom. Everything before her was shrouded in a gauzy grey.

'Go on then, go and join the others.'

Her grandmother pushed her forward towards the group of girls cooing and pecking at each other like excited fantail doves. They stopped their chatter as she approached and stood apart to accept her, a sad little blackbird among their bridal white.

This was her first Solemn Communion, but she was furious with God and she didn't know why she'd been made to come here, in front of all these people, in these hateful black clothes, the thick veil down to her waist, as if she was being made invisible, inhuman. How she'd argued with her grandmother.

'I won't go. You can't make me!'

'Shush, child. Your poor mother would be ashamed to hear such wickedness. This is one of the most important days of your life. Of course you must go.'

So here she was, black against the white. As she processed with the others along the shining marble, feeling the faithful looking at her with their unwanted pity, she fought back tears behind the veil. Too bereft, too confused to grieve, these were tears of incomprehension, tears of rage.

Christmas had been such a strange, unhappy time. They were at the Palace Hotel in Poperinghe with her grandparents as usual. There were only two distractions at the Palace: the company of Simone, and the cinema next door. Of her eight aunts and uncles, some lived and worked in the hotel, others had shops or establishments of their own in the town. It was a tight family, focussed on their web of businesses. Uncle Charles, the eldest, ran the cinema. When she was staying there sometimes, she managed to sneak in to see the films he brought in from Brussels. Her favourites were the lively ones with swearing and soldiers' songs. Even better, there were cards with the words of the songs on, for the audience to sing along to. She would stand at the back, unseen by the smoking, beery men, slipping in and out behind the velvet curtain in case Uncle Charles caught her.

The only other young person at the Palace was her aunt Simone, the youngest of her mother's siblings. With less than eighteen months between them they'd grown up together, but there was difference and distance too. Elaine wanted to be friends but Simone sometimes made this difficult. She didn't speak English and would stamp and pout if Elaine forgot her Flemish. As the youngest of nine, she was spoilt and used to having her own way. The lonely only child envied her this and found it hard to understand why it didn't make her a nicer person to be with.

That Christmas the atmosphere at the Palace was more tense than usual. Her mother seemed unwell, Mémère was fussing round her all the time and her father was mostly absent. When he did come back, there was shouting. They'd returned to Ypres to reopen the Prince Albert for New Year, but the shouting didn't stop.

Then, a few days into 1934, just before she was due to go back to school, she was woken at night by a different sound. She knew the screams were her mother's and it frightened her, but she crept out to the attic landing and crouched there, hugging the banisters as she had done when she was much younger and wanted to know what was going on. Odd words and phrases erupted from the floor below.

'Dear God … make it stop! Lal, fetch Mama!'

Voices, urgent, on the telephone in the bar. Doors opening and slamming shut. Her father's voice, trying to reassure, but with an unmistakeable edge of panic. He came out on to the landing and caught sight of her.

'Go back to bed. Mummy's sick.'

She'd never seen him so agitated.

'Can I see her?'

'No. Go back to bed.' He hurried away.

She lay in bed, still and straining for every voice and footstep, until there were no more screams, no more voices. A door opened, then closed quietly. She slipped into sleep.

In the morning, all was quiet. She went down to the big kitchen for breakfast as usual. Mémère was there, but no one else. This was strange: the kitchen was always busy, full of people cooking and serving breakfast for customers coming and going from the station. On any other day she would be invisible, a useless adjunct to the morning's proceedings. Today, for the first time, she felt curiously exposed.

'Hello Mémère, why are you here? Where's everybody? Is Maman better? Can I see her?'

Her grandmother turned from the stove, red eyed, and spoke to her in Flemish.

'Sit down, chick.'

This was when Elaine knew she was about to hear something terrible, unforgivable.

'Your maman has gone to live with Jesus.'

This was what people said when someone had died. But how could she mean her maman? In incomprehension and disbelief, all she could manage to say was: 'Why?'

'Why? Because Jesus called her and when He calls, we have to go to Him.'

This was no answer at all. She didn't seem to be having a rational conversation with her grandmother but her head felt so tight she thought it might burst. She couldn't think straight.

'But Jesus doesn't need her! I do!'

'I know, Elaine love, but you'll have to be a brave grown-up girl and manage without her. We all will.'

As if that concluded the emotional business, her grandmother turned to practical matters.

'Now then. There's a lot to do. We have to close the café for the time being and make arrangements. It's best if you come and live with us at the Palace for a little while.'

'But I have to go back to school. And what about Daddy?'

'There's no school for you for a week or two, and your father will have to look after himself. We must go out today and buy some mourning clothes for you.'

It suddenly occurred to Elaine that there might have been a terrible mistake.

'I want to see her.'

'Later, when she's ready, we'll go and say goodbye.'

෯

The weeks passed but the hurt in Elaine's head did not ease: incomprehension at what had happened blocked her ability to grieve. The funeral must have taken place but she couldn't recall any of it. She hated being at the Palace. No one had any time for her when she most needed comfort and reassurance. Mémère was always busy in the kitchen, Pépère was in the brasserie and Uncle Charles looked at her crossly, as if she was a nuisance and shouldn't be there. It wasn't her fault; she was bewildered and angry. Nothing made any sense. Why did Maman die and leave her? Where was her father? She'd heard him say something terrible to Pépère: '*I don't want her. She looks too much like her mother.*' Even being compared to her beautiful maman didn't soothe the shock and hurt of rejection. Surely he'd want to be reminded? Did this mean he didn't love her any more? And why wasn't she allowed to go back to school? She was wanted there, loved even. Well, Billy Crouch had told her he loved her. He might forget her if she didn't go back. She missed Rene and Dorothy and being able to laugh and talk in English.

She was given no answers and no say in the plans now being made for her future.

෯

The thing she hated most about her new school was the uniform, a hideous dun-coloured overall reaching nearly to her ankles over thick black stockings. After the British Memorial School, the uniform and everything else about the convent was stifling, drained of all colour and comfort. Here she was a stranger in a foreign land, with sniggering girls, stupid lessons in French and spiteful nuns instead of helpful teachers. It seemed as if she was being punished – by her father, her grandparents and by God. But for what, she had no idea. Everything familiar and comforting had been snatched away. She'd been abandoned by everyone she loved and who she had thought loved her. Maman had left her, suddenly without apology or explanation. Daddy didn't want her, he'd said so. Her grandparents obviously didn't care whether she was happy or not. She was alone in the world and would have to make her own way. Well, so be it. If no one else would fight her cause, she'd have to fight it herself, and there was enough anger in her to drive it on.

She had to get away from this suffocating convent and back to the Memorial School. So she set about getting herself expelled. The hated uniform was to be the canvas for an audacious display of disobedience: she took a pair of scissors to the overall, cutting it – not remotely straight – to well above the knee. The thick black stockings got the same treatment, converting them to crude ankle socks, in the process revealing a shocking expanse of bare leg and thigh. Her defiant appearance in the classroom flaunting these illicit modifications got her sent straight to the Mother Superior. Her grandparents were sent for with instructions to come and remove her from the school forthwith.

The family was furious but Elaine was not in the least bit sorry. To her grandparents or to anyone else. She'd made her feelings known and taken back some control over her life.

౷

The iron gate between St George's Anglican Church and its Presbytery opened on to a paved playground with a strip of grass at one end and a modest single storey neo-Georgian building at the other. The British Memorial School looked as if it should be sitting in a London suburb, not tucked in among the Flemish houses here in the middle of Ypres within sight of the cathedral and the Cloth Hall.

Familiar playground noise greeted her as soon as she turned into Elverdinghe Street and as she swung the gate open to join her old friends her heart nearly burst. Her few weeks away had felt like a term of imprisonment and now she savoured release. This was the nearest thing to a home she'd known and it was more important to her now than ever.

She'd been coming here since she was five and knew every inch of its two bright interconnecting classrooms and the elegant Pilgrim's Hall next door, where she would be taught by Mr Allen when she went into the seniors. She loved the picture of St George and the Dragon in this room, and the dress uniform in a glass case that belonged to Field Marshal Plumer, a famous soldier from the war and one of the school's founders.

She knew it would be just as she'd left it: the smell of polish and plimsolls and the soup Mr Godden the caretaker made for them at lunchtime; the board with the names of the men from Eton; the pictures of women in saris picking tea; her precious books still in her desk with the lid that squeaked; her coat hook still with her name over it. Everything else in her life was in flux and she was in mourning black instead of her school uniform, but she still felt waves of relief as children mobbed her in the crowded playground.

'We *have* missed you, haven't we Rene?'

'We heard you'd gone to a convent school over the border. I bet it was horrid and you had to pray all the time. You poor thing.'

Revelling in the unaccustomed attention, Elaine swung her arms in nonchalant windmills.

'Oh, I'm alright.'

Billy Crouch pushed through the crowd and gave her a friendly dig in the ribs.

'You're back then. That's good. I've got some Jacks. Fancy a game at break?'

Being back among the familiar icons of her previous life almost overwhelmed her. Here she wasn't forgotten, she hadn't been abandoned. Though the fierce anger that had driven her campaign to get herself removed from the convent had subsided, she was still bewildered by the peremptory removal of both parents from her young life, but at least she had the comfort of the Memorial School restored to her.

At the end of the day, Mr Allen drew her aside.

'Welcome back, Elaine. What a very sad time you've had. Never mind, we're all here to help you. You can talk to me and Mrs Allen about anything that's troubling you, just come round to the flat for a cup of tea and a chat after school. Tell your grandparents you're getting on a later train. We want you to be happy here, so that you can do your very best.'

Later, he said to his wife: 'That Madden girl. There's something about her. The other kids can see it. And she's bright. She's going to be somebody.'

'Elaine?' Mrs Allen replied absently from behind the *Daily Express*, 'Yes, a striking looking girl. Such lovely, dark hair. She's going to break some hearts.'

That wasn't altogether what he meant.

Every day at the British Memorial School was a joy to Elaine, especially once she had progressed to Mr Allen's senior class. Here the twenty or so pupils enjoyed the exclusivity of gathering in the Pilgrim's Hall, away from the younger and duller children, and in the company of St George and Field Marshal Plumer's dress uniform. Here she immersed herself in books, revelled in English history and discovered an aptitude for algebra.

Mr Allen, a navy man in the war, left them in no doubt that they were special: literally in a class of their own. They were British, in Belgium by invitation and so had a duty to show respect to local people and an example to other children. They were bright and had a responsibility to use their talents for Britain and to help others. Discipline, selflessness, teamwork, these were the things that would make their country proud.

She thrived in an environment that encouraged competition, initiative and success but where those who tried and failed weren't punished but encouraged to try again. In a school of 120 pupils that catered for children of every ability from the age of five to sixteen, trying to achieve any kind of academic consistency was a nonsense. It was therefore to their sense of Britishness, and their unique position at the centre of a foreign city-cum-war-shrine, that Allen appealed to bring the school together in a sense of common purpose. The public school model of 'houses' in competition, the celebration of heritage through ritual and performance, incentives to excel, were all grist to his mill.

Like her classmates, Elaine loved competing for the honour of winning the Plumer Cup for the house with the most merit points at the end of each term. The fact that there were only two houses only served to increase the intensity of the contest and the sweet taste of triumph. She cheered her best friend (and Mr Allen's favourite girl) Rene as Britannia at the Empire Day parade, so splendid with her enviable blonde hair, shield and trident. She loved performing in the historical pageants and little displays they put on for parents in the playground at the end of each summer term. Rene's mum and dad were always there and took care to include Elaine in their praise. But there was no one from her own family to watch and congratulate her: her grandparents were always too busy at the hotel and her father was too distracted these days – or maybe too drunk – to make the effort.

'Why couldn't they come, just once?' she asked Rene.

But Elaine was not short of attention from other quarters. The slight girl with the mass of dark hair was still small for her age but already matched older children in her physical and intellectual maturity. She had her mother's good looks, calm and serious, yet compelling. In the autumn term of 1936 Mr Allen appointed her an elder, one of eight prefects led by the school captain. She was fulfilling the promise he had recognised in her some time before. Her ability and popularity were now formally acknowledged: still only thirteen, she was officially a leading member of the British Memorial School.

Alongside her in the photo of the headmaster, the school captain and his elders stood Billy Crouch. He'd moved on from offering her a game of Jacks to offers of trysts in secluded places – to what purpose she could only imagine. She was thrilled and alarmed at the prospect and resisted his escalating inducements. She had learned to play rudimentary tennis with borrowed racquets. Billy, whose father was well off, had two. One of them was on offer if she would meet him behind the cathedral. She enjoyed playing tennis and she liked Billy a lot but neither quite overcame her worry that a kiss might result in a baby. So they continued their innocent flirting, much to the chagrin of other boys in her class who envied him Elaine's attentions.

രൗ

Just as school life grew more exciting and fulfilling with adolescence, home life was causing Elaine increasing unhappiness. If she was hardworking, happy and popular at school, she couldn't help but be a different person at home: sulky and withdrawn. Larry was proving unable to look after himself adequately, let alone run a busy café and a home for his daughter, so he'd employed a housekeeper. Elaine didn't like her or the way she tried to order her and her father about. The Prince Albert was even less of a home these days. With the housekeeper's nagging and her father's long periods at the bar with his cronies, there was no comfort, no companionship, no stimulus.

She spent more and more time at the Palace in Poperinghe with her grandparents. This was little better, though at least she had the company of Simone. Though the younger girl, Elaine could still have been mistaken for the elder of the two in maturity. Previously aloof, Simone had lately become rather more interested in her bright little niece and sought her out for confidential chats about kissing and boys. Glad to have someone to talk to, Elaine welcomed the attention, but there was still a gulf of difference between them.

It wasn't just that Simone didn't speak English. She had the run of the hotel and appeared to do no work, where Elaine was expected to help out wherever she was needed when she was there. Uncle Charles petted and fussed and indulged her as his youngest sibling but he always seemed to be scowling with resentment at Elaine. It was as if she wasn't really part of the family.

This didn't seem to matter much at the time. She'd lost her family when she lost her mother and hadn't expected anything to be right in that part of her life after that. But she couldn't understand why Uncle Charles seemed to dislike her so much, especially now that Larry had all but disowned responsibility for her and Charles had recently been appointed her legal guardian. She suspected that money might be involved in it somewhere.

୭୦

In 1936, the same year that Elaine became an Elder at the British Memorial School, Poperinghe had a celebrity visitor, though not a wholly welcome one. There were elections in Belgium and the star of a newly formed party was looking for somewhere to hold a public meeting and a place to stay afterwards. The cinema next door to the Palace Hotel was the largest venue in Poperinghe and Uncle Charles was very keen to oblige. Egide Duponselle wasn't so sure.

'I don't like his politics. He's been talking to those madmen Mussolini and Hitler. Warmongers. We don't need people like him, not here. Let him go somewhere else. He's trouble.'

'This is business Papa. I've already done the deal.'

So the posters went up around the town. Leon Degrelle, charismatic leader of the Rex Party, was coming to Poperinghe.

Elaine was intrigued. What little she understood of politics came from her father and grandfather, both liberal in outlook. But she was only too aware of the bitter rivalry between French-speaking Wallonia and Flemish Flanders. Degrelle was a Walloon but he was never out of the local papers and here he was canvassing – and getting – support among the Flemish. She wanted to see this man and find out why.

Just as she'd done as a young girl when she crept behind the velvet curtain, she slipped in among the crowd standing at the back. The cinema was packed with men and women and even some older children, so she didn't stand out. The mood was unlike anything she'd seen when Uncle's films were playing. The crowd was alert, expectant, ready to be charmed. Rexist followers in black shirts lined the front of the stage and filled the first few rows.

A small group of men took their places on the stage. No one was interested in the local candidate. All eyes were on Degrelle and he knew it. Elaine wove her way through the standing crowd to get a better view. He had considerable presence. A good-looking dark-haired man with strong features and a smart suit, he wore a black shirt like his followers. As he launched into his manifesto, his performance – because that was what it was – worked up to a crescendo of passionate rhetoric.

Even Pépère wouldn't have disagreed with what he said, quietly and reasonably at first about equality among people and working together for the good of the country. But as his voice rose it gained an arresting stridency, like a gramophone record you can't turn off. Dramatic arm gestures matched the scale of the voice and seemed to fill the stage. The crowd was mesmerised. Elaine didn't understand much of what he was saying, but she recognised a charismatic performer and she saw how he held his audience spellbound. Then, the magic was shattered.

'Fascist! Hitler's lackey! Go home to Germany where you belong!'

The heckling came from a small group of men standing in the aisle near the front.

'Communists', people around her murmured to each other. The crowd shifted uneasily as the black shirts moved in as one to strong-arm the dissenters, struggling and shouting obscenities, from the cinema. Degrelle, smiling, resumed his performance. His audience, chastened by the unexpected display of force, listened more obediently than before.

Elaine had heard and seen enough. Troubled by the change of mood and thinking she might be missed at the Palace, she eased herself back through the crowd. The black shirts, brushing dust from their dark clothes and smoothing down their hair, passed her, laughing, in the foyer as she left the cinema. Out in the empty street, she saw the 'communists' stagger, bloodied, into a nearby bar.

◌◌

Caroline Duponselle had taken out an insurance policy that would, in the event of her death, benefit her only child to the tune of one million Belgian francs. Elaine was unaware of its existence until a simmering row between her father and her Uncle Charles came to a head.

'I'm her guardian. The money should come to me until she's of age.'

'To hell with that! That's Caroline's money. I'm her widower and I'm Elaine's father.'

'Really? So why is she living at the Palace, sponging off us? I'll tell you. You're not fit to run a station bar, let alone take care of your daughter or her legacy. Elaine won't see a penny of it. I know you, Larry Madden, it'll go on drink and the horses. We've taken the girl in and we're paying to keep her. It's clear to me where the money should be.'

Finally it went to court. The judgement stunned Charles. The money went to Larry.

Simone relayed all of this with relish and not a little outrage on behalf of her big brother. Elaine didn't think much of her father; he was weak but he wasn't a bad man. Uncle Charles on the other hand she saw as a malign presence. She feared him. Simone was keen to share her brother's disgust at the outcome.

'You'll never see your money now!'

'I don't care. He can spend it how he likes for all I care. I'm leaving school soon. I'll get a job and earn my own money.'

It was true. She was sixteen and waiting for the results of her School Certificate. After that she'd have to leave the British Memorial School. It didn't take anyone on to Higher Certificate, the really bright pupils had to go back to England to do that. The prospect of being denied her safe haven and all her friends filled her with sadness. Billy Crouch had found someone else to lure behind the cathedral but she was still fond of him and they still flirted together. She was uncertain about what her future held but she knew she had to get away from the Palace Hotel, Simone's sticky embrace and the uncle she'd now begun to loathe.

൭

She hated to admit it, but Uncle Charles was right about the money. It ran like quicksand through her father's fingers. The racetrack at Ostend proved irresistible. The windfall drew in new pals with powerful thirsts and expensive tastes. The housekeeper became a lover. Elaine was by now living full time at the Palace, unable to bear the atmosphere and chaos at the Prince Albert, the rows and the extravagant makings-up.

The largesse didn't last long. By the middle of 1939 Larry was bankrupt. What was left of the money disappeared one day with the housekeeper. The Prince Albert was sold but this didn't help Larry – it was already Duponselle family property. He'd been the architect of his own misfortune, or so it seemed to Elaine. But then she only got the Duponselle side of the story from Simone.

'We're *so* fed up with your Papa. Charles is going to have to pay him off to go back to England. He's been nothing but a burden to this family.'

The subtext to this little outburst was only too clear to Elaine. Simone was parroting what she'd heard from her brother. Like father, like daughter: Elaine too, was nothing but a burden, and Charles couldn't wait to be rid of her. Well, it was mutual. She couldn't wait to get away. She almost wished she was going to England with her father.

When Larry came to the Palace to say goodbye, she found it difficult to know what to say to him. She was clever enough to know that his situation was probably more complicated than Simone's black-and-white account, yet she couldn't overcome her emotional response to him as a failed father who'd abandoned her when she needed him most and was abandoning her completely now by running away to England.

He looked terrible: usually so dapper with neatly clipped hair, now he was rough shaven and untidy. Short and sturdily built, he'd lost weight and it didn't suit him. Once so chipper, the Aussie spark and cheek had gone out of him. But at least he was sober.

The meeting was a surprise and a shock for both of them. Larry hadn't seen his daughter in six months or more and seemed taken aback at the sight of the attractive sixteen-year-old who looked so much like the girl he'd first seen in the bar of the Palace Hotel.

'My God, Caroline ...' he muttered, then regained his composure. 'You've grown up a bit since I last saw you. How's my girl, then? I hear you did good in your School Certificate. Well done. Your old dad's proud of you, y'know.'

The praise was welcome but too late.

'What are you going to do, Dad?'

He relit the end of a roll-up with a single shaking hand.

'Thought I might rejoin the army. They'll need blokes with some experience. Things don't look too good here. Not for me, or for Europe either with Adolf on the rampage'

'What about Australia?'

'What about it? I left there in a hurry in 1915 and I'm in no hurry to go back. Not yet anyways. Look, Elaine love ...'

She wasn't sure if she could take an apology. She couldn't bear it if he started crying.

'... I know I haven't been a great father to you since your mother ... and that bloody insurance policy ...'

'Please Dad, don't. I'm alright. I can look after myself. I'm leaving school soon and I can get a job. You don't have to worry about me.'

'But I need to explain. I loved you and your mother so very much. I just went to pieces …'

'I know.'

'… that's why I couldn't bear to look at you after she died. You're the spit of her – even more now – it would just have reminded me all the time. But I love you and I'm proud of you. Whatever happens in the future please remember that.'

He hoped they would stay in touch. He'd send a forwarding address. If nothing else, he wanted her to maintain contact with her Madden family in Australia, Auntie Elaine in Sydney, people she'd never met but who she knew her father corresponded with. Then he stood up very straight, as if to attention.

'You're a Madden, don't forget. We may have rough times, but we're from tough stock. We always come back, fighting.'

'Goodbye, Dad.'

He kissed her on the forehead and left.

Afterwards she wondered, should she have wished him luck?

◌◌

Elaine's final weeks at the Memorial School were sad and desultory. Her best friends Rene and Dorothy had already left, so had Mr and Mrs Allen, their four-year contract up. The school didn't seem quite the same without them all. At the end of the summer term she said goodbye to Mr Yorath the new headmaster and the other teachers and went through the playground with its ghosts of past pageants, out by the side of St George's Church, shutting the iron gate on her childhood haven. She was an adult now and needed to start thinking about her future.

Uncle Charles was ahead of her. Elaine was now an attractive young woman with his sister's fine features, beautiful dark brown hair and brown eyes. A handful, it was true, but marriage and children would settle her. She'd make a good match and he owed a friend a favour. It would be a good solution all round.

'There's someone I want you to meet.'

Her uncle didn't usually trouble to speak to her, much less engineer social introductions. 'He's a nice young man, son of a doctor friend of mine. You'll like him.'

She doubted that. She'd had limited contact with Flemish boys at the Memorial School, where they were separated by language and religion. Though she was Catholic and spoke Flemish, they had nothing in common. She'd never given a thought for the local boys with their crude country ways and pudgy faces.

She went with bad grace to be introduced to the boy and his father. It was a stiff first meeting in the front bar of the Palace. After the introductions, the men turned away to discuss their respective businesses, leaving the two young people trying not to look at each other. With some effort, Elaine made what she thought might pass as polite Flemish conversation, to which the boy responded in terms. She could tell by the way he looked at her that he was interested. She looked at him more closely. Not pudgy. In fact quite presentable.

As they exchanged information about each other, the awkwardness eased. He was eighteen and about to go into the Belgian Army. His name was Luc and they seemed to get on alright. Elaine relaxed and talked about herself, her old school, even her father going to England to join the army. They found common ground and were soon laughing. The men nodded to each other and looked pleased with themselves. An outing to the cinema was arranged.

∽

The summer passed more pleasantly than most because of her new companion. Simone was fiercely jealous but that didn't stop her from wanting to know every detail of their burgeoning relationship. Had he kissed her? Had he tried anything else? What would she do if he did? In fact their courtship – because that's what it was fast becoming – was entirely innocent. She liked him, she looked forward to seeing him, but she didn't know if she loved him. What did it feel like to be in love? Surely she'd know if she was? Though she liked Luc, she couldn't dispel the feeling that she'd really rather be with Billy Crouch.

If she learned little from Luc about lovemaking, he taught her something about what was happening in the outside world. Since the Degrelle meeting, she'd become more aware of growing support for his fascist Rexists in Flanders. They'd done surprisingly well in the 1936 election, much to Pépère's disgust. Luc explained that Belgium had to safeguard its neutrality and that meant sending more troops to defend its borders. As he saw it, Hitler wouldn't stop at recreating his Greater Germany by reclaiming lands 'lost' to the Treaty of Versailles. Belgium, Holland, even France itself were vulnerable and he for one was prepared to defend his country to the death if necessary.

Elaine couldn't imagine it would come to that and she didn't want to. Luc now offered her the chance to make a new life away from the Palace Hotel and for the first time in ages she was looking forward. Now she just had to find herself a job. So the news that her grandparents had made plans for her to go back to school – in England – came as a shock.

'But I've only just finished school. Why would I want to go back?'

'This is different. It's a private college for young ladies where you'll learn bookkeeping and commercial subjects. Things you need to get a good job.'

It sounded deathly boring.

'But why England? There must be places here where I can do that.'

'You'll be staying with your Aunt Alice in London. With the situation here at the moment it's safer for you over there. St Helen's is just round the corner from where they live. It's all arranged. You start in September. Not long now. You'd better start thinking what you'll need to take with you.'

It wasn't the escape she'd envisaged. And Luc would be so disappointed. But the thought of London excited her. She'd always dreamed of seeing Piccadilly Circus with Eros and all that colour and bustling traffic. *The Heart of the Empire.* It's where she felt she belonged. Her Aunt Alice was the second eldest, next to Charles, of her eight aunts and uncles, and had married an Englishman after the last war. They didn't come to Belgium often so she didn't know them very well. They lived somewhere in London called Streatham. She hoped it wasn't far from Piccadilly Circus. Perhaps she could get a tram or a bus there. What were they like? What would they think of her? She was less keen on the idea of St Helen's. It couldn't sound more different from the Memorial School. Surely she'd be the oldest girl there? And she'd never heard of any saints called Helen.

As she suspected, Luc was devastated when she told him her news.

'But we've only just got to know each other.'

'I know. I'm sorry. It's a shame, but I can't do anything about it. I'm going to London in a fortnight.' She sounded final because she had assumed that this meant an end to their friendship. She'd be in London and he'd be in the army. So she was astounded by his response.

'Let's get married!'

'What? I can't. I'm going back to school in London.'

'I don't mean now. I mean when you get back. You won't be there forever, will you?'

'I suppose not. Yes, I'll be back for the Christmas holidays.'

'Well, maybe then, or soon after that. Whenever you finish school. We love each other, don't we? So let's get married!'

His excitement was infectious. Escape, permanent escape, was still a possibility.

'We'll need permission from my father.'

'He'll give it, won't he?'

He pulled her to him.

'Enough excuses. Just say yes.'

'Alright then. Yes!'

FOUR

LONDON AND POPERINGHE

SEPTEMBER–DECEMBER 1939

At first, everything about England seemed even bigger and brighter in the late summer sunshine than in the pictures and posters at school. The white cliffs, the hop fields of the Kentish weald, the oast houses with their pointed hats sitting so comfortably in the rolling landscape, it was all as she'd imagined. It gave her a thrill of excitement to know that she was on her way to London and the first adventure of her grown-up life. Even better, she was away from the Palace Hotel where she felt so unwanted and ill at ease.

But as the train from Dover wound its way over the viaducts of south London, the sun went in and the colour leached out. She looked down, fascinated, into yards and back gardens with their ramshackle sheds and lean-tos, abandoned armchairs, bikes and prams, wigwams of runner beans the only green relief in a jumble of smoky greys. Would Streatham be like this, so dirty and crowded? Following the endless rows of Edwardian terraces with their big pubs on every corner, everything covered in a sooty film, she grew disheartened. This wasn't the heart of the Empire she'd been told about at the Memorial School. Then she heard someone point out London's new landmark, the huge and half-completed Battersea Power Station, and they were crossing the River Thames into the long, busy approach to Victoria Station.

The train was packed and she'd been lucky to get a seat, but nothing prepared her for the chaos in the station as she shuffled with the crowds through the ticket barrier. She was meeting Aunt Alice under the clock. She could see the clock but it would be an assault course to reach it.

The concourse was a swarm of children dressed up in winter coats despite the heat, loaded with shoe bags and all kinds of luggage, cardboard boxes strung round their necks and name labels tied in their lapels. Harassed teachers and uniformed ladies shouted instructions and chivvied crocodiles of infants through the throng towards distant platforms. At every ticket barrier tearful mothers waved encouragement and farewells with their hankies.

Victoria was a babel of tannoy announcements, shouts of '*Keep together Tooting Juniors!*', excited chatter and muffled sobs. Elaine had never seen or heard so many people all in one place and in the sweaty mayhem she felt apprehensive. What was happening? Why were all these children apparently leaving London just as she was arriving?

Several hundred others had also chosen to meet 'under the clock' but through the shifting lines of different shapes and sizes, she could at last see Aunt Alice waving to her. It had been a while since Elaine had last met her aunt, but even so she hardly recognised the woman, smartly dressed for town in her costume, hat and gloves, but thinner and greyer than she remembered.

'What a day to arrive!' As if it was her fault. A quick peck on the cheek. 'Let's hope St Helen's hasn't decided to evacuate by the time you get there. Never mind, you're here now.'

As they wove their way through the moving lines of children to the Streatham train, Elaine looked up into the cavernous canopy of the station. Despite the less than warm welcome, the sense of wonder and elation had returned. So different from everything she knew in Belgium, this was a world of noise and activity, of promise and possibility. A new month and the first day of her new life in London. She'd remember this day: Friday, 1 September 1939.

∞

Streatham wasn't as bad as she'd feared. There were Edwardian terraces in Deerhurst Road, it was true, but they were terraces of comfortable three-storey family houses just across the Common from the station, and No. 23 was right at the end. The first house she'd ever stayed in. No guests, no bar, no brasserie, just a home. A nice area, Aunt Alice said, they were lucky to be near a green space in London. Not exactly London, thought Elaine, it was nowhere near Piccadilly Circus.

The Common itself was wide, open and treeless, on high sloping ground with distant views, but even here were signs that normal suburban life was giving way to war: concrete-lined trenches and piles of sandbags, temporary huts and cordoned-off sections of green for mysterious military purposes. She now had a cardboard box of her own containing a gas mask, a hideous rubber thing with a metal snout that was suffocating to wear. Her father had talked about gas in the Great War and how it had burned and blinded men, so she supposed she'd have to put up with it. At Deerhurst Road, yards of thick black material waited to be fitted to the windows and a corrugated iron shed, half-buried in earth in the back garden, was meant to shelter them from bombs.

She was surprised by all the preparations. People had been anxious in Belgium, certainly, but the determination to stay neutral – and, perhaps, a widespread denial among older people that war could return within a generation – meant a reluctance to prepare for one. Here in London, everyone was expecting war. And now that Hitler had invaded Poland, they said, it was only a matter of time.

Barely forty-eight hours after she'd arrived at Victoria she was sitting in the air-raid shelter with her aunt and uncle, gas mask at the ready, waiting for the bombs to come. Almost immediately after the prime minister's solemn announcement on the radio that morning, air-raid warning sirens started wailing over London. Elaine had escaped Poperinghe and found herself in a war zone. She didn't know what was going to happen but she wasn't fearful. This was where she was meant to be.

After the excitements of early September, life at Deerhurst Road settled into routine. St Helen's was a small private establishment of a vaguely Anglican character run by Miss Burgess and Miss Pratt from a Victorian house on the north side of the Common, just five minutes' walk away. The kindergarten and juniors had been evacuated so the senior girls had the run of the place. Here Elaine and a dozen other sixteen year olds were instructed in 'commercial' subjects: shorthand, typing and bookkeeping. She found keyboard practice tedious but was intrigued by shorthand and the idea that you might conceal your writing in a secret code known only to a privileged few. And she loved using the comptometer, the magic shoe-box that calculated complex sums as her fingers flew up and down its keys.

She learned fast and got on well enough with the south London girls and their broad humour. She joined in with their chat about boyfriends, film stars and the latest dances down the road at the Locarno ballroom. This was quite different from the Memorial School but she was enjoying learning new things. She wasn't sure who was paying though. It certainly wasn't her father, who she hadn't heard from since their parting. Uncle Charles in Poperinghe she supposed, or perhaps her Streatham uncle. They were childless and seemed to live comfortably enough on his pension as a former Guards officer. No matter: once she'd mastered keyboard and comptometer she could go out and earn her own living until she married Luc. The thought brought her up sharply. Surprised and rather guilty, she realised she wasn't missing him at all.

∞

London seemed prepared for a war that wasn't happening. Life went on and, in the absence of the expected mass air attacks, many of the children who'd thronged Victoria and the other mainline stations in September had returned to their families.

Autumn turned to winter and Elaine spent sedate evenings at home behind blackout curtains with her aunt and uncle and the BBC Home Service. There were some food shortages and prices had shot up, but the skies were so far clear of enemy bombers and, apart from the occasional false alarm, it was difficult to believe the country was at war. Yet Mr Chamberlain's government was still behaving as if attack was imminent.

In this phoney war she noticed that people had started to 'forget' their cumbersome gas masks when they went out and grumble about the petty restrictions that made life more difficult. The blackout was a nuisance and a danger on dark winter evenings: trains and buses were unlit, women were vulnerable in the dark streets and traffic accidents soared. The girls at St Helen's never went to the Locarno at night in packs of less than six.

Things were calm enough on the Continent for Elaine to return to Poperinghe for Christmas where everyone was talking about the *drôle de guerre*, the 'funny war'. No Allied offensives had been mounted against Germany and despite some border skirmishes, Belgium remained uneasily, watchfully, neutral.

At first, everything seemed much the same at the Palace. Her grandparents were too busy in the hotel to take much interest in her. Simone clamoured for information about the latest dances and what people were wearing in London. But the atmosphere, always strained, was more tense than usual. There were rows between Charles and her grandfather and she knew they were about her. Charles made a point of starting them when she was within earshot.

'This can't go on, Papa. We've just had another bill from the Streatham place and now she's come back demanding new clothes.'

Not true. She needed a winter coat for London, but she'd asked Pépère very politely.

'Who else is there? She's our responsibility now Larry's gone for good. You talk about the girl as if she's not part of the family.'

'What about Alice and George? They're well off and have no one but themselves to look out for.'

'You know Alice isn't well. They shouldn't be expected to pay her college fees.'

'I don't see why not. Anyway, why does she need to go to that place at all? She'll be married next year. Just as well. She's sponged off us long enough. Dear God, what was Caroline thinking, getting herself involved with that waster? And that girl's the living proof of her biggest mistake.'

That was enough for Elaine. She came out of the shadows, small and fierce, and faced her uncle.

'Talk about me all you like. I'm used to it. I know you hate me. But don't you dare talk about my mother and father like that! I won't have it!'

Charles sneered at her.

'You're in no position to dictate terms to me, Madam. Not whilst you're under this roof and we're paying for you.'

'Then don't! I'll leave and get a job. I'll pay for myself. It'll be a pleasure to get away from you and this place.'

'Oh yes? And what job might that be? The only thing you're fit for is to lie on your back …'

'Charles! That's enough.'

But he wasn't done yet.

'... that's right. You're only fit to be a whore!'

Such venom that Elaine had no words of reply.

'The sins of the fathers, they say, don't they? Well it's certainly true in your case, Elaine. Do you think Caroline would have hitched up with a loser like Madden if she hadn't been carrying you? They had to run away to London to get married, did you know that? In disgrace. And then you arrived barely five months later. Larry ruined her and then he killed her.'

'Charles, will you stop?'

'You know why she died, don't you? She'd miscarried and then it turned septic. My beautiful sister. Your mother died in agony and your father was responsible!'

Elaine wanted to kill him, scratch his eyes out, gag that vile mouth forever, but she was stopped in her tracks by the vivid memory he'd so painfully revived of that night when she sat on the stairs listening to her mother's screams. Shaking with anger and distress, she walked away.

There was to be no return to Streatham and St Helen's in January 1940. Her fees remained unpaid. She hadn't learned enough for a secretarial qualification and in any case there were few such jobs available in a small Belgian town like Poperinghe. She felt more trapped than ever. Her options had fatally narrowed: she must endure more months of torture at the Palace until Luc could ride to her rescue.

FIVE

FLANDERS

MAY 1940

Elaine wasn't expecting anything special for her seventeenth birthday on 7 May, so she wasn't disappointed. A small cross and chain from Mémère and Pépère, hankies from Simone, a card from Luc covered in kisses. She felt her mother's absence more than ever today, her seventh lonely birthday. What she'd give to be ten again, taking tea with Rene and Dorothy at Dunn's in her dear company.

The weather was unusually warm and still for early May, the air heavy as if in anticipation of a summer storm. Though there was now the delicious possibility of a different kind of life away from the Palace Hotel, she felt a weight of unease settle in her about the wider world and what everyone around her referred to as *the situation*.

She wasn't clear what was happening with the war. Perhaps nothing much was. The London she'd left at Christmas was sandbagged and blacked out and peppered with barrage balloons, but there'd been no air raids and people were starting to wonder if there ever would be. Marshal Petain was convinced the mighty Maginot Line would stop German ambitions on France along their mutual border in the south. But on the wrong side of the Line in the lightly defended north lay neutral Belgium, soft as butter. There was plenty of support for Hitler in Flanders: she remembered the Rexist meeting in the cinema and what happened afterwards. Those who remembered the carnage of 1914–18 and said it couldn't be allowed to happen again now weren't so sure. Becalmed in this sea of uncertainty, people shared an unspoken dread of old horrors lurking, ready to resurface at the first gunshot.

The atmosphere in the hotel, quiet after the Easter holiday, was more suffocating than ever. In her room, the day over, Elaine fastened the cross and chain around her neck and considered her own situation. Well, she wouldn't have to put up with life at the Palace for much longer. She was going to marry Luc.

It hadn't been easy: she needed her father's permission and he'd run away to England and was probably in the British Army by now. Her pleading letters to the last address he gave her went unanswered. In his absence they'd had to apply to the courts. After what seemed like eternity, permission was granted and a provisional date set for early June. It would be a quiet Town Hall affair with a modest reception in the Feestzaal at the Palace afterwards. That was one expense Uncle Charles was only too happy to sanction. He couldn't wait to see her off the family's hands.

She no longer cared. Luc was her future now. He was young but he adored her and would look after her. It was enough. The knot of anger, resentment and frustration inside her for so long was starting to unravel. If only the situation beyond Poperinghe could be resolved somehow, she might even feel optimistic about the future.

∽

The uneasy calm was short lived. Little more than forty-eight hours later, on Friday, 10 May, news reached Poperinghe that German Panzer divisions had stormed through the Netherlands, breaching the Albert Canal and capturing Fort Eben Emael on Belgium's eastern flank. Hour by hour the news worsened: now they were breaking through the Ardennes in the south-west. Everyone said its forests and deep river valleys were impregnable but the German Army had crossed the Meuse, completely skirting the Maginot Line, and were now pushing into France through Belgium's back door. No more uncertainty, no more neutrality. They were at war.

The effect was immediate. French and Belgian troops flooded into Poperinghe in transport columns, on foot and leading strings of horses. As they mustered in the wide market square outside the Town Hall, the scene looked to Elaine horribly like the photographs her father used to show her of the town in 1914.

By the evening of that first day, the hotel was full and her aunts were putting camp beds up in the Feestzaal for the overflow. Every able-bodied family member was drafted in to help feed the guests and keep the beer flowing for the hordes of military occupying the bar at all hours. The Duponselles hadn't seen such business since 1920 when Larry Madden first stepped through their doors.

Within days the town was fit to burst with refugees fleeing from the east. They camped out in parks and cemeteries, on pavements and in shop door-ways. Uncle Charles was compelled to open up his precious cinema and they slept between the seats. It was as if the whole population of Belgium was passing through Poperinghe in search of a safe haven: young and old, student and peasant, families carting tearful children and loaded-up prams, every one exhausted and fearful.

Even locals had started to join the trek westwards. Poperinghe was a cauldron of rumour; it seeped from every bar and penetrated every street-corner huddle.

'It's obvious, they're going to blast us to buggery in revenge for 1918.'

'I heard a woman in Wytschaete had a German parachutist land in her garden. He unpacked this little folding motorbike and rode off, cool as you like.'

'They're coming disguised as nuns with machine guns under their robes!'

Elaine pressed close to the wireless every evening at six o'clock and again at nine London time for the BBC French service. There was nothing about nuns and parachutists but the news was grave: King Leopold had made a stirring call to arms and Belgian troops were putting up a brave defence, but the German advance – so swift and on so many fronts – seemed unstop-pable. Winston Churchill had just succeeded Mr Chamberlain as British prime minister. She remembered her father's stories about how Churchill had loved Ypres and all it stood for. Perhaps he would come to its rescue again now?

Luc was still at the barracks in Poperinghe but he wanted to see her urgently and she could guess why. On the third day and with a heavy heart she went to meet him behind the town hall. He was there waiting, a boy in a man's uniform, nervously grinding his cigarette into the ground. She tasted the tobacco as they kissed.

'Why are we meeting in this awful place?'

'You've seen the town. It's crazy. I wanted somewhere quiet.'

Elaine shivered despite the heat. No one ever came here, except perhaps on Armistice Day, a dusty enclosure with a battered hop pole standing in one corner. A place of execution from the Great War, inhabited by the ghosts of men found wanting in the hour of battle. She'd never seen Luc so anxious.

'I haven't got much time. My unit's leaving in an hour and God knows when I'll be back.'

'Our wedding. You'll be back for that?' Hopeless, stupid question, she knew.

He took her hand and kissed it. 'My beautiful Elaine. We will be married, I just can't say when. You heard the king. We've got to try and hold the bastards back, they'll be here within days if we can't stop them.'

'They'll have to get past the BEF first!'

It was her father talking, full of false bravado.

'Oh yes, the British.' He was dismissive. 'They're in all the wrong places and turning up too late to be any damn use. We're on our own and the Boche are getting closer all the time.'

He took off his signet ring and tried to put it on the ring finger of her right hand. It was too loose so he moved it to the middle finger.

'Look after this for me till we can be together again. You can give it back when we're married. And keep yourself for me. Promise?'

She looked at the gold ring, engraved with his initials, symbol of her dashed hopes.

'I promise.'

She forced a brave smile even as that old familiar knot tightened. She wanted to cry, to scream and shout but no tears, sounds, words came.

'I have to go. Wish me luck.'

They parted with a fierce kiss. So quick, and she'd said nothing of the tumult inside her. He was gone and she was alone in that place of pain and ghosts with the taste of his tobacco still in her mouth.

෬෩

Air-raid alarms made the following nights uncomfortable. The cellars of the Palace Hotel were damp but they were safe. Elaine pitied the people out on the streets and in the parks. Where would they go for shelter? The days grew desperate as food ran short. Supplies were diverted to the army and transport for food deliveries commandeered for war materiel. Hardly anything was reaching the town to restock empty shelves. The hotel soon exhausted its reserves and could no longer feed its many official and unofficial guests. People started pilfering from shops and looting larders in abandoned homes. Elaine ventured out as little as possible; she couldn't bear the pleas of the women who followed her, begging for food for their crying children. She had nothing to give them. The men were worse. There was a new air of menace on the streets, as if people were slowly going mad with hunger.

A few days later, as the family finished their meagre supper, there were raised voices by the back door. A young man, dishevelled and unshaven in his army uniform, appeared in the kitchen accompanied by an agitated Pépère. Elaine was shocked to see her Uncle Louis, just twenty-one, looking so dirty and defeated.

'I'm not going back. It's suicide.'

'Duponselles aren't deserters, son.'

'You don't understand Papa, there's nothing to go back to. The whole unit's gone. Captured. Dead. Deserted. The Meuse was a rout, a bunch of boys with pea-shooters against their Panzer tanks. We did our best, we weren't cowards, but we had no ammo, no air cover. We were sitting targets with nothing to fire back at them. I tell you, we haven't got a hope in hell. Get everyone out now while you can, Papa. Go to France, England, anywhere. Belgium's lost.'

❧

On Friday, 24 May at 2.15 in the afternoon, two weeks to the day from the start of the invasion and with no warning, Poperinghe was bombed for the first time.

As the Duponselles scrambled to the cellar, Egide made up his mind: they would pack up the hotel and move out to relatives in the country.

But not Elaine. Her father was Australian, a British subject, and so she was too. He took her aside, out of earshot of Mémère and the aunts.

'You've got British papers. You're more at risk than any of us. If the Germans get hold of you, you'll be interned. Or worse.'

What did he mean? What could be worse than prison? He lowered his voice.

'I know soldiers and I know war. I'm talking about rape, Elaine. You must get to the coast, it's less than thirty kilometres. Find a boat. Go back to Alice in London where it's safe.'

But someone had been listening. Simone was soon by their side.

'Let me go with her! Please, Papa.'

'Absolutely not. It's too dangerous. And you're too young.'

'But that's ridiculous. Why is it too dangerous for me to go but not for Elaine? And anyway, I'm older than her.'

The truth was that Elaine was the more mature, the more capable of the two. Egide thought there was a fair chance Elaine could look after herself; he wasn't so sure about Simone.

'Your mother would never hear of it.'

But Simone was determined. She had her own reasons for wanting to get away. Now she saw her chance, she realised that persuasion not petulance was more likely to win her father over.

'Mama will do whatever you say, Papa. Just think about it. I don't like the idea of Elaine going by herself and I'm sure you don't. She might be vulnerable alone on the road. We can look after each other. Two is better than one, don't you think? And it will be one person less for you to feed and worry about here. Because I'll be safe in London with Elaine.'

Egide wasn't happy but he couldn't argue with her logic.

'What do you think, Elaine?'

She'd hardly had time to absorb the idea of setting out for London herself, much less with Simone in tow. She thought quickly. They weren't exactly soul mates, but they'd rub along and two *would* be safer than one. It would be good to share the journey. She'd just have to take the risk that Simone wouldn't turn out to be a liability.

'OK. We'll go together.'

෨෧

In the eerie quiet following the raid they went back up to check the damage. Windows were blown in and a glass roof was open to the sky, but the hotel was intact. The Duponselle men set to work boarding up windows as their women hurried the children away to start packing.

Desperate for air after hours in the dank cellar and with a fatal curiosity, Elaine and Simone stepped outside into the street. The town was barely recognisable. Black smoke wreathed the Town Hall's Gothic tower. Here and there, fires burned in the shells of shops and houses. Charred lace curtains fluttered at gaping holes, exposing neat wallpapered interiors. Scraps of clothing flew like ragged pennants from lamp posts. People were lying down in the street and everything looked wrong. In the air, above the smell of burning, there was a note of something unfamiliar, sickening.

With handkerchiefs over their noses, the girls stumbled, slow and speechless through the market square into rue de l'Hopital. Shell-shocked figures emerged like dusty ghosts from houses and basements. Now it was all too obvious that the people lying in the street were dead. Women and little children, blackened and ravaged, and in the detritus of rubble, rags and glass, bloodied shapes no longer human.

They stopped, mesmerised by something in the gutter. A man's head, the skin obscenely bloated and blistered. They were still staring at it as civil defence wardens arrived to gather up the dead; the men waved them away, shouting at them to get off the streets. They moved back from the gutter shaking, sickened by what they'd seen and by their own gruesome, ungovernable fascination.

Mute, Elaine pointed to where they'd come from and led them through the back streets, away from the carnage. Near the hotel they saw a neighbour leaning against the wall of his house, looking at the smoking ruin on the other side of the narrow street. With relief to see someone, something familiar in all this chaos, Elaine found her voice.

'Mr Rynhaert!'

When there was no response, she moved closer. He was upright and his eyes were open but he was stone dead.

After that first raid on Poperinghe, the wardens counted 150 dead and over 400 injured, many of them refugees. There would be more to come.

෨

On Saturday, 25 May in the lobby of the Palace Hotel, as the family prepared to leave for the country, Pépère handed Elaine an envelope full of francs.

'Stay in the cellar till you're ready to leave. Stay together and don't let anyone separate you. Good luck and God Bless.'

They exchanged filial kisses. To embrace would signify a parting that might be final, and the Duponselles were not a family given to displays of unwarranted emotion.

In her room, Elaine squeezed some favourite books into her bulging suitcase. One in particular was precious: a poetry anthology Mr Allen had given her at the Memorial School. The jewel box would have to go to make room. She tipped the tinkling shower of trinkets on to the bed and picked out the little flower-basket brooch – a tenth birthday present from her mother – and pinned it to her dress. With her cross, Luc's ring and now Maman's brooch, she felt a little overdressed for an arduous journey. But they were her good-luck charms, talismans from people she cared about, and who she hoped would watch over her.

Encamped in the cellar, their cases by the door and ready to leave at any moment, the two girls waited for cover of night and a lull in the bombing to make their escape. After more than three days of raids with barely a chance to sleep or scavenge for food, they decided it was now or never. Just before dawn on the morning of Wednesday, 29 May they joined the straggle of refugees on the road to the coast, leaving Poperinghe still smouldering behind them.

෨

Footsore and burdened by their heavy cases, they had covered barely eight kilometres by the time the sun was up. Simone wanted to rest but Elaine was cautious, rumours of dive-bombing still fresh in her mind. It had been quiet on the road so far, apart from the occasional Allied troop convoy pushing them on to the verge, but the countryside was flat and open. They needed shelter.

Outside Roesbrugge they peeled off from the column and made for a barn standing back from the road. Inside, it smelled of manure and old animal feed but it would have to do. They threw down their cases, eased off their boots and settled as best they could in the sour straw. After less than an hour's uncomfortable dozing, they were woken by the swoop of Stukas grazing the sky above them, heading for Poperinghe. The girls comforted each other: whatever they thought of it, now they'd have no town, no home to go back to. They were refugees like everyone else on the road. It was a little before seven in the morning. Elaine was tired. They had hardly eaten or slept for the past five days. Strangely, having Simone with her made her feel older, stronger, more in control than she really was. Alone, she might already have crumbled under the weight of her youth and vulnerability.

After a bare few hours of uneasy sleep she woke up shaking. It took some minutes before she realised that it wasn't her body shaking but the floor of the barn beneath her. Outside, a mechanical snort and a low rumble, then silence. Tanks. They must be near the French border, and in greater danger than she'd thought. She leapt up.

Sure enough, in fields behind the barn there they sat, squat and incongruous in the sprouting maize like giant grey-green toads, their gun-turrets poised, the Iron Cross visible in the morning light. She roused Simone and they scrambled to rejoin the dismal column on the road, unaware of the eyes following them from behind armour plating.

Hitler's 'sickle stroke' invasion plan was all but complete. The Allies were surrounded, cut off from reinforcements and supplies, forced back into a shrinking pocket on the Channel coast. The Battle of Belgium was over. Before long France too would fall.

ତ୬

Back on the road a desperate sense of community pervaded the stream of fleeing humanity heading for the coast. Most were too exhausted or dispirited to engage in conversation; those with the strength to talk spoke of horrors left behind and those still being wrought by the advancing German forces.

'You've come from Pop? I heard the Luftwaffe and the Panzers between them have put it to sleep. No point going back there now. Not two bricks left standing on top of each other.'

'Ypres too, so I hear. The Menin Gate blown up. Cloth Hall badly damaged. It's a crying shame.'

Elaine feared for the Memorial School and her old friends, Rene and Dorothy. Had the war graves families managed to get out in time?

There was news too, none of it good. King Leopold had surrendered the day before and the British were getting out through Dunkirk, the only Channel port still in Allied hands.

The girls stayed quiet, concentrating on putting one blistered foot in front of the other, their step broken every few minutes by motorcycle outriders weaving through the crowd or by armoured vehicles grinding by. Civilian or military, they were all going in the same direction, to the coast, with military policemen at every junction directing the traffic, sometimes sending them separate ways. What was it her father used to say? *Organised chaos*. Being part of such a crowd lent a false sense of security. They hadn't yet been fired on or dive-bombed, but there was plenty of evidence that others had. All along the road they passed burnt-out vehicles pushed haphazardly into ditches, roads pitted with shell holes and blanket-covered shapes in pitiful rows on verges.

'Oh God, how much longer is this going on? I'm starting to wish I'd never come with you.'

Simone's low resilience to discomfort was starting to get on Elaine's nerves. 'So why did you?'

Simone looked taken aback. 'What do you mean? I told you. So we could look after each other.'

'That's what you told Pépère. But that wasn't the real reason, was it?'

A thoughtful pause. 'Alright. I had to get away from that place. So small town, small-minded. I know I can do better. When I heard you were going, I took my chance.'

'And the boy in London?'

'Whatever do you mean?'

'Oh come on Simone. I know you were seeing a BEF lad. He'd been sent back, hadn't he? And now you're going after him.'

'Of course not. How could you suggest such a thing?'

But Simone's sulky demeanour told Elaine everything she needed to know.

They continued trudging in uneasy silence. As they approached a British Army truck stopped in a lay-by, Elaine was distracted from her irritation with Simone by a shout in distinctive, wonderful, welcome English.

'Hey, girls! Want some chocolate?'

Two travel-worn young squaddies were throwing sweets to the passing crowd. Her reaction was immediate, instinctive: she shouted back: 'A lift would be even better!'

There was intrigued consternation in the truck as the girls drew closer and the two parties eyed each other up. A sergeant, stocky, perhaps the same age as her father, stepped down from the cab to inspect them.

'Well, this is a turn up. You're *English*?'

Elaine scrabbled in her shoulder bag for her identity card with its distinctive red bar.

'Yes, I'm English. My name's Elaine Madden and these are my papers. This is Simone, she's Belgian. We've come from Poperinghe and we've been walking for hours. If you're going to the coast, please can we have a lift?'

He looked at the card, then at the pretty face, streaked with dirt from the road.

'We can't take civilians, love. But …' He looked at her more carefully.

'How old are you?'

'I was seventeen on the seventh – just before the Germans arrived.'

'I've got a daughter at home your age. Wait here.'

There was a muttered conference in the truck before he returned with the verdict.

'We'll take you', he said to Elaine. 'It's strictly against regulations, but you're British, we can't leave you behind. But I'm afraid we can't take your Belgian friend.'

She turned to Simone, waiting anxiously a few feet away. Though she hadn't understood the words, she'd caught the tone and the gravity of the situation. There was fear and panic in her face as she whispered to Elaine:

'*Verlaat mij neit.*'

Don't abandon me.

It was so tempting to carry on without her. Here was the perfect excuse. And she might lose the lift altogether if she insisted. But she remembered her grandfather's instruction. *Don't let anyone separate you.*

'She's not my friend, she's my aunt. My mother's youngest sister. She doesn't speak any English. I can't leave her – she's the only family I've got left.'

Not strictly true. In fact not true at all, but Elaine knew when a lie could be a lifesaver.

'Please! We have to stay together.'

A painful pause, their fate held in the balance. The sergeant still looked serious.

'Alright then, Elaine Madden, get yourselves up there. But you're going to have to keep quiet and tuck right in at the back where no one can see you, or I'll be shot.'

Relieved that their nightmare might soon be over, the girls threw their cases up into the high canvas-covered truck and large hands helped them clamber over the tailgate. The Bedford lumbered on its way.

Swaying with the rolling movement of the truck, Elaine asked the young corporal for news: 'We saw German tanks at Roesbrugge today. What's happening?'

'It's chaos, Miss. We're on what they call a fighting retreat. Advancing backwards, ha ha. Jerry's cut us off left, right and centre. The BEF is a busted flush and we're getting out. Got the order to go to Dunkirk this afternoon. Home in time for tea with a bit of luck.'

With a sigh of relief, Elaine conveyed the news to Simone. They'd be on their way to England soon.

'Thank you, God', she breathed aloud. And so the girls made the acquaintance of Smudger, Knocker and Gary of the Dorsetshire Regiment.

'Now then, what are two nice girls like you doing in a shithole – sorry ladies, *predicament* – like this?'

Denied respectable female company for too long, Knocker and Gary revelled in the novelty of their new travelling companions, even though one of them could only nod and smile. As they made halting progress along the clogged roads, Elaine told her story: Ypres, the war graves, her father in the Australian Imperial Force, the Memorial School, her mother's death, the hotel and that first horrific bombing raid on Poperinghe. Knocker, the young corporal, was a good listener. She realised she'd never put her life into words before; it gave her a surprising sense of release and lent the past perspective. They in turn told their stories. They were all regulars, their sergeant, Smudger, had even been in Flanders in 1916. Knocker and Gary had joined up in '37 and '38, still boys then. Jobs were hard to find and the army was recruiting – the army had made men of them. But now they'd been cut off from the rest of their unit, picking up the evacuation order late. This wasn't what they expected or wanted: the British Army didn't retreat.

Late into the afternoon and now under steady rain, they came to a full stop. Dripping, Smudger came round to the back of the truck with the unwelcome news that they could go no further: the road was shot to pieces with shell holes. They'd have to walk. With army greatcoats now over their flimsy dresses to keep off the rain, the girls climbed down, struggling with their suitcases.

'Leave those, we're travelling light. Essentials only.'

While Simone fussed with her case, Elaine didn't hesitate. Stuffing the poetry anthology and a pair of knickers into her shoulder bag she did a quick check: papers, money, hanky, photo of Maman. All there. She had everything she needed.

They were in open country in pouring Flanders rain with no building in sight; there was no option but to march in step with Knocker and Smudger while Gary went ahead to recce the chance of picking up new transport. As they trudged on, following the path of the cratered road, the only wheeled vehicles that passed them were bicycles, their riders pedalling like the devil towards the smoking horizon.

Gary returned, sodden but cheerful. He'd found 'a nice little Morris' abandoned in a ditch but mercifully unsabotaged. It'd fix up a treat and they'd be on their way.

No sooner were they back on the road when they found themselves caught in crossfire from roadside trenches outside the town of Bergues. They'd unknowingly hit the BEF's 'outer perimeter' – the line holding German forces back from the evacuation now in full flight from Dunkirk. To the crunch of gears going into reverse and some furious effing and blinding from Knocker, they map-read their way out of trouble with a tortuous detour in the direction of the Bergues canal.

The canal, when they finally got there, was impassable: the bridge had been blown. Smudger was stoical. He'd seen it all before.

'Bugger me. The sappers got here before us. Never mind, we'll just have to walk on water.'

'*What?*' Elaine looked at him, incredulous. They were already soaked through but she didn't fancy getting any wetter. Gary, the fresh-faced private, winked at her.

'You're with the Dorsets now, Miss. We work miracles.'

The girls watched open-mouthed as the men put their shoulders behind three abandoned flatbed trucks and pushed them in smooth succession into the shallow canal. They had a bridge.

Bone-weary and shivering as she was, Elaine couldn't help but cheer this display of inventive gallantry, just like Sir Walter Raleigh laying his velvet cloak over a muddy puddle for Good Queen Bess to walk on. She took Simone's hand and, with the soldiers' help, they launched laughing on to the nearest truck.

They soon stopped when they saw what was on the other side of the raised canal. The road, identifiable only by a line of semi-submerged vehicles, was under a foot of filthy water. The sluice-gates had been opened to impede the Panzers' progress. The girls slumped down on the canal bank, dispirited, but the lads were undaunted. Smudger led the way into the water.

'Come on girls, a little footbath won't do you any harm.'

Weighed down by their sodden greatcoats they waded, stumbled and paddled on, half-supported, half-dragged by their soldier companions, till they reached higher ground. Almost at once, Simone collapsed, crying, into the mud.

'I can't go any further, leave me here. Just leave me. I want to lie down ...'

The men, embarrassed, busied themselves over a map. With some effort, Elaine crouched down beside her. She had twisted her ankles badly over the rough terrain and was in agony but she wasn't going to tell Simone that.

'Come on Simone. Remember the reason you're on this journey. You can't give up now, we're nearly there.' She guessed, judging by the increasing piles of abandoned materiel by the roadside and the pall of smoke rising from the northern horizon, that they must be within ten kilometres or so of Dunkirk. 'We're bound to meet a main road soon, and we can hitch another lift.'

'You go on. I'll be alright.'

With difficulty Elaine stood up and offered Simone a small, wet hand.

'We stay together, and we carry on together. Come on. You owe it to yourself and to these lovely men who've been so good to us today.'

'Oh for pity's sake Elaine, you're so damn British about everything. It makes me sick.'

But she took Elaine's hand and struggled to her feet. They carried on.

Burnt-out vehicles, piles of jettisoned equipment, potholes, shell holes, blown bridges and opened sluice gates: they'd overcome every kind of obstacle on their journey so far. But in the failing light of dusk outside a small French village, they came across a massacre. Bodies littered the road and spilled lifeless out of lorries. Soldiers and civilians indistinguishable in death. Those not fatally wounded by blast were shot up with bullets.

Smudger, the battle-hardened sergeant fazed by nothing, could hardly get the words out.

'Good God … Somebody's had a fucking field day here.'

He'd heard rumours about the Waffen-SS, the military wing of the Nazi Party, who took no prisoners and were no respecters of the Geneva Convention. They'd been brutal in Poland in 1939. This looked like their work.

There was no alternative but to pick their way through the charnel house, the girls wincing as they stepped around, over, sometimes on, the dead because there were so many of them, and in such concentration, that they could not be avoided. In the half-light of a dreadful day that was not yet over, Elaine now accepted what she'd been struggling since Poperinghe to deny: that their nightmare wasn't nearly done. Like the worst nightmares, it had barely started.

❦

In the back of another British Army lorry, three exhausted men from the Dorsets shared cigarettes with a few battered stragglers from the Warwicks and West Kents. The presence of two bedraggled figures, too petite to be soldiers but wearing British army greatcoats, went entirely unremarked. They were all stunned to silence, unable yet to process the horrors they'd seen but conscious that they had, somehow, so far, been spared. For what further horror they knew not.

To the accompaniment of Stuka fire and shelling, the ragtag convoy made its way into the outskirts of Dunkirk, their destination indelibly marked against the late evening sky. Here inside the inner perimeter the refugee columns had long melted away, diverted elsewhere to their fate. This was now a military zone.

The silent company stirred into life at the sight of a town engulfed in flames and the stink of cordite invading the night air.

'Bloody hell, we're not going into *that*?'

Smudger, the older experienced man, steadied them. 'Eyes on the prize, lads, eyes on the prize. On the other side we'll have those lovely white cliffs and the prospect of a nice lie-down with our wives and sweethearts.'

'May they never meet', came the weary chorus in reply.

Then a shout from the back of the cab: 'Anyone here know the way to the docks?'

The mood itself caught fire as they veered into the heart of the inferno. Through a maze of bombed and burning streets, the driver turned and turned again to avoid the wall of flame outfacing them at the head of every diversion.

'We're going round in fucking circles!'

'Tell the fucker to turn back or we'll be burnt alive!'

The vehicle erupted in frantic oaths and exhortations, unheard above the din of collapsing masonry and the shower of screaming shells.

Elaine had been soaked, starved and shaken to the core by being in such close proximity to death, but until that moment it had never occurred to her that she was in the slightest danger of losing her own life. Now she gripped Simone as the world around them collapsed into flame.

'Hold my hand! Pray!'

She shut her eyes, their mouthed prayers lost in the heat and fury of the moment.

An explosion, a blinding light and a timeless, airless, drifting blackness. A vacuum. Nothingness.

She came to, her mouth full of smoke and khaki. She was lying on top of Knocker. He pushed her off, groaning and checking himself for damage.

Bizarrely, they were still trundling along through the flames. Regaining composure of a kind, the occupants scrambled to their feet and looked back to the source of the conflagration. Barely 400 yards away, the truck behind them was sticking end-up like a Dinky toy in a smoking crater. The shell had exploded right between them.

After the panic of being lost in flaming hell and the shock of their near miss, by luck or by judgement, they found themselves at the harbour entrance. Here, beyond the barrage of abandoned vehicles, were the massed and swelling ranks of what was left of the British Expeditionary Force and their allies, a scene of Biblical exodus backlit by burning oil tanks and the flaming town, intermittently illuminated by shelling and tracer fire.

Smudger stopped the girls from scrambling down from the lorry with the others. Even in the semi-darkness and chaos, they were too conspicuous.

'Get those helmets on and make sure you're covered up. We're in a military zone. If you stick close to us, you'll pass in a crowd, but if they see you're civilians they won't let you in. If we get separated and you're challenged, say you're with the Dorsets.'

The greatcoats bulked them out and skirted their ankle boots, the tin helmets covered their hair and obscured their faces. The men fell in close to form a protective triangle. Moving as one, in the early hours of the morning of Thursday 30 May, they joined the throng milling through the gates of the inner harbour, oblivious to the Luftwaffe still wreaking havoc from the air.

Knocker let out a low whistle as they took in the scene. Ahead of them, through the crowd, Elaine could see a swaying mass of men in the inner harbour being marshalled on to one of the two moles, the long, thin stone-built breakwaters that made Dunkirk's outer harbour. In the harbour and along the moles, half sunk, burning and burnt-out vessels poked incongruously from the water, smoke pouring from their funnels. At the end of the mole men were being taken off by boats large and small: destroyers, trawlers, pleasure boats, every kind of craft moored alongside or straight into the mole wherever there was a gap.

To their right a few miles up the coast and lit up by burning oil tanks, the sand dunes of La Panne were black with waiting troops, the beaches scored with lines of men like rivulets running into the sea. In the Channel waters small boats bobbed, plying to and fro to the lines, scattered now and then by strafing planes, only to regroup almost immediately. On the horizon, visible in the refracted firelight, the low grey hulks of bigger ships moored or moving.

Could this really be the same place where she paddled with Maman in sunny peacetime? Now its dark magnitude took her breath away. She'd seen nothing like it, not even in the films in Uncle Charles' cinema. But something about the scale of effort here stirred her. It was heroic. Organised chaos.

But then, a hoarse command in French to halt.

'Who've you got there? Civilians? Show me.'

The French military policeman must have caught sight of the girls' ankles, but Smudger decided to bluff it out.

'*Non, non, ne civil. Militaire.*'

Knocker and Gary instinctively moved in closer. Elaine, brought back sharply from her childhood reverie, bit back the instinct to plead for mercy in her perfect French. Smudger weighed up the risks: the chap was getting agitated in that annoying way the Frogs had. If he attracted the attention of a British officer they'd be sunk. They'd be on a charge, and who knew what would become of the girls. Better to finish it now. The sound of the blow barely registered in the milling crowd of khaki. The policeman reeled back winded and they took their chance.

'Go go go!'

They melted into the darkness and one of the anonymous groups waiting to be called to the mole. Elaine whispered, appalled, to Smudger.

'Have you killed him?'

Smudger feigned a breezy confidence.

'Nah. Just gave him a nasty shock in the bollocks, that's all.'

The mood of mild hysteria soon passed into one of exhausted compliance as they shuffled with infinitesimal progress towards the mole, moving like a phalanx of zombies to barked instructions from the marshalling sergeants. Now and then in the heat of an air raid, mad or desperate men broke ranks and tried to jump the queue, to be shouted at then shot by officers wielding pistols, these summary executions raising barely a murmur from onlookers.

Finally they were on the narrow mole. Sleepwalking now, Elaine was held upright by the crush, the pain in her ankles anaesthetised by exhaustion. Regular drenching from shells falling into the water on either side failed to shake her fully into consciousness. She hadn't eaten or slept for days; the last twenty-four hours she'd been caught in an endless switchback ride of good humour and gross horror. Now, at what might or might not be near the end, they could be close to rescue or close to death. Elaine no longer cared. For self-preservation she had entered a second state of mind, detached from herself and from the reality of her perilous situation. She wasn't on that puny pier with bombs dropping around her amid the distant screams of dying men. She was lying in the Ramparts cemetery in Ypres, though whether on the soft turf among the English cottage garden flowers or beneath in the dark earth, she couldn't yet tell.

∽

Every so often the queue came to a standstill while breaches in the long mole caused by shelling were hastily repaired. The three-abreast shuffle would finally resume, then trickle into single file across wooden planks exposed to the sea on both sides.

Jolted back into reality, Elaine summoned her last reserves of concentration as she faced the planks, encouraged at each end by Gary and Knocker.

'Come on girl, you can do it.'

Was she hearing men's voices, or were the words coming from inside herself?

No one there on that night had any concept of time, but just before first light on the morning of Thursday 30 May Elaine and her small party finally reached the head of the queue. An iron ladder led down to a trawler moored unsteadily on the retreating tide below.

Ever the gentleman, Smudger waved them on first. Elaine put a foot on the ladder, praying that her ankles wouldn't fail her now. Shouted instructions assailed her from below.

'Chop chop, soldier! There's another 700 behind you.'

And then, when she was about six feet from the rolling deck of the trawler, a new voice, authoritative, amused.

'Well, well, well. What *have* we here? *Ladies'* legs!'

Half-jumping, half-falling the last few feet, she winced with pain and turned to see a British naval officer looking at her sceptically. Elaine panicked.

'Yes, but I'm English!'

Surely they wouldn't be turned off the boat now? But his attention was distracted by Simone coming down behind her.

'*More* ladies legs! What *is* going on here?'

Pulled to one side by the officer, Elaine produced her papers. There was no time for a proper interrogation but there were proprieties to be observed: they were to be secured in the skipper's cabin, safely away from the men. Even there and then, this struck Elaine as absurd. They'd just spent the last momentous eighteen hours in the intimate company of three squaddies who'd shown them nothing but gallantry and good humour. Now they wouldn't even have the chance to thank Smudger, Knocker and Gary or to say goodbye.

Guided through a mass of battle-stained soldiers, smoking, standing, sitting or lying wherever they could find a space, they were taken below deck to a grim cubbyhole with a single bunk, decorated only with photographs of under-dressed women. To the girls, who hadn't seen more than a canvas camp bed in a fortnight, it was more welcome than the Ritz itself. They flopped on to the filthy bedcovers and curled up together, too tired to celebrate their extraordinary deliverance or to hear the key turn in the lock. They were safe.

So too, by the end of the Dunkirk evacuation five days later, were almost 200,000 British and 140,000 French troops. They were aided by luck, fine weather, the bravery of the soldiers of the Allied rearguard who held the perimeter at the expense of their own lives and freedom, and perhaps above all by the heroic efforts of the 'little ships' which crossed the Channel to rescue so many from certain disaster.

SIX

LONDON

JUNE 1940–DECEMBER 1943

They landed in the south coast seaside town of Eastbourne. The cabin door stayed locked until the trawler's bedraggled cargo of men had all disembarked. When the girls finally emerged blinking into the light, still wearing their army greatcoats and stinking of sea water, it felt to Elaine like they'd landed in heaven. They were safe and the sun was shining. Everything was calm and people were talking in English. There were no Stukas, no dead bodies, no flames. The nightmare really was over.

But the welcome party that met them looked far from friendly. Plain-clothes policemen escorted them to a police station. It seemed that after all they'd been through they were to be interrogated as enemy aliens. Who were they? Where had they come from? Why were they in Belgium? *Sprechen Sie Deutsch*? How did they get on the boat? If they were who they said they were, was there anyone in England who could identify and vouch for them?

Elaine did all the talking, as she had to. Light-headed from hunger and exhaustion, she did her best to answer, about her Australian father, her Belgian mother, their life in Ypres and Poperinghe and their horrendous journey through France and Flanders to the coast.

'There's my aunt, Alice Stone, who lives in London. She can vouch for us. She's married to an English officer in the Guards. They're on the phone but I can't remember the number. I can give you the address in Streatham. She'll identify us. She's Simone's sister and my aunt.'

Someone was dispatched to check. The policemen – if that's what they were – talked in low voices among themselves.

'Isn't this a job for MI5, sir?'

'Don't think so. They won't thank us for adding to their burden, vetting all the flotsam and jetsam coming in from Dunkirk. No, they look kosher enough to me. Cheeky monkeys, hitching a lift with the BEF. Top marks for initiative though, eh? Get them a cup of tea while we wait to see what this Mrs Stone has to say.'

Several cups of tea later, they were free and on their way back to Streatham with Aunt Alice.

Word spread fast. Within days of their return they were a source of neighbours' curiosity and amazement. The Stones had never entertained so many visitors, come to look at the 'girl soldiers' who'd escaped from Dunkirk with the BEF. The press were soon on to the story. A *Daily Mirror* reporter arrived on the doorstep with a photographer.

'I think we'll have you outside, sitting in a deckchair together, nice and cosy. Our readers'll love it. God knows we could do with some good news. That's right, you'll need to cuddle up close. You're sisters, aren't you? Yes, lovely. That's it. Hold tight. Smashing.'

The flashbulb eclipsed even the June sunshine as they sat posing together in the back garden, two smiling young women in summer dresses hand in hand. Even they had difficulty believing that the week before they'd been stepping over dead bodies in Belgium.

But this wasn't what the reporter was most interested in. This was a good news story of deliverance – and romance.

'Now then, tell me all about our brave lads who rescued you. And, by the by, have you both got boyfriends, fiancés?'

When the report came out a couple of days later, Elaine read it out to the assembled company, laughing as she read the headlines.

'Listen to this, we're famous! *"Shapely ankles gave girls away. They joined B.E.F."* '

'Go on, then. What does it say?'

'Elaine, who is now at the home of her aunt, Mrs Stone, of Deerhurst-road S.W., fingered the gold ring given to her by her soldier fiancé as she told her story. "It brought me luck", she whispered. "We might have been burnt to death when we reached Dunkirk. We drove through the burning streets in a lorry. We did not know the way to the docks. Suddenly we came upon a stream of soldiers waiting to

embark. Our luck had held." I'm sure I didn't say all that. Not in that soppy way, anyway.'

Soppy or not, Elaine was secretly thrilled by the attention, of which she took the lion's share. The *Mirror* report inevitably lost something in translation into Flemish. Simone, unhappy not to be able to share the limelight, and not yet in touch with the boy she'd followed to England, had to be content with mute smiles. It was Elaine who told their story and Elaine who answered the questions of enthralled enquirers after their welfare.

The Dunkirk evacuation was a strategic catastrophe skilfully translated into a propaganda victory for the English-speaking world. Elaine was unwittingly part of that effort. As far away as remote Western Australia, the *Albany Advertiser* carried the story of the plucky 'Australian' girl whose father had fought in Flanders with the Australian forces in the last war, who'd braved bombs and Stuka fire to escape with the troops from Dunkirk.

҈

By the middle of June the unfolding disaster in France had wiped what good news stories there were off the front pages. Hitler had taken Paris apparently without resistance; Petain capitulated soon after. France was now divided into an occupied and a 'free' zone and Axis powers controlled practically all of continental Europe. It looked as if the British government's fears of invasion, so derided by its population only weeks before, were well founded. There was no grumbling about the blackout and petty rules now: everyone was on full alert and only too aware of their country's perilous position. The enemy was only a narrow stretch of water or an hour's flying time away. Britain's allies had melted away; she was alone.

London was now on a proper war footing: barrage balloons clouded the sky like toy Zeppelins, many theatres and cinemas were still shut and rationing was starting to bite. Evacuation of schoolchildren started all over again, especially from London and the south-east coastal towns. Streatham Common looked very different from when Elaine had last seen it in December 1939. A great central section was now turned over to allotments, a barrage balloon station occupied the corner by the church and public shelters fringed the High Street side. The girls watched as Civil Defence workers took down road signs at junctions and sawed off the 'S. W.' from the end of the street sign in Deerhurst Road. It seemed absurd that these puny measures could stymie an invasion. Surely the Germans would have maps?

Fear, uncertainty and an acute sense of vulnerability made Londoners watchful and newly suspicious of anything – or anyone – unfamiliar. Their cheerful tolerance of incomers and different nationalities deserted them. Mobs attacked Italian restaurants and Austrian patisseries. Even Jewish refugees, who'd fled from the Nazis to what they saw as a safe haven in Britain, were reviled, rounded up and interned. The public mood had darkened: no one now believed a British victory was a racing certainty. Agents of the enemy were perhaps even now in their midst preparing for invasion.

Simone's Belgian accent and halting attempts at English soon drew sharp looks and unfriendly comments. Even half-hearted jokes could be wounding.

''Ere, you're not one of them fifth-columnists are you?' was almost the first English phrase she learned, and she soon tired of hearing it. After being shouted and jeered at by a group of schoolboys when she tried to buy bread, she refused to go out alone. This was a bind for Elaine, who longed to explore the area on her own or just go for a walk around the Common, but she knew she had to stand by Simone until she was able to stand up for herself.

'Don't be ridiculous, of course she isn't. She's Belgian, she's my mother's sister and we've just escaped from the Germans.'

Belgian, German, it was all the same to suspicious Londoners. They were all damn foreigners and most likely up to no good.

It was something they just had to put up with for the time being. And they had a new priority now. They couldn't expect to live for free at Deerhurst Road for the duration. They had to look for work.

∽

In the unusually hot summer of 1940 the country was transfixed by the air battle going on between the RAF and the Luftwaffe in the skies above southern England. British shipping in the Channel, airfields, aircraft factories and radar installations were all targets. Hitler, they were told, needed to gain air supremacy before he could launch an invasion. This was nothing less, Mr Churchill said, than the Battle of Britain. If it was lost, invasion was certain.

Bombing raids on London had been predicted and prepared for since the outbreak of war but the newspapers, newsreels and radio reports presented a stirring picture of David beating back Goliath in the air, so it was a shock in the middle of August when the first bombs were dropped in a daylight attack not far from Streatham, on Croydon Airport. It was an isolated raid but a small harbinger of what was to come. Not much further into the war, bombs would drop not just a few miles away but a few hundred yards away from Deerhurst Road. But by then Elaine would be long gone.

By early September, with the battle for air supremacy all but won and Churchill exultant, Londoners could afford a little optimism. But there was no let up in the war effort. During the frenetic months since Dunkirk, thousands more men had been mobilised and war production cranked up to the point where many factories were operating twenty-four hours a day.

There were now more jobs than men to fill them. Women's labour was in high demand. Two young girls lately arrived from Belgium had little difficulty finding work, even if one of them struggled with her English. They were both taken on by the British Relay Wireless Company at their headquarters in Aldwych, central London, Elaine as a Stores Clerk, Simone in a more menial job where good English wasn't essential.

It wasn't particularly interesting work and Elaine wasn't using many of the skills she'd started to master at St Helen's, but it was a job and the money they earned meant they could contribute to their board and lodging at Deerhurst Road. Together with their train and tube fares into town each day, this left little for luxuries, and there were few to be had except at inflated prices from the spivs exploiting the commercial opportunities of a growing black market.

But the real attraction was being in the centre of town. At last Elaine was within striking distance of Piccadilly Circus and she could see for herself the heart of the Empire she'd looked at, fascinated, on her classroom wall. She walked there in her lunch hour whenever she could, just to sit with her sandwich or mingle with the crowds. It was just as colourful, brash and bustling as she'd hoped. There they were, the Guinness is Good for You clock and the big Bovril sign. She caught the last glimpses of Eros before he disappeared for the duration, sandbagged and boarded up and covered in posters for War Savings.

The city, soot stained as it was, held a magic for her. Yes, it was dirty and crowded, but not in the same way as those miserable terraces she'd seen from the train when she first arrived in what seemed a lifetime ago. Here, everything had purpose, everyone was going somewhere to do something useful. Inside each monumental building and office block there were people with lives and histories working away. Despite the grime of decades of smoking chimneys that cloaked even the most distinguished of buildings – Buckingham Palace and the Tower of London were just as black as everything else – there were splashes of colour everywhere from the buses, pillar boxes, gaudy advertising hoardings and bright summer dresses of the women passing by.

Now she could put on a little rouge, powder and lipstick and pass for a proper Londoner, taking buses, trams and the Underground, window shopping in Regent Street (such shops as she'd never seen in her life) and treating herself and Simone to the occasional tea and toasted teacake at a Lyons Corner House. And she was earning her own money, almost independent at last. She still had Simone to look out for, but she'd get her chance soon enough. Life was about to change at Deerhurst Road, and for all Londoners.

On Saturday, 7 September as Elaine and Simone took an early evening walk around the Common after a particularly hot late summer's day, they noticed a pulsating glow to the north-east. It was bright enough to rival the dipping sunset in the opposite direction and gained in brilliance until it lit the darkening sky. Far too big to be a single fire, it looked as if London itself was ablaze. Memories of their descent into a burning Dunkirk all too recent, the girls held on to each other in wonderment and fear.

'What is it?'

'It must be a fire, but it's so big, it can't be an ordinary fire. Whatever it is, it must be miles wide.'

'Oh God, Elaine, it looks just like …'

'I know. Don't say it. Come on, let's go back and see if there's anything about it on the news.'

The bombing had finally begun. What the girls could see was Woolwich Arsenal and all the docks along the Pool of London ablaze. In the nine days and nights that followed 'Black Saturday', hundreds of enemy bombers laid waste great swathes of the East End. The rest of the capital was spared, though stray bombs fell in the central area, and Buckingham Palace itself was hit. Radio and press reports played up the bravery and resilience of East Enders and minimised the dreadful carnage. Few outside the East End knew the extent of their suffering, but on their tube journeys to and from work, Elaine could tell something was very wrong. From the earliest days of the bombing, at Holborn where they changed for the Aldwych spur, there were weary people on the platforms, on the escalators and in the tunnels between platforms carrying bundles of bedding. They were exhausted East Enders who'd obviously been trying to stay in the deep station all night to shelter from the bombs.

A massive air attack on 15 September was designed to deliver the knock-out blow in preparation for invasion, but in the many dogfights over the south-east of England people cheered as the RAF destroyed twice as many enemy aircraft as it lost. Mr Churchill declared this a decisive victory in the Battle of Britain. Invasion – for the moment anyway – was no longer imminent.

Despite the brief rejoicing no one was in any doubt that this was just the start of Hitler's revenge for the RAF's success. Without air supremacy he'd had to delay – and within weeks abandon altogether – his invasion plans. Instead he'd bomb Britain into submission. The capital, centre of power and key to Britain's national morale, would be his first target. Elaine and Simone, who'd seen his military machine at close quarters, knew better than most what it was capable of.

If London had just begun a horrific new chapter in its long history, Deerhurst Road was soon to suffer its own small convulsion. Though it was never spoken of, Elaine knew her Aunt Alice must be gravely ill: already thin and prematurely aged, she'd begun to look sallow and every movement was an effort. She would rise late and go to bed before the evening news on the Home Service, the bulletin that nobody missed if they could help it. Her deteriorating condition was hard to ignore and the girls were worried, but it was impolite to ask her directly what the matter was. When they expressed their concern, Uncle seemed embarrassed and told them little.

So it was a shock when within weeks Alice died, the cause unmention-able but undoubtedly cancer. The girls' lives – so eventful in the past six months – were about to take another dramatic turn. Perhaps he couldn't be blamed, but the bereaved widower lost little time in introducing another, much younger, woman into the household. Ostensibly employed to run the house, it soon became clear that she was to be a more permanent fixture in his life. The girls felt increasingly awkward in this new situation and it brought back for Elaine unwelcome memories of her father's disastrous dalliance with his housekeeper. The dynamic had changed; they knew that sooner or later they would have to move on.

'I think it's time for you girls to strike out on your own', Uncle announced one day. 'Alice and I gave you a roof while you got settled but you're earning now and old enough to stand on your own feet.'

It was hardly news to Elaine and Simone.

'I've been in touch with an old friend from the Guards. They live in the City. Nice people, got two girls of their own, a bit older than you I think. Anyway, they'll put you up for a while until you can get digs of your own. You'll be much nearer to your work there.'

This was unexpectedly welcome news. Elaine was intrigued.

'The City? I didn't think anyone lived there. Isn't it all banks and offices?

'You'd be surprised. Quite a few people live in the City. There's a lot of old churches there and he's a church warden for one of them. It's in Fleet Street and that's where they live, just off Fleet Street.'

Off Fleet Street. With some excitement, Elaine explained its significance to Simone. Fleet Street was only a short bus ride along the Strand from Aldwych. They'd be proper Londoners, living in the heart of the city where everything was happening. Streatham was alright but their lives there were quiet and it felt so distant from the real London. She kept the last bit to herself: Fleet Street and their new digs could be the stepping stone to the full independence she craved. It was an energising prospect. It never occurred to her for a moment that this meant they'd be moving from the relative safety of the suburbs into the eye of the storm.

᎚᎚

The East End was being battered day and night during September and early October but there were no pictures of dead bodies in the newspapers and the radio never gave casualty figures or specified where bombs had caused most damage. Newsreels showed bomb-wrecked terraces but always ended on an upbeat note with a house still standing and cheerful cockneys going about their normal business.

Despite the censorship there were horrific rumours coming out of the East End: rubbled streets littered with corpses, thousands homeless, crowds packed into dank, unsanitary shelters with only an earth bucket and a bit of canvas sacking for privacy, looting of abandoned homes and riots outside shelters, the people desperate, civil society near to collapse.

Elaine could believe it. After the move to Fleet Street, they were living so close to their jobs in Aldwych – she could walk there – she didn't need to use the Tube so much but it was hard to ignore the transformation underground. People from bombed communities in the east were swarming into the deep Central and Piccadilly Line stations every night now to sleep. If the girls had an evening out in the West End to go to the pictures, the platforms were always packed with sleeping families on their return to Holborn or Chancery Lane. The authorities, no longer able to prevent the crowds determined to stay in stations after they shut, had relented and the people flooded in night after night. To Elaine, the Underground now stank of sweat and piss and weary desperation. Like other passengers trying to reach their destinations hampered by these squatters, she was initially dismissive of their plight. Weren't there shelters for them? Why did they have to clog up the Tube?

Attitudes soon changed as the bombs started to drop nearer home. From mid-October, the Luftwaffe changed tactics to night-time only raids to avoid the RAF fighters. The pounding anti-aircraft guns made a reassuring backdrop to the drone of enemy aircraft, but in truth did little to affect the nightly assault. Now it wasn't just the East End: every military and civilian installation in the capital was a target.

Their hosts, Mr and Mrs Ashford, lived in a narrow town house tucked away in one of the eighteenth-century courts. It was like something out of a Dickens novel with an entrance from Fleet Street so discreet it hardly made its presence felt at all. Elaine explored the area's cramped passages and alleyways fascinated: its crowded medieval street pattern was even more hemmed in than ancient Ypres. Away from the main thoroughfare and the striking new black and chromium facade of the Daily Express building, it was full of mysterious nooks, crannies and dead ends with century-worn names like Hen and Chicken Court and Hanging Sword Alley.

Evening trips into town soon stopped for Elaine and Simone. At dusk each night the air-raid warning wailed as reliably as an alarm clock. There was no Tube station immediately nearby and neither was there yet a public shelter, so they went down to the cellar. Most houses in the area had a cellar, though, as Mr Ashford cheerfully observed as a raid was happening at full tilt above them, this wasn't much good if the house fell in on top of you. *In extremis*, he said, they'd have to go into the crypt of St Dunstan's. This prospect didn't fill the girls with confidence: even the smelly Tube or a crowded public shelter would be better than a spooky undercroft among the bones of the long dead.

As winter nights drew in the government's propaganda machine fought a losing battle for Londoners' morale. The night-time raids were incessant and it was increasingly difficult for the press to play down major disasters and obvious bomb damage when the results were so plain to see. Balham Underground and St Pancras Station took direct hits, West End department stores were gutted, and mains services and transport disrupted. Bomb craters in roads and razed buildings became regular features in the city landscape. In each morning's count of the night's carnage, hundreds of lives and homes were lost, hundreds more made homeless.

It was dispiriting and frightening by turn, a constant round of battling to work, sheltering at night, checking the damage and clearing up in the morning. Simone, who wasn't used to working much at anything, was finding life under these conditions particularly trying. Her English was improving but not enough to make her life easier in these testing times. As they manoeuvred round the previous night's mayhem in the Strand and the small civilian army of people clearing up, she sighed and tutted with irritation.

'How much longer is this going on?'

'Don't ask me. Only Hitler knows for sure.'

'I can't stand much more of it. It's getting on my nerves.'

Elaine bit her tongue. There was a lot she wanted to say.

'It can't last forever. And d'you think we'd be any safer in Poperinghe with the Germans?'

'At least we'd be in familiar surroundings without bombs dropping on us every damn night. It's horrible here. I hate it. I miss Mama and Papa and the hotel.' The petulance gave way to genuine distress. 'What's happened to them all, Elaine?'

'Don't worry, they'll be safe somewhere, I'm convinced of it. As for the Palace, who knows?'

Who cares, she might have added, I don't. She remembered Luc's ring on her finger and hoped he wasn't in danger. And her father, where was he now?

෨෦

Even as Simone grew increasingly alienated from her new surroundings, Elaine relished them more. Now the war had come much closer to home there was a different mood as people were brought out into the streets to survey the night's damage and help each other salvage precious belongings and clear up the mess. After the shock and chaos of the first weeks of the Blitz, central, local and voluntary services had started to work together and people felt more confident that help was at hand. That in turn made them more willing to help others. A brief respite in November and December, when German bombers turned their fire on Coventry and other English cities, gave London vital breathing space to regroup, plan and re-energise.

In the close courts of Fleet Street, the broad streets of the City or the busy West End, Elaine could feel a new strength and solidarity of purpose. Everywhere on bombed-out shops and houses people had chalked up their own messages of defiance: *Down But Not Out* and *Hitler's Bombs Can't Beat Us.* They cheered each other up: 'Mustn't grumble, things could be worse' they said, though everyone knew things were bad enough. Now, the giant government posters matched rather than chafed against the public mood. *Your Courage Your Cheerfulness Your Resolution Will Bring Us Victory* suddenly looked inspiring rather than patronising. But it wasn't clever propaganda that brought about the change of heart. It was Hitler's bombs.

Going to and from work, Elaine watched the civil defence workers, the nurses, firemen and air-raid wardens, tired and dirty, toiling away in the rubble. She envied them. Like her, they had full-time jobs during the day but here they were doing something off their own bat and in their own precious time. They were part of something valuable for the war effort, for capital, king and country. She remembered Mr Allen and the Memorial School, and how she had felt saluting the flag on Empire Day and singing 'I Vow to Thee, My Country' all together in Assembly: a warm feeling of pride and belonging. She longed to feel part of something so solid, so worthwhile again now.

'I'm going to join the WVS.'

Simone was aghast.

'What? You mean those frumpy women in green who pour tea and boss people about on bombsites? Whatever for, it's not compulsory is it?'

'No, but I want to do something.'

'You're mad. It'll be dirty and dangerous and the uniform's hideous.'

'I know! But at least I'll be doing something useful. All this going on around us and all I'm doing is stuck behind a desk all day and stuck in shelters all night. I can't stand by and let other people do all the dirty work. They're crying out for volunteers, haven't you seen all the posters?'

'Well, rather you than me. Life's hard enough as it is without volunteering for more.'

That was good then. Free of Simone and her dismal pessimism, she'd be able to carve out her own little corner of independence where she could use her initiative, meet new people and make her own small contribution. She was on her way.

The Women's Voluntary Service for Civil Defence 'training' amounted to little more than a couple of pep talks and some instruction in rudimentary first aid. She needn't have worried about the green uniform: there weren't enough to go round. A thick brown overall and an armband had to do. She was soon assigned to a group of air-raid wardens close to the Strand, her duties were to assist them before raids in getting people into public shelters and then to give immediate help to the bombed out and the walking wounded and alert the emergency services if more help was needed.

In the brief lull between mid-November and Christmas the nightly bombardment was reduced to sporadic raids so it wasn't the baptism of fire she might otherwise have faced. Nevertheless when the raids did come, she didn't expect to feel quite so inadequate in the enormity of destruction they wrought.

It was so much worse than anything they'd seen during the bombing in Poperinghe. In the frenetic aftermath of a raid in which whole buildings were burning, facades collapsed into rubble and craters opened up in the roads to swallow buses whole, it was no longer enough to guide dazed householders through the flames and leaking fire hoses to their rest centres or calm their screaming children with a bandage and a sweetie. Behind her in the chaos were dozens more she couldn't help: the badly injured trapped by falling masonry; those still lying beneath smoking wreckage waiting for the Heavy Rescue and Disposal squads to do their grim retrieval work.

'Leave 'em, love. They're for the heavy mob', the ARPs and firemen told her all too often, even as the injured and dying cried out to her. All she could do was try to stay calm and assure them that help was on its way, even when she knew it would probably be too late for them.

She felt shamed by her own feeble efforts in the face of such suffering. There had to be more she could do. By Christmas she had enrolled with the Red Cross to train in first aid and home nursing. It wasn't much but it meant she could at least tend the housebound and the injured in rest centres with some degree of confidence and professionalism. More important, she would be able to give immediate help – even hope – to those in their most urgent hour of need.

※

Christmas had been just business as usual in her family's hotels, so Elaine's first Christmas in London was a novelty in all kinds of ways. She was in a house – a real home – for one thing, something she'd always dreamed of. There was a war on, but this only added interest and excitement despite the many inconveniences.

On Christmas Day the girls went to church with the Ashfords, ignoring Simone's fears that she'd burn in hell. Elaine told her not to be so stupid: God wouldn't mind, especially as these were exceptional circumstances. No stranger to Anglican worship herself, she'd often gone to services in St George's because it was next to the British Memorial School and part of its life.

There was a decorated tree in the house, and a small artificial one in the cellar so that it still felt a bit like Christmas during raids. After all, Mr Ashford said, if shelterers could have trees on Tube platforms, he was sure they could have a tree in their own little shelter.

She missed the church bells though. No bells had rung in Britain since September 1939 and no one wanted them rung because that was the invasion signal. Christmas Day without bells was a curiously subdued affair. Dinner was a meagre joint saved up from several weeks' rations. A slightly musty Christmas pudding set aside from the previous year was served with something masquerading as cream that Mrs Ashford called 'evap'. They pulled crackers and exchanged small gifts and gave grateful thanks for what they had. For the moment, they were safe.

The past couple of months had been relatively quiet, though in early December they'd had had a night of terrible fires when the Luftwaffe bombarded the capital with thousands of incendiaries. That's what first set Elaine thinking seriously about the Red Cross. If it was going to carry on like this, she'd need to be able to give proper help. By the end of the year and the Second Great Fire of London she knew she'd made the right decision.

On Sunday, 29 December at 6 p.m. the siren wound up to its familiar wail over the ARP station in the Strand.

'There we go. Titfers on and into the fray. Christmas truce is over!'

The ARP chaps had a fatalistic humour wrought, she assumed, during their time in the trenches in the last war. They were all too old to be called up. Father figures, they called her *girlie*, *love* or *ducks* but they didn't take liberties, especially after they'd heard her Dunkirk story. In their eyes she was some kind of heroine but she shrugged this off, embarrassed. To her *they* were the heroes, going out into the dangerous night not knowing what they might find or whether they would come back. If only she'd been able to look up to her father in the same way … Never mind. Work to do. She grabbed her tin hat and went to follow them out.

'No love, this one's not for you. Jerry's going for the City, if it's anything like the last lot it'll be hell in there tonight. You sit tight here till the All Clear. That's when you'll be needed.'

She darned stockings in the half-light of a Tilley lamp, wishing she was out there with the men. When eventually the drone of bombers and the familiar crump crump of high explosives ceased and the All Clear sounded she took her tin hat and ventured out into Fleet Street.

Even during raids Fleet Street was never deserted: night-time was when the presses rolled and the night editors prepared for the next day's news, vans poured out of print works and messenger boys scurried from offices on bikes. Tonight fire engines and ambulances added noise and motion. Above all the sight and smell of fire was unmistakeable: the City was burning. Elaine followed the fire engines east. Ludgate Circus was as far as she could get before a Special Constable barred her way and the heat of the inferno ahead hit her in the face. Looking up Ludgate Hill with eyes smarting, she could just see the dome of St. Paul's rising above the smoke and flames. Everything around it was on fire.

'Emergency vehicles and personnel only, Miss. You wouldn't want to be up there tonight, I can tell you.'

'I'm WVS, can I help?'

'There's a tea van round the corner by Blackfriars Station. They'll be run ragged. I expect they could do with an extra pair of hands.'

'Thank you, I'll do that then.'

'Mine's plenty of milk and three sugars.'

She turned back to him with a smile as another fire tender screamed past.

'You'll be lucky.'

At the WVS refreshment van a small crowd of smoke-stained firemen and exhausted workers slumped on the ground sipping from tin mugs. For the next couple of hours she served tea and fetched water from a standpipe until it ran to a trickle and then stopped altogether.

'You won't get anything more out of that, love. The main's buggered.'

The fireman was barely visible in the shadows in his dark uniform and blackened face, sweat-streaked now.

'The lads up at St Paul's have been wading in the mud trying get water out the river for the hoses but the tide's too low tonight. I've never seen it so bad. We're running out of men, we've never had the right equipment and now we've even run out of sodding water. I'm gasping for another cuppa, too.'

'Sorry, I didn't see you there. I could probably find you some cocoa. There's plenty of dried milk left.'

'No love, you're alright. You can stay and chat for a bit though. You're a sight for sore eyes tonight, I can tell you.'

She sat down beside him.

In the time it took to share a furtive cigarette, she learned a lot about firefighting, about firestorms and what the men had to put up with as they battled to save London from the flames. How the bombs kept rupturing the mains and their back-up systems so often failed. How they relied on the Thames but the tide had to be high enough for the hoses to reach. Jerry had obviously studied the tide tables tonight … And the effects on the men of being in such hostile conditions: sometimes so desperately dehydrated they even drank river water. Even with hundreds of auxiliaries drafted in, there still wasn't enough manpower to deal with the fires incendiaries caused. Impossible decisions had to be made about what to try and save and what to leave to burn. Tonight there was only one instruction: save St Paul's. Everywhere else the fires were left to rage out of control. She listened, enthralled and horrified.

The fireman put his tin mug down and wiped the muck from his watch. 'Tide's on the turn. It's been nice talking to you, Miss. Keep up the good work.'

He got to his feet, gathered the rest of his crew and went back in the direction of St Paul's. Good work? She resolved to start doing some.

Elaine got to bed, exhausted, better informed and not a little inspired by what she'd seen and heard, barely a few hours before she had to be up again for the start of the new working week.

Fires burned into the following day, and the next, but the damage was already clear to see: among the smoking wreckage London's medieval Guildhall was a gutted ruin and more than a dozen historic churches had been destroyed. St Dunstan's was left unscathed but all that was left of St Brides at the eastern end of Fleet Street was Wren's magnificent tiered tower, its bells turned to molten metal in the heat. The ancient area around the Barbican and Moorgate was razed to rubble, the last timbered vestiges of the old medieval city gone. The wind had carried the flames as far as the South Bank where a mile-long stretch of riverside wharves and warehouses burned to blazes.

By God's Providence and superhuman effort St Paul's had been saved, the flames kept back from its churchyard by the firemen as volunteer fire-watchers threw live incendiaries from its roof. For Londoners and for the watching world, London's cathedral stood proud as a symbol of hope in hell, faith in the face of evil. But this was the worst night of the Blitz so far: hundreds of civilian casualties, fourteen firemen dead and 250 injured. By the first day of 1941 it was clear that more of the City had been destroyed than in the Great Fire of 1666.

∾

The early weeks of 1941 offered no immediate prospect of relief. A little beyond St Paul's to the east, less than a mile from Fleet Street, six of the City's major thoroughfares intersect where the impressive bulk of the Bank of England dominates this busy hub. Here, on the evening of 11 January, shortly before 8 p.m., the booking hall of Bank Underground station took a direct hit. The blast tore down the escalators, through tunnels and on to the platforms, killing 111 people and creating a crater so massive that army sappers had to build a temporary bridge over it to keep the traffic flowing.

Less than forty-eight hours after the bombing Larry Madden could be found in this crater wielding a pickaxe with motley comrades from 97 Company, Pioneer Corps. They were clearing rubble, looking for salvage, and hoping not to find too many bits of bodies. Larry had seen enough of those in Flanders.

His fellow workers were a rough lot. Just like the lads on the war graves in 1920, the Pioneers attracted all sorts: the workless and the work-shy, aliens who'd managed to avoid internment, ex-cons, misfits and rejects from every other service for every other reason. Their mission was demolition, clearance and salvage. Lately, the salvage tended to be human, dead or barely alive.

They were an undisciplined rabble and they always got the dirty jobs, but he was a beggar not a chooser. When he'd signed up in March 1940 he was working as a casual labourer, too old at forty-one and too short at five feet four to fight. He needed a steady job and Britain needed manpower. The Pioneers welcomed him in.

The Corps' 97 Company started its war in East Anglia building concrete and barbed wire coastal defences, but was drafted to the capital as soon as it became clear the Blitz was going to be a long and messy business. They were based at Finsbury, just north of Bank up the Moorgate Road. It was a lot livelier here than Great Yarmouth. They'd already rescued survivors from a bombed-out public shelter in Stoke Newington, excavated a bomb crater at Mount Pleasant sorting office and dug out bodies from a collapsed Peabody tenement in Farringdon Road.

The Second Great Fire at the end of the year spread to their patch north of Moorgate and destroyed many of their billets in the nearby terraces and tenements. The lads lost precious equipment and personal belongings, which hadn't improved morale any. After that little lot, he was lucky not to be living in a bell tent on the artillery ground with the other lads. At least he still had a roof over his head and a few precious mementos of a happier life, photographs of when he still had a family and Elaine was his little girl. Such a pretty little thing, he'd take her to the Last Post. She loved that small cemetery by the Ramparts with the ducks and the willow trees. They were good times, before everything went awry.

He'd had no contact with his only child since early 1939. Was she still at the Palace with the Duponselles? He hoped not. Perhaps she'd managed to get away with the war graves families – he'd heard somewhere that they all got out to England just before Dunkirk. It might have been in the papers, though he rarely saw a newspaper these days. They hadn't parted on the best of terms: it was a bad time, but what could he do? He owed money, Charles was on his back. There was nothing for him in Belgium, he had to get away. Hacking away at the rubble in bomb craters gave him too much thinking time. He'd lost Caroline. Had he lost Elaine too? Where was she? How was she? Did she ever think of him?

၆၀

Elaine's new friend grasped her hand. 'I'm so pleased you could come.'

'It's an honour to be invited.'

'Don't be silly, *cherie*. It's a pleasure to have you with us. I can't tell you how glad I am to have another French-speaking friend in London.

I love those Red Cross girls, but gossip and slander just isn't the same in English somehow!'

Elaine knew what she meant. She always thought of English as her first language, but she was just as at home with the fluting cadences of her mother tongue. She didn't use it much these days, and she'd never been much good at written French – apart from those terrible weeks at the convent her education had been entirely in English – but it brought back fond reminders of Maman, so she was glad to have found this new friend and, it seemed, such a well-connected one.

Perhaps more than any other voluntary service, the Red Cross drew in women from all walks of London life. Elaine was surprised to find herself working alongside double-barrelled debs one day, rough diamonds the next, nice middle-class girls from Pinner the next. She found companionship, laughter and new purpose there. She also discovered a new social life. The Red Cross opened a door, not only to the rich variety of London life in wartime, but to its burgeoning expatriate communities recently fled from occupied Europe.

A very tall and serious soldier called de Gaulle, who someone said looked as though he'd swallowed his sabre, was trying to rally 'Free French' forces and was swanning about London as if he was president-in-exile, although nobody seemed very interested and few expatriates trusted him. Elaine's new friend was a diplomat's daughter whose father had chosen to stay on at the French Embassy in London after Petain sacked all its pro-British staff. Disgusted by Petain's capitulation but suspicious of the upstart de Gaulle, they now operated a kind of embassy in exile, maintaining a social and political *salon* to which Elaine found herself invited from time to time. This evening, however, was a very special occasion. The elegant crowd were at their most glamorous and instead of the usual tinkle of polite conversation an air of excitable anticipation energised the concert hall.

'It's so exciting! To have her here, just for us!'

'And I hear she's come specially from Switzerland … by rights we should be entertaining her in the Embassy. *Our* Embassy, occupied by the enemies of France. It's despicable.'

'… Here she is! How lovely she still looks!'

A wave of applause greeted the elegant figure in full-length evening gown taking her place by the piano. Striking, Elaine would have said, rather than lovely, the great French actress and singer Françoise Rosay had to be getting on for fifty but her commanding presence soon stilled the hall. Elaine had seen her films of course, *Carnival in Flanders* and *Les Gens du Voyage*, in her uncle's cinema in Poperinghe. She was famous throughout the French-speaking world and in Hollywood too. Here she was in London, playing to a privileged audience of which Elaine could hardly credit she was part. She should have felt out of place. Instead it felt entirely right that she should be there, a part of something exciting and extraordinary.

Rosay's familiar repertoire of recitations and operatic songs held the audience rapt throughout the evening. If the siren had gone it would have been ignored. Nevertheless, no one was prepared for the impact of her finale.

'My compatriots, I thank you for your invitation to London, and for listening. I have one last song for you.'

The familiar opening bars galvanised the audience as she launched into a full-throated rendition of the workers' song, *L'Internationale*, and the refrain that begins '*This is the final struggle ...*'

It was a personal message of resistance that needed no explanation. At every chorus the hall erupted with Gallic pride and unabashed tears. After many encores and a defiant *Vive la France!* Rosay finally left the stage to ecstatic applause. Elaine hugged her friend, caught up in the high emotion of the occasion.

'Thank you so much, what an unforgettable evening! So inspiring! She makes me want to go and storm those imposters in the Embassy right now!'

They laughed together with tears in their eyes. This too was part of her heritage. She had much in common with these people anxious to fight the oppressor in Europe to regain their lands. Madame Rosay had made her realise that she was part of something bigger and more powerful than even the propaganda posters proclaimed.

◌

Elaine now threw herself into her extended role for the WVS, her Red Cross training enabling her to help bridge that critical gap between finding injured bomb victims and the professional medical and rescue services arriving to take over. There were still far too many she had to leave behind but now she knew from basic triage training how to distinguish those most likely to benefit from her help from those whose cause was hopeless.

Since the Second Great Fire, she'd taken on a new, more personal task, inspired perhaps by her conversation with the weary fireman that terrible night in December. But her colleagues did their best to stop her.

'Elaine, for God's sake! We haven't had the All Clear yet. There are still bombs out there!'

She carried on filling flasks from the ancient kettle in the ARP station.

'It'll be alright. None have got my name on them tonight.'

And even if her breezy confidence was misplaced, she thought, what of it? If I go, I go. She'd seen enough of death by now to know that life was precarious. You could be lucky or unlucky. Most of the time she felt lucky and she would carry on till that luck ran out. So off she went into the glowing night, clutching her tea flasks and tin mugs, often as bombs were still falling, to look for the nearest fire crew in need of refreshment.

For some reason she couldn't fathom, she was insouciant in the face of the big bombs; it was the little ones that terrified the life out of her. 'Butterfly bombs' sounded pretty but were a lethal prototype of cluster bomb. They looked like large tins of food with 'wings' on the end of a stalk. Dispersed from much larger containers they'd float down to earth to land in trees, catch in the crevices of buildings or hide in shrubbery. The slightest vibration would cause the can to release its explosive charge, killing or maiming anyone unfortunate enough to be within striking distance.

Elaine was so scared of these little horrors that she avoided walking anywhere close to the huge plane trees lining London streets in case she set one off. It was irrational, she knew, when she was out most nights serving tea to firemen while raids were still on. It was a bit like not stepping on cracks in pavements or walking under ladders. Or like wearing Luc's ring for luck when she gave him hardly a thought from day to day. She was a fatalist who didn't want to put temptation in Fate's way.

There was soon another opportunity for good work. An old friend of her father's, a Canadian now living with his family outside London, had read the *Daily Mirror* report and got in touch. They were glad of his invitation to get away from the city to visit them in the leafier suburbs.

'Have you heard from Dad at all?'

'We had a telephone call to say he'd arrived in England and was planning to join up. That was more than a year ago. Nothing since then.'

'Perhaps he's been posted abroad somewhere.'

'Maybe, but he's getting a bit long in the tooth for active service, so I doubt it. He talked a lot about you, you know Elaine. If he gets in touch again, shall I tell him you're here in London and would like to see him?'

He could read her hesitation.

'Just tell him I'm alright, will you? I expect we'll be moving digs soon and I don't know where I'll be. Everything's so uncertain at the moment, isn't it?'

'Sure.' He knew when to take a different tack. 'So what are you doing with yourselves in London town?'

Elaine told him about her boring job, her more rewarding voluntary work and her recent *debut* into French expatriate society.

'You may be too busy but if you're interested, I may have something else for you.'

'Oh yes?'

'We've started a kind of club in town for our airmen. Nothing fancy, just tea and buns, somewhere for them to kill time, meet fellow Canadians, relax. We've got a few young lady volunteers but we could do with more. Pretty faces are good for morale but don't worry, the boys are pretty presentable, no riff-raff. You'll be perfectly safe. Come and help out from time to time when you have a spare couple of hours after work. What d'you think?'

She didn't hesitate.

'Sounds like fun. I'd love to.'

It wasn't so much a club, more a testosterone-charged tearoom. Instead of chintz and old ladies there were scrubbed tables, battered leather chairs and a fug of tobacco smoke. Above the buzz of laughter and lively conversation a young blonde woman with a modish 'do' beckoned to Elaine from behind the counter.

'Ah, our new volunteer! Glad you found us. Welcome to the madhouse. I'm Susan, by the way.'

'Hello, yes, I'm Elaine. I wasn't sure this was the right place. It's tucked away, isn't it?'

Heads turned, the buzz subsided as she squeezed around the tables.

'And what heavenly cloud did you just step off, Angel?'

Elaine could feel the blush rising from her neck.

'Give the girl a chance, lads. She's only been here ten seconds. Ignore them Elaine, they might go away eventually. Here's an overall. Shockingly unattractive, I'm afraid. We all dress like Mrs Mopp here, it helps keep these naughty boys at bay.'

'Don't believe a word of it, princess. We're perfect gents. Wouldn't lay a finger on ya.'

Susan smiled at the new girl. 'You'll get used to it. They're perfectly harmless, really. We'll have a cup of tea, then I'll show you the ropes.'

She did get used to it, and she loved the raucous atmosphere of the club. The boys were cheerful, polite and generally respectful. There was the odd joker, but she learned to swat away unwelcome attention with a smile and a firm refusal. Now in her nineteenth year, she could look after herself. Faces came and went. If someone hadn't come in for a while she soon learned not to ask why. She got plenty of offers, but took Susan's wise advice not to form close attachments with any of the boys. Susan conducted her own love life well away from the club. During quiet times they would share confidences over tea and cigarettes.

Susan Heath was the perfect example of independent womanhood to which Elaine aspired. She was perhaps a couple of years older and already renting her own flat. She obviously came from a comfortable middle-class family but supported herself from a good job in a reserved occupation. It was never clear to Elaine exactly what but she seemed to have a lot to do with Americans, and she enjoyed a social life full of dinner dances and shows in London's most glamorous and exclusive venues. In turn, Susan was enthralled by Elaine's background among the war graves and the story of her flight from Flanders.

Here was another new friend, someone she felt a connection with, one who boosted her confidence and made her feel welcome. Elaine now felt properly at home.

෬෨

If only things were as congenial in Fleet Street. Simone clearly resented Elaine's increasing independence but didn't seem prepared to carve out any for herself. She hated going out alone, was petrified during raids, and used her limited English to whinge about the hardships and privations that everyone else by now took for granted. This was wearing on Elaine and worse for the Ashfords, who had been kind hosts in difficult circumstances. Their house wasn't large and, though their daughters were away in the services, two extra mouths – even with their ration books – put an additional strain on the household. A sulky house guest was a dampener at any time but at a stage of the war when a positive outlook was seen as essential psychological armour for survival, it was deathly.

Mrs Ashford was frequently exasperated.

'Really, that girl is the absolute limit! Whose side is she on? Anyone would think Herr Goebbels had sent her over here specially to undermine morale. For goodness sake, Elaine, can't you do something with her?'

'She's been a bit spoilt I'm afraid. It's what sometimes happens when you're the youngest of nine. I'll talk to her.'

But Simone was unrepentant. She was sad and homesick, she missed her parents and familiar comforts. It didn't help that the boy she was sweet on had apparently disappeared into the maw of the army and hadn't been in touch. She felt cut off from everything she knew and held dear. Elaine did her best to cheer her up with small treats and trips out, but the problem was more intractable than just a passing mood: Simone was jealous. Elaine was everything she was not: outgoing, risk-taking, at ease with herself and others, and most annoying of all, apparently in love with London.

She had established a rapport with Susan Heath and her social circle who introduced her to the surprisingly active nightlife that flourished in London even through the worst of the Blitz. Though cinemas and theatres had closed at the start of hostilities, many had reopened in defiance of the bombing and there were more than enough places of entertainment open in the West End around Soho and Piccadilly that were below ground and considered immune from raids. Susan knew most of them.

In March 1941 they were invited out on the town by some boys from the airmen's club. Susan suggested the subterranean Café de Paris between Leicester Square and Piccadilly Circus, a large glitzy place, rather posh before the war but now full of uniforms and a lively mix of social classes. Ken 'Snakehips' Johnson's band was in residence and she loved the dancing to their brand of 'swing'. So it was disappointing to find, when they arrived at the street-level entrance, that too many others had the same idea. It was full to bursting. No one else was being let in.

'Never mind. There's plenty of other places round here. I know where we can go, it's just round the corner. And there goes the siren. Perfect timing.'

They enjoyed an evening's dancing a block away well below ground, music and jollity drowning out the sound of falling bombs and ack-ack guns above. They emerged in the early hours to pandemonium in Coventry Street, where stretchers and people in blood-stained evening dress were still being taken from a bombed building. The street door to the Café de Paris was no longer there. Almost as a reflex Elaine crossed herself.

'My God! That could have been us!'

'But I don't understand it, they always said it was the safest place to be in a raid, three storeys down ...'

A passing rescue-worker interrupted.

'Pure fluke, Miss. A high explosive went straight down a ventilation shaft. Went off right on the dance floor. It's a bloody mess down there. Johnson's had it I'm afraid. Apparently his head was blown clean off.'

'God, how awful! Is there anything we can do? I've got first-aid training.'

'Too late I'm afraid. Just thank your lucky stars it wasn't you down there tonight.'

She did. My number's not up yet then, she thought.

 ଚ∾

Life in Fleet Street was becoming increasingly untenable as the bombardment continued into the spring of 1941. The area was badly damaged and the Ashfords made the difficult decision to move further out, putting the girls on notice that they should find somewhere else to live. This posed a dilemma for Elaine, who still felt responsible for Simone yet was desperate to get away and live her own life.

She'd already had a tempting offer.

'Come and share with me in Bayswater. There's a broom cupboard of a room you could have. It's not exactly Knightsbridge, but it's cheap and handy for town and we could share the bills. It'd be fun. What do you say?'

Sharing with Susan was everything she could have dreamed of, but …

'What about Simone?'

Susan had heard all about Elaine's trials with her young aunt.

'The broom cupboard won't stretch to two I'm afraid and, honestly, do you really want her trailing after you forever? She's a big girl now. Isn't she older than you?'

'By eighteen months, though she acts as if she's about twelve sometimes.'

'There you are then. The decision's yours of course. The offer's there. Think about it.'

Elaine thought of nothing else and had almost made up her mind but she owed it to Simone to talk it through. Somewhere public was the place to have a calm and rational discussion about their futures. A favourite haunt of theirs for Saturday treats was the Lyons Corner House in Coventry Street, scene of the carnage she'd so recently escaped. It didn't cross her mind not to return: if you took that attitude you'd have to avoid practically every street in London. That Saturday it was packed as usual with summer dresses and service uniforms, cigarette smoke and chatter as if the tragedy a few doors away had never happened.

Elaine poured the tea and got down to the business in hand. French seemed the right medium for this private, and potentially difficult, conversation.

'We need to talk about somewhere else to live.'

'Have you found us something?'

It had to be done.

'I've had the offer of a flat-share in Bayswater.'

'Oh? That's good, then. What's Bayswater like? Better than Fleet Street I hope.'

'It's just me, Simone. The flat's only small. It's with my friend Susan at the club. I'll help you look in the evening papers for somewhere nice for yourself, perhaps nearby.'

The familiar pout.

'But I don't want to be by myself. You can't leave me, I can't manage on my own.'

'Don't be such a baby. Of course you can. We've been here a year now and your English is pretty good.'

'I know why you're doing this. You want to be on your own so you can have boyfriends there. How could you? It's shameful, what would Mama and Papa say? And what about poor Luc?'

Though their conversation was incomprehensible to many on nearby tables, its tone was unmistakable. Heads turned. A young chap in a uniform bearing the insignia of the Free French Army seemed particularly interested. At the next table an older man looked up briefly from his crossword. Being the centre of attention was the last thing Elaine wanted.

'Shush. Keep your voice down. People are looking.'

'I don't care! You're abandoning me. I'm an inconvenience to your love life!'

Elaine wanted to laugh, but she knew there was a grain of truth in Simone's hysterical accusation.

'Of course I'm not abandoning you. We'll still meet up and do things together.'

'It's not the same and you know it. You're so selfish, you don't care what happens to me, and you've never cared about our family!' By now she'd caught the eye of the young man in uniform. 'But if you don't, I do!' She flounced from her seat and went over to join him.

Elaine followed her. 'Simone, for goodness sake, what are you doing?'

The Free French soldier seemed glad to have the unexpected company of two young women who spoke his language, even though they seemed to be in the middle of a row. Gauloises were offered. Simone accepted with a coquettish smile. 'So sorry about that, Monsieur. My big sister and I are having a minor disagreement.' Elaine took a cigarette and looked at the ceiling: it was pointless to correct her. 'But I think you may be able to help us with something.'

'At your service, Mademoiselle.'

'This is the thing. We had to leave our home in Flanders when the Germans came last year. Our parents were left behind. We miss them terribly and want to make sure they're alright. Do you know how we can find out? Maybe get in touch with them?'

The young man looked thoughtful.

'The Red Cross, perhaps? An ordinary letter won't get through, I know that. Where are they?'

'We're not sure exactly. But they run the Palace Hotel in Poperinghe. They're called Marie and Egide Duponselle, and my name's Simone Duponselle.'

'Very good, Simone Duponselle. Where can I contact you if I find out more?'

It might have been an entirely innocent request but just in case, Elaine intervened. 'We don't have a permanent address at the moment. But you've been very helpful, thank you. We'll enquire with the Red Cross. Thanks for the cigarettes, we should be going now.'

He shrugged an *au revoir*, disappointed that the encounter had ended so abruptly, and they returned to their table to finish their tea and get the bill. On the way to the cash desk they passed the man with the crossword. Idly glancing down to see how far he'd got, some jottings in capitals caught Elaine's eye. By the side of the puzzle as if to crack an anagram or solve a clue, he'd written PALACE, POPERINGHE, DUPONSELLE.

∽

Within a matter of days, Elaine received a worrying telephone call from the wife of the Canadian who ran the airmen's club.

'You need to be careful. My husband is mad at you. He's heard you've been … you've been a bit too free with your favours with the boys at the club and now you're moving out to somewhere you can, let's say, entertain them. He won't want you there if you're going to behave this way. I must say I'm surprised at you, Elaine. I thought you would have more sense.'

'But it's not true! Who told him this?'

'Someone who knows you well enough to know your plans, obviously.'

'Well, I can assure you it's absolutely untrue. It was one of the first things Susan Heath said to me: "Don't get involved with the boys." And I haven't. It would be stupid, and I have more self-respect. And anyway, I'm engaged.'

Who would want to spread such horrible lies? In whose interests would it be if her reputation was discredited, she was removed from the club and from her friendship with Susan Heath?

This was the end. She'd tried hard to be a friend to Simone, perhaps her last link with the Duponselles, for Maman's sake if nothing else, though God knows it hadn't been easy. If Simone thought this was the way to keep them together, she had another think coming. The girl's vindictive betrayal of trust was an unexpected gift: there was now only one possible outcome.

The parting, when it came, was calm and greeted with sullen silence.

'I'm not going to have a row with you, and I don't want to hear your pathetic excuses. I just want you to know a couple of things. I've spoken to Dad's friend at the club. He accepts that what you told him was nothing but spiteful lies. And I'm moving to Susan's this afternoon. Goodbye, Simone and good luck. You're on your own now.'

By the time Elaine had gathered her few belongings together and said a grateful goodbye to the Ashfords she was no longer even angry. As she walked through the maze of courts for the last time, north to Chancery Lane Underground station, she felt light, relieved of a burden. Simone was now out of her life. She was being hard-hearted about it, she knew, but it was the only way. Simone had repaid her help and support by betraying her trust. That she could not forgive.

❧

Bayswater Court wasn't actually in Bayswater, though to be fair it was within striking distance of Whiteleys department store. Well to the north of the Bayswater Road, in what originally must have been a gracious stuccoed square, St Stephen's Gardens was now bedsit-land, bisected by a busy road, with the gardens at the opposite end. The Blitz had created rubble-filled holes where houses and whole terraces used to be but the west of the city had generally fared much better than the central area and the East End and it was possible, during daytime at least, to imagine there wasn't even a war on.

Elaine had pictured a lofty redbrick mansion block like those in the West End, or perhaps a modern Art Deco building, but Bayswater Court was in fact a grubby terrace of flat-faced early Victorian houses now carved into flats, the views uninspiring and the rumble of trains from the main line into Paddington a constant backdrop. Nevertheless, it was bliss. No. 24 was small but comfortable, with a rudimentary kitchen and its own bathroom.

'My dear, I couldn't share facilities. Think what you might find nestling near your toothbrush.'

Susan was a relaxed flatmate and entertaining company who welcomed the opportunity to share with Elaine the delights of the capital known only to knowledgeable habitués. 'Come on', she'd say, 'Jerry's napping tonight, let's go up West.'

The reason for Jerry napping became clear in June with news of the German invasion of the Soviet Union and the resistance being put up by Britain's new ally. It was the first good news of the war and especially welcome for Londoners to know that Hitler's attentions were for now mainly directed elsewhere. Cautious optimism spawned a new lightness of mood just as the summer warmth brought out a flush of cheerful vegetation on bombsites. Growing tall, delicate and pink from sturdy green leaves, *London Pride* bloomed everywhere among the rubble, to be forever yoked with Londoners' Blitz spirit in that summer's hit song by Noel Coward.

Relieved from the constant round of nightly raids, London resumed much of its colourful nightlife and the new flatmates took full advantage. The long working day was tiring and travelling from one side of London to the other was often a tedious business full of disruptions and diversions, but in the evenings and at weekends there was always the cheering prospect of a dinner dance or a nightclub outing on the arm of a man in uniform. Susan knew all the places favoured by the officer class and with her dark good looks, Elaine was never short of a presentable companion, but she chose carefully and her choices were respectful. Her uncle's cruel jibe and Simone's lies only made her more determined to prove them wrong. She was no good-time girl. She would make her own way in the world and keep her self-respect. At the same time, Luc and her promise to him now seemed to belong to another life altogether. She'd heard nothing from him though she'd been careful to leave forwarding addresses after every move. Their estrangement seemed complete.

America's entry into the war at the end of the year gave Britain a further boost and offered the girls at 24 Bayswater Court new social opportunities. Elaine knew and liked the Canadian lads at the club, but the Americans were a different sort and they didn't seem to share the same language. As more poured into the capital in the early months of 1942, she had her first exposure at a party organised by the Red Cross to welcome the new arrivals.

She was chatting to a small group of officers when one of them launched into a story about how he'd found himself at Waterloo Station late at night.

'So here I was, alone with a bunch of crazy-looking bums …' The officer stopped dead when he saw Elaine blanch with distaste. 'What did I say?'

They all turned to look at her with interested amusement. She blushed, not sure how to answer.

'Well, we don't usually talk about bums at cocktail parties.'

'Huh? Why not?'

'I'm not sure what it means in America but here it means … something different.'

She didn't know the American equivalent and she wasn't even sure of the polite word in English, so she patted her backside. To her consternation they roared with laughter, so different from her polite Canadians and painfully reserved Englishmen.

'Well, thank you Ma'am, for our first lesson in English etiquette. What did the great man say: "two nations divided by a common language"? How true. So, tell us about yourself, Miss Madden. Have you always lived in London?'

Embarrassment over, they were off. She had a great story to tell and, if asked, was proud to tell it.

'Gee, that's quite a tale. You must meet our Belgian producer friend, Henry. He'd love you.'

ഏ

There was something about London in wartime – of course she knew it at no other – that made life extraordinarily intense. To come to terms with the idea that you, your friend, lover or neighbour might not survive the next night, young people especially adopted a cheery fatalism and a relaxed attitude to risk. Life had to be lived to its limits, no opportunity wasted. But contrary to a general abandonment of moral standards Elaine found that – in the circles she moved in at least – the men she met were looking for fun, companionship, diversion, rather than sex. If offered it was unlikely to be refused, but relationships could be based on mutual attraction without ending up in bed with someone. She knew girls who slept around but most had steady, or at least serial, boyfriends – some of them, as she discovered, surprisingly well connected.

There was still gross inequality between the haves and the have-nots: money could buy everything and influence in high places still counted. But the 'equality of hardship' endured by Londoners during the Blitz and the coming together of all classes for voluntary work out of business hours provided previously unheard-of opportunity to meet all kinds of people.

Elaine kept up her WVS work with the air-raid wardens and her personal mission of mercy with her tea flasks. Though London's post-Blitz lull lasted for much of 1942 and 1943, the capital was still on full alert. She was now attached to a new warden station where another WVS girl had a boyfriend in the RAF.

This wasn't unusual, but the boyfriend was. Elaine met him quite a few times when he came to the station to meet the girl from duty. Introduced as Wing Commander Gibbs, he was a playboy charmer in his early thirties who flew Spitfires and was now something very high up in RAF Command. But he had a marked German accent and Elaine could have sworn she heard him speak Dutch – so similar to Flemish she could even understand much of what he was saying. He sometimes turned up with a suave French-speaking friend in the uniform of the Irish Guards who he simply introduced as 'John'. These visits were always accompanied by much giggling and nudging by the other girls and a certain amount of irritation by the wardens. It was obviously something more than a routine wartime romance.

She didn't know the girl well and didn't want to ask her direct, but she thought something wasn't quite right.

'Who *is* that man?' she asked one of the wardens. 'I can't believe his name is Gibbs.'

'They call it a *nom de guerre* I believe. Don't tell a soul, but he's really a prince.'

'You're pulling my leg.'

'As I live and breathe. Prince Bernhard of the Netherlands.'

'It can't be. He's married to Princess Juliana. They've got two little girls.'

'So I understand. But they're in Canada, aren't they, and while the cat's away …'

'But that's awful!'

'My dear girl, that's wartime for you. They don't make much effort to be discreet about it. Been going strong for some time, apparently. And while we're on the subject of minor continental nobs, that chap tagging along is the Grand Duke of Luxembourg. A pretty pair of chancers, if you ask me. Just think, if any of our Royals got up to those kinds of tricks …'

Elaine's eyes were opened. She'd been naive. London society was more intriguing and morally compromised than she'd realised.

∞

The Yanks' producer friend Henry was a charmer of an altogether different stripe. In his fifties, avuncular, portly and Jewish, he was Belgian by birth but American by immersion. Elaine understood that he was well known in Hollywood and was now in London making newsreels for use by the US Army. Her new American officer friends introduced them over lunch.

At Henry's insistence, they all went to an expensive restaurant in the Strand. Henry rubbed his hands in anticipation of a good meal.

'I love this place. Came here often before the war. So English. Great food and in portions a Belgian-American is used to!'

So the menu, when it came, was something of a disappointment.

'Hey, Henry. Mutton cutlets? Pig's trotters? I thought you said this was a decent place?'

'This can't be right. Where's the chariot of roast beef? And what's this five-shilling limit? A man can't eat for five shillings!'

Elaine was apologetic. 'I'm sorry, chaps. It's the rationing rules. Every restaurant is the same I'm afraid, whether you go to the Ritz or Woolworth's. Nobody can have more than three courses or spend more than five shillings a head.'

'Well, that's a damn shame. We'll be wasting away over here.'

'It's only fair. It would be horrible if some people could buy the best food whilst others went hungry. There'd probably be riots or something.'

'Yes, the revolting English. *Trotters a la mode* it is then. Waiter!'

Henry turned his full attention to their guest.

'Now then, my dear Miss Madden, how would you like to meet Clark Gable?'

She certainly would and within days she did. Gable was attached to the US Army Air Force and was in England making a propaganda film for the troops, *Combat America*. At Henry's spacious apartment in one of London's more fashionable squares, she was introduced to Hollywood's greatest star. Handsome and charming of course, but thinner than he appeared in his pre-war films. It was said he was still grieving the tragic loss of his wife Carole Lombard in an air crash the previous year. But now he was throwing himself into the war effort, in combat as well as on the screen.

They chatted briefly about the war – the news from North Africa that spring was hugely encouraging and everyone was starting to talk about a turning point in the Allies' fortunes. He asked, though not in an accusatory way, why she wasn't in uniform. Essential occupation, she said hurriedly, not wanting to go into detail about her humble job at British Relay. He tapped his nose. Something hush-hush perhaps? Oh no, she said, nothing like that. And then Henry came up and took him by the elbow to make a new introduction. The King of Hollywood gave her an apologetic smile and moved on.

Over those magical months of 1943, whenever a big American star was passing through London, Henry would telephone to invite her to a party at his flat to meet them. Susan was beside herself with envy: 'Clark Gable, Jimmy Stewart, Carmen Miranda! My autograph book has never been so star-studded. Whoever next, you lucky thing!'

Yes, she was a lucky thing. Her number still wasn't up, but quite apart from matters of life and death, she'd made her own luck by grasping every opportunity wartime life in London had to offer. There were so many interesting people passing through and she had been privileged to meet some of them. If her work life was boringly routine, her leisure hours were often an intoxicating mix of glamour and danger. It was a heresy to think it, but some days she wished the war could go on forever.

SEVEN

LONDON

JANUARY–FEBRUARY 1944

Throughout the Blitz and in the sporadic raids that followed, the British Relay Wireless building stood its ground, steadfast and stone-faced on the northern flank of Aldwych, where the City ends and the West End begins. Opposite, the BBC's Bush House suffered a couple of direct hits and the Gaiety Theatre on the western end, dark since the start of the war, was looking much the worse for wear, but her place of work remained stubbornly upright and open for business.

In the lonely fastness of what her elderly boss liked to call her 'domain', her erstwhile colleagues long called-up, Elaine was starting to think this was rather a pity. Though she loved being in town, she longed for something to happen that might offer release from her tedious daily intercourse with comptometer, invoice and ledger. A couple of stray incendiaries when the building was empty, perhaps?

The only alternative in prospect was a visit to the Holborn Labour Exchange to sign up for the British Army's Auxiliary Territorial Service. Now twenty, she'd already had two deferments. Her boss had told her not to worry. He wasn't letting her go just yet. She was absolutely indispensible to the war effort right there. How did they think they're going to get their precious radar parts if she didn't make out the chitties? It was alright for him, he'd been recalled from retirement like most of the few remaining men in the company. But now her luck was out. She'd had her call-up papers for a third time and there was no escape.

It wasn't that she didn't want to do her bit, but she knew so many ATS girls who'd got stuck in a storeroom in Aldershot or behind a typewriter in some anonymous office and were never heard of again. Four years into the war, her call-up options had narrowed; the ATS now had an insatiable appetite to draft every eligible girl left in London.

Their propaganda was everywhere. The latest poster all over the Tube showed a perfect English rose, the butter-wouldn't-melt type. That certainly wasn't her.

There had to be something else she could do. For much of her time in London, she'd been living a kind of half-life. The working day was dull and, as far as she could see, pointless in the fight against Hitler. She came alive at night, on duty during raids, aiding the injured and helping bombed out mothers with their children, taking flasks out to the firemen and serving tea and sympathy to the boys at the airmen's club. That was proper war work. Work with meaning and an outcome she could see in people's faces.

There was Bill, too. He was part of her freelance war effort. Starry-eyed, she loved meeting the celebrities who passed through Henry's apartment but Bill was her ballast. He kept her feet on the ground – well, on the dance floor in fact. He was a splendid dancer and good company; she always enjoyed their time together. They'd met at the airmen's club, quite soon after she started there.

'Any chance of a cup-a-coffee?' The young Canadian looked so hopeful, Elaine was almost sorry to have to disappoint him. He had such an open, appealing face.

'We don't serve coffee here I'm afraid, even if we could get it, which we can't. There's tea. Or there's cocoa, but I wouldn't recommend it. Tea's the lesser of the two evils on offer, believe me.'

'A mug of your British brew then, honey.' He winked. She was used to being chatted up by her customers, it was part of the reason she kept coming, but this chap appealed to her in a different way from the others.

That night was quiet and he was on his own so she chatted amiably back as she poured his tea from the big double-handled teapot.

'Just arrived in London?'

'Well, someplace called Northolt, which is out the back of beyond.'

There it was, that distinctive way they say 'out' that sounded more like 'oat', that she quickly learned distinguished Canadians from the Yanks.

'I got a lift to a station at the end of the red subway line. It's taken me several days to get here, which is why I'm dying of thirst.'

'Oh yes?' she said, with a sceptical smile. 'And you'll be starving too, after your long journey, so you'd better have an Eccles cake.'

'What in the hell are Eccles and are they safe to eat?'

'Perfectly. Though these have been hanging about a bit. Probably best to dunk them first.'

'Dunk them?'

'Yes, you …'

He interrupted her.

'It's OK, only teasing. I know all this stuff. Mom came from Bolton. I'm Bill, by the way, Bill Hardy.' He stretched his hand over the counter. Elaine took it.

'Very nice to meet you, Bill. I'm Elaine.'

There was only a momentary pause.

'Say, Elaine, I don't suppose you ever …'

'Almost never', she cut him off, laughing.

He smiled, a nice open smile, she thought.

'I'm looking for a dance partner, not a girlfriend. My lovely fiancée back home would take that amiss. The fleshpots of Northolt look mighty tempting, but I'm going to be faithful to her.'

It wasn't often they told her about their fiancées within two minutes of meeting, and he sounded sincere.

'Well, I could perhaps make myself available to accompany you to the occasional hop. To protect you from the rampant hordes of British woman-hood. Nothing more, mind.'

'Absolutely.'

'Then it's a deal, Bill Hardy. That'll be tuppence for the Eccles cake.'

So whenever he was on leave he came into the club and if she was on duty they would make a dance date. He taught her to jitterbug, she taught him the rather more sedate Lambeth Walk and together they learned the Palais Glide. There was nothing more to it, but they enjoyed each other's company. As she got to know him, he encouraged a correspond-ence with his fiancée. This reassured them all: Bill that she knew he was behaving himself; his fiancée that he had some warm but unthreatening female company; and Elaine that they all knew there was nothing in it but friendship. Elaine wasn't a great letter writer, but when she did settle down to it, her letters were long, descriptive and frank. No letters to Bill's fiancée survive but, during the sporadic raids of 1943, they might have read something like this:

Darling Cora,

I'm such a terrible correspondent, I know it's been months since I last wrote, but I have a pretty good excuse – Jerry has been playing up again and much of my so-called "spare" time has been taken up with what we Londoners call our "war work". That is, helping to clear up the mess he makes when he sends his bombers over to give us something to do with our evenings … but it isn't all blood and gore and tragedy by any means. We are determined not to let him spoil our fun. Imagine if you can, our once-fine capital city, now a sad landscape of smouldering bomb sites like rotten teeth among the lovely old build- ings. At night, we go about like moles in the black-out, feeling our way in the dark. But underground, it's a different world! Not the dirty old Tube where we go to shelter from raids, but all the lovely places where Bill and I go to keep our spirits up. Every big hotel in town has its ballroom below ground and some of the best clubs and dance places are several storeys under the street. Here there's light and music and laughter and to-hell-with-Jerry … Bill is such a sweetie, you are a very lucky girl and I'm doing my best to keep him safe for you. I'm not dating at the moment, but I'm on the lookout for a good'un …

There may have been no one special, but dates were never in short supply, her flatmate Susan's close connections to the higher echelons of the US military saw to that. The one Susan arranged in the early weeks of 1944 was especially welcome as Elaine was anxious and unsettled about her call-up, but otherwise, it didn't promise to be out of the ordinary in any way.

'By the by, I've fixed us up a double date with Army Man for tomorrow night'.

'Oh, good-oh! Let's hope we get taken somewhere smart and expensive. I've lived off toast all week.'

They loved the US officer they called Army Man. His no-strings rela- tionship with Susan suited them both and Elaine had the bonus of his excellent company, his good taste and a succession of presentable escorts.

On this dreary January night, after a mediocre film at the Empire Leicester Square's early house, they hurried through the chilly blackout to Piccadilly Circus, so different now from the vivid picture, *The Heart of the Empire*, she remembered from her classroom wall in Ypres. Now the famous neon advertisements for Wrigley's and Bovril and Gordon's gin were mere ghostly tracery against darkened buildings. Traffic, such as it was, crawled blind around the boarded-up stump where once Eros danced.

They arrived for supper at the Criterion, its warm gold-leafed interior an opulent contrast to the bleak cityscape outside.

'It feels like a Sultan's boudoir', said Elaine as they took their seats beside a mirrored alcove.

'Shouldn't that be Sultana? I'm not sure Sultans have boudoirs.' Even US Army majors from Albuquerque could be surprisingly erudite.

'Or a Raisin, perhaps?' the New Man chipped in. They all laughed politely. He was struggling to match his buddy's practised ease with these two attractive British women. 'So', he turned rather too quickly to Elaine, 'what do you do?'

'Oh, nothing much. I work for a wireless company off the Strand as a stores clerk. It's pretty frightful. I could bore you for hours with my wide knowledge of valves and modulators.'

'Is that what they call a Reserved Occupation then? I'm surprised you girls aren't in uniform.'

Susan took a sharp intake of breath: 'Ooh, careful. Touchy subject.'

Elaine smiled apologetically.

'I've just had my call-up – for the third time. But I'm damned if I'm going to go into the ATS, which is about the only choice I've got left at this stage of the game. I really don't want to spend the duration stuck out in some godforsaken army camp somewhere. Give me a desk job here in good old Firebomb Alley any day.'

'Hey, such passion! But don't you feel you ought to be doing something more useful for king and country?'

His tone, she thought, was unnecessarily provocative and it chafed against her unsettled mood. She rose to the bait.

'You bet I do! I'd *love* to do something more useful. After all, French is practically my mother tongue and I speak Flemish and Dutch as well.

Surely those skills must be needed somewhere? There *must* be something more I could be doing for the war effort. I've got a reasonable brain and I really do want to help win this war. I'll consider anything, but I'm damned if I'm going into the bloody ATS!'

A WAAF at the next table turned round and smirked at her. Elaine blushed, embarrassed.

'Sorry chaps. It sounds so ungrateful, I know. We're jolly lucky to be here in this marvellous place, alive and in such good company, and here am I moaning about poor me. Give me a cigarette, someone. I need something to shut me up.'

New Man proffered his pack of Lucky Strike and Susan came to the rescue.

'Look! Rabbit pie on the menu! Let's order – I'm famished.'

'Great idea', said Army Man, and the evening proceeded on an altogether lighter note.

The following Sunday evening, there was a telephone call to the flat. Elaine picked up the receiver.

'Bayswater 0011.'

'Hi there!'

Only Army Man said 'Hi there!' on the telephone without announcing himself. 'We sure enjoyed your company on Friday. Hope you both had a good time?'

'We did, thank you very much. Though I think I spoiled it rather at the restaurant. Never mind, we still had a lovely evening. I'll get Susan for you …'

'It was you I called for, Elaine. Can you meet me for lunch on Wednesday?'

This was unexpected. She had to be clear about the rules of engagement.

'You mean with Susan, or just me?'

'Just you. Don't worry, this is business. There's something I want to talk to you about.'

'Well, I only have half an hour for lunch. It'll have to be somewhere near Aldwych.'

'The bar at the Waldorf then. A quarter after one. Don't be late.'

Intrigued but uncomfortable, she was there early, settling herself in a corner where she hoped she'd be unobtrusive. Without the protection of a man or a uniform, there was always the risk of unwanted attention. An unaccompanied civilian woman in the bar of a London hotel was fair game. He arrived, apologising, a few minutes late.

'Sorry. I had calls to make.' He lit her cigarette and his own. 'Thanks for coming. This won't take long. Gin and It?' He signalled to the boy waiter and carried straight on. 'What you were saying on Friday …'

'Oh, that. I'm so sorry. What an embarrassment I am, you can't take me anywhere.'

He ignored her apologies.

'Are you serious about wanting to do something useful?'

No flippancy now.

'Deadly.'

'And you would be prepared to consider anything?'

'Absolutely.'

'What about going back to Belgium?'

Well of course she'd love to go back to Belgium when it was all over, if only for extended visits.

'Certainly.'

'Then I might be able to help. Your languages are wasted at that wireless place and we need good people now more than ever to finish this thing off. Let me talk to some people. There may be diplomatic issues. Susan tells me you have something of a chequered background. Are you Belgian or British, or what?'

'British. Through my father. He was – is – Australian. My mother was Flemish. She died when I was ten.'

Their drinks and a plate of delicate, barely filled sandwiches arrived and she told him something of her story, how she'd grown up in Ypres and escaped with the BEF through Dunkirk in 1940. He listened carefully, quietly. This wasn't an interrogation. When she'd finished, there was a thoughtful silence. She was even more intrigued now.

'What did you have in mind?'

'Don't know yet. Might come to nothing. I'll be in touch.'

As she crossed Kingsway on her way back to work, she wondered what it might mean. What were these 'diplomatic issues'? Was she being lined up for a job at the American Embassy? That would certainly be better than the ATS but it still wasn't quite … well, what *was* she looking for? She couldn't honestly say. She only knew that she was marking time. Her destiny lay elsewhere.

ᕢᕣ

A week later, she found herself in what had recently become dubbed Little America. Since early 1942, the US military had colonised most of the gracious neo-Georgian buildings around Mayfair's Grosvenor Square. Today she was meeting Army Man at No. 20, diagonally opposite the US Embassy at No. 1, across what used to be pleasant gardens but, since the Blitz, was a scruffy collection of huts housing a barrage balloon station.

The lobby of No. 20 bustled with military types. Elaine waited as instructed, admiring their stylish uniforms and confident manner. The Americans always seemed so much taller and better looking than the British, never mind the Belgians. She was aware too of covert but admiring glances coming back in her direction. Army Man appeared, waving from the back of the crowd. Taking her elbow, he escorted her smartly back out into the square.

'What's the matter? Did I cause an international incident or something?'

'We're taking a walk. Just half a block.'

There was no brass plate outside 70 Grosvenor Street to indicate what might lie within. On an upper floor Army Man knocked on a numbered door and ushered her into a smoky office where another American uniform rose from his desk with outstretched hand to greet her. With a whispered 'good luck' Elaine's escort retreated.

'Lieutenant-Colonel ...'

She didn't catch the name. Or perhaps he didn't say it clearly enough to catch.

'Miss Madden, pleased to make your acquaintance. Please sit. So. You're keen to help us win the war. I'm told you're a linguist.'

'Well, you had to be where I grew up, in Flanders, or you didn't survive.'

He asked her some not-very-testing questions, some of them in less than perfect French, to which she replied, she thought, satisfactorily. Then he asked: 'Have you heard of the US Office of Strategic Services?' He made it sound as exciting as the Ministry of Paper Clips.

'No, I don't think so. Should I have?'

'No. That's just fine. We're recruiting for some specialised work, certainly using your languages, perhaps with travel overseas. I think you might fit the bill, Miss Madden, but I shall have to clear it with the Brits before we go any further. We don't want to be accused of poaching their talent, do we?' He laughed. Elaine laughed politely too, but wondered what he meant. 'The Brits' hadn't been interested in her for the past four years so why would they be bothered now?

Forty minutes later she emerged, puzzled but excited, into the streets of Mayfair and began the walk home to Bayswater Court to save her Tube fare.

It didn't take very long before she got another call.

'It's no-go with OSS I'm afraid.' She had to stop for a moment to understand what Army Man was saying: the Americans didn't want her. 'Those diplomatic issues got in the way. But we're not done yet. There's someone else who might be interested in you. I've arranged a meeting. You should get on just fine. A charming chap, as the Brits would say. He's a Belgian.'

So, late on another winter afternoon she found herself in another gracious square – this time in Belgravia. She knew the Belgian embassy and its government in exile were around here somewhere and she eventually found them in a grand stucco mansion at the junction of Belgrave Place and Eccleston Street.

The Belgian was indeed charming. He introduced himself in French by saying she didn't need to know his name at this stage, but that he held the rank of major in the British Army. The interview continued in French, moved to vernacular Flemish until, after thirty minutes or so of intensive questioning about her knowledge of Belgium and the Duponselles in Poperinghe (he didn't seem at all interested in her father's side of the family) he said in perfect Received Pronunciation: 'Alright then, Miss Madden, very good. I expect you'd like to continue in English?'

She was surprised to find that she enjoyed talking about Ypres and Poperinghe in the languages of her childhood and adolescence. It brought the landscape and her old friends back to her. She suddenly saw herself with her father in the Ramparts cemetery overlooking the moat.

'I really don't mind. Yes, if you like.'

'So. When the chips are down, are you British or are you Belgian?'

If this was a trick question, she'd have to fall headlong unthinking into it because the response was immediate, intuitive.

'I'm British. I mean, I've always felt British, and that's what it says on my papers. There never has been any doubt. I grew up in Flanders, but that's slightly different. Of course I feel devastated that Jerry is there now, stamping his jackboots all over it. When I think about the Menin Gate and all our war cemeteries it makes my blood boil … We must kick them out as soon as possible. And we're working as one with the Belgians to do that, aren't we?'

The major looked inscrutable.

'Quite so.'

She had no idea whether this was the right answer, but it was *her* right answer. She couldn't dissemble on something as fundamental as her allegiance. It was all rather frustrating, this interview business. This one, like the last, gave her no clues at all about what she was being interviewed for. The major continued.

'We'll be making enquiries about your family in Belgium and as soon as we have the answers, we'll be in touch with you. It's alright to telephone you at this Bayswater number, is it?'

And then she was out again into the sharp cold of the February evening.

Susan was as intrigued as she was by the recent turn of events, but at least she had heard of the Office of Strategic Services.

'It's to do with intelligence and security but goodness knows what they actually do. Spying perhaps? Your mysterious Belgian must be involved with a similar outfit on the British side. It's got to be pretty hush-hush if they won't even tell you their names.'

'Yes, that is a bit unnerving. And why do they need to know so much about my family in Poperinghe? I don't even know if they're still there. Or even if Poperinghe is still there, come to that.'

'All will be revealed, my dear, in the fullness of time.'

'It had better be sooner than that – I've been summoned to the Labour Exchange next week. This is serious, Susan. I'm about to be press-ganged into the ATS.'

∽

Away from the gracious squares of Mayfair and Belgravia, in an anonymous office block on Baker Street along the road from the fictional abode of Sherlock Holmes, Major Ides Floor congratulated the newly appointed Head of the Special Operations Executive's Belgian Section.

'Lieutenant-Colonel Amies, sir. Or would you prefer "T"?'

A large, suave Englishman in his mid-thirties with perfectly slicked-down hair and a uniform whose fit was so immaculate it must surely have come fresh from Savile Row, stood to greet his Belgian colleague.
'Hardy will be perfectly serviceable Ides, as it always has been. Do sit.'

Amies opened a silver cigarette case as Floor continued.

'Excellent news though, that you've been properly made up. You really should have got it when Johns was brought in.'

'We both know, dear boy, that Johns was a first-class "T". I was only ever keeping the seat warm for him.'

'Nevertheless, you've got the seat back now. You're head of the firm's Belgian operations.'

Amies sighed. 'Yes. I suppose they thought a suburban frock-maker perfect for the job of fomenting death and destruction across north-western Europe … But I couldn't have achieved such dizzy heights without your good offices, smoothing the way with our colleagues in the Belgian Sûreté at Belgrave Square. Now then, what news on recruitment?'

'Tricky. We've been through every expat in the country, every last man in the Belgian military, we're even reduced to trawling Boy Scout troops. We've pretty much exhausted the usual channels in our search for suitable agents.'

'And now you're going to tell me about the unusual ones?'

Floor looked apologetic.

'I suggest it's time we consider recruiting women.'

Leaning back in his chair, Amies blew smoke at the ceiling.

'Oh dear, I thought this was coming. Go on then.'

'You know F Section has successfully deployed women agents since '41. They've proved their mettle in the field. Some have been quite magnificent in the face of danger. With the invasion coming up, we desperately need more people on the ground to support the Resistance networks. They needn't all be men. And women … how can I put this? … have their own distinctive talents.'

Fully engaged now, Amies leaned forward, elbows on the desk, cigarette between clasped hands.

'God knows we need more bods – but France is a different kettle entirely. Belgium is small and exposed and crawling with bloody Gestapo. Far fewer places to hide. We've managed without the ladies till now. I'm windy about women in the field, Ides. They're a liability.'

Floor raised an eyebrow: 'No more of a liability than some of the men turned out to be.'

How careless of him. He'd walked into that one. They both knew what and to whom Floor was alluding. Incompetence, stupidity, venality, betrayal: T Section of the Special Operations Executive had seen them all since 1940.

Amies relaxed.

'Alright. Fair point. You've almost convinced me. Who have you got?'

'Enquiries are continuing, but we've just had a clean report from MI5 on a rather promising girl I saw a fortnight ago. Grew up in Ypres, Belgian mother, British schooling … Australian father, but we shouldn't hold that against her. Not twenty-one till May, so we wouldn't be able to send her out till then. One of their chaps heard her and another girl in the Coventry Street Corner House apparently, asking a Free French chappie about contacting their people in Poperinghe. She's keen, no doubting where her allegiances lie. Plucky kid. Seems she dressed up as a Tommy and escaped with the BEF at Dunkirk.'

'Boudicca in battledress, how thrilling. Who referred her?'

'Grosvenor Street.'

'Ah, our esteemed colleagues in the OSS. So they have their uses after all. Attractive?'

'I should say so. Dark, petite, lovely girl.'

Amies brushed an imaginary speck from the uniform he'd skilfully adapted by his own hand to suit his particular requirements and impeccable taste.

'Alright then. Bring her in.'

EIGHT

SOUTHERN ENGLAND

MARCH–JUNE 1944

In early March 1944 Elaine had a call from the Belgian major, who now identified himself as Ides Floor. He asked her to meet him at an address in Baker Street close to the headquarters of department store Marks and Spencer. Perhaps now she might find out what kind of organisation she'd be working for and what she'd be doing. When she got to the heavily sandbagged address, there was no name plaque on the door, but the reception area was bustling with people in and out of uniform.

'I have an appointment with Major Floor.'

'Identity card, and sign in, please.'

'I know this sounds a silly question, but where am I?'

The woman at the desk referred to her male colleague who gave her the briefest of nods.

'This is the Inter-Services Research Bureau.'

It sounded only marginally more interesting than the British Relay Wireless Company.

The Belgian officer greeted her formally with a small bow.

'We meet again, Miss Madden. Do make yourself comfortable.'

A meaningless courtesy: the room was bare except for a desk, a telephone and two functional chairs of the sort one would expect to find in a church hall.

'Well, we've made some enquiries about you and your family in Poperinghe and everything seems to be in order. We'd now like to put you through some further tests, if we may, to see if you're suitable for the kind of work we have in mind. This will involve a short residential course. Mostly practical, I think you'll enjoy it. You'll be with French-speaking Belgians and some classes will be conducted in French. But first we have to get you into uniform. We'll be enrolling you in the FANYs.'

'The Fannies?'

'The First Aid Nursing Yeomanry.'

'Oh.' This wasn't what she imagined at all. Perhaps there'd been a mistake or some misunderstanding. She tried to overcome a rising panic. 'Well, I suppose I have my Red Cross training in first aid and home nursing … I didn't realise … What exactly will I be doing?'

Floor laughed, as if she had been the one who'd misunderstood.

'You might well find your first aid comes in useful, but it isn't the object of this exercise. These days FANYs do practically everything *except* nursing, but don't worry too much about that. The work you'll be assessed for is very specialised and will take particular skills and aptitudes. Perhaps above all, it takes a particular state of mind … I'm sorry not to be able to give you more precise detail at this point in the proceedings. You'll understand why later. But I can assure you that, if you pass the course, and the training that follows it, you'll be doing absolutely vital work for the war effort, for Britain and for Belgium.'

This sounded more like it. But she still had only the sketchiest idea of what she'd volunteered for.

'Take this chit and pick up your uniform from the outfitter in Piccadilly. There'll be more kit when you arrive for your course. You'll get another call shortly instructing you where and when to report. We tend not to write things down here, so any future instructions will be verbal only. And from now on for reasons of security whilst you're with us you will not use your own name. You'll be known as Elaine Meeus, and you will use *only* this name, do you understand? Don't share with other students or anyone on your course any details of your own life, family or background. And finally, please don't discuss with anyone else where you've been, where you're going, or what you'll be doing.'

He stood up and offered his hand.

'Well, Miss Meeus, good luck.'

What was there to discuss with anyone else? What little she'd learned from Major Floor made no sense at all.

Lillywhites department store on Piccadilly Circus was familiar to her. She'd never had cause to go inside, but the Circus was a favourite haunt from her first arrival in London and she knew every well-worn inch, hoarding and shop window of it by heart. The uniform, to her surprise, was beautiful. She'd imagined something serge, scratchy and hideous. Instead she was fitted with a smart single-breasted barathea jacket with a wide leather Sam Browne belt. The assistant affixed a burgundy pip to each shoulder.

'What are they for?'

'You're a cadet ensign, Madam.'

'Really? What does that mean?'

She seemed surprised.

'Don't you know? It's like a lieutenant. You're a junior officer in training, Madam.'

A commission in prospect already, and she'd only just joined the service. This was an unexpectedly encouraging start. Khaki shirt and tie, a nice plain skirt, a peaked cap that didn't obscure her lovely dark hair too much and sensible shoes completed the dress uniform, the distinctive round FANY badge on cap and lapels. She looked at herself in the fitting room mirror: a slight girl in civvies transformed into a purposeful young woman, proud and prepared to serve her country.

'And finally the trousers and Aertex shirts, Madam. For the training, I understand. Sign here, please.'

'Yes, of course. Thank you for your help.'

The older woman, grey and professional, handed over the packages at last and looked her in the eye. 'Good luck, dear.'

That was the second time today. She must need it.

She'd hardly struggled 500 yards up Regent Street with her Lillywhites parcels when she saw an excited young WAAF making a beeline for her.

'I don't believe it! Elaine Madden!'

She recognised her old school friend Dorothy Charlton at once, though it must have been more than five years since they last met in Ypres.

'Dorothy! How lovely to see you in London! And in uniform, too!'

'Are you in a hurry? Have you got time for a cuppa? Such a lot's happened since the Memorial School and I want to know *every single detail*. I've got a million things to tell you. Have you seen anything of Rene?

I hear she's got a little hairdressers in Sussex with her sister … You look as if you're about to expire under that load. You *have* been on a spree, I wish my coupons stretched that far. You'll have to show me *everything* you've bought.'

'Oh, it's boring things, nothing special. There's a Kardomah round here somewhere. I've got half an hour if you have.'

'Come on then, give me some of those parcels. I can't wait to hear what you've been up to.'

They settled in the café and Elaine lit their cigarettes while they waited for their tea.

'So you managed to get out of Belgium in time then?'

'Yes, we got away with other war graves people from Poelkappelle. Pretty hairy on the road to the coast I can tell you. Stukas all the way. People shot up and mutilated. Ghastly. Then some rusty tub of a boat across the Channel. Mines and yet more bloody Stukas. It's a miracle we got here at all. We had to ditch our papers at the dockside and of course we were treated like spies when we arrived, rather than refugees. It's been quite tough for Mum and Dad since we got here though the Commission has helped where it can. I joined up and both my sisters are in the ATS. What about you?'

She didn't know why, but Elaine hesitated. Perhaps it was Major Floor's injunction to be discreet, or recalling Dorothy's delight in gossip and exaggeration when they were at school.

'Oh, I managed to get away with my aunt, Simone. Much the same way as you. But tell me what you're doing in the WAAF. You're looking so smart.'

'*Well!*' She moved closer, conspiratorial. It was obvious she was dying to disclose some great confidence. 'I've been doing weather reports till now, but something rather exciting has cropped up. I shouldn't be telling you this, but I'm about to be transferred to a different sector. Frightfully hush-hush.'

'Really? Do tell!' The more Elaine could engage her about this secret, the less she'd be tempted to share her own. Dorothy prattled on with some story about being sent to France to help the Resistance. Really, it sounded so outlandish she doubted it could be true. She feigned fascination until Dorothy eventually ran out of steam.

'Anyway, what about you, Elaine? You can't have spent the whole war shopping, surely? How on earth have you managed to dodge being called up?'

There was a new edge to Dorothy's tone that grated. The temptation to match her friend's ridiculous boasting was almost too much. She hoped Major Floor wasn't listening.

'I haven't, actually. I've just signed up with the FANYs. They're sending me on a training course for some kind of special assignment.' She pointed to the packages. 'I've just been to pick up my new uniform.'

'Oh yes? How exciting. What kind of special assignment?'

'I don't know. Haven't had my marching orders yet.' She couldn't resist teasing Dorothy just a little: 'Maybe it's something frightfully hush-hush!'

She looked at her watch, took a last gulp of tea and stubbed out her cigarette. 'Goodness, is that the time? It's been marvellous catching up, but I really have to go. We must do this again.'

'You can't go yet, you haven't told me whether you're engaged or married or …' A quick peck on the cheek, '… and your address?'

But Elaine was already halfway to the door.

On the tube she had to stand all the way to Notting Hill Gate surrounded by her packages. Tired but exhilarated, she rehearsed her eventful day. At last she was on the way to her destiny, whatever that might turn out to be. But she'd passed the first small self-imposed test. She'd managed to divulge far less to her inquisitive school friend than she otherwise might have done under normal circumstances. It was naughty of her to rush out like that without leaving even a telephone number, but Dorothy was a careless talker. Elaine didn't trust her with details of her mildly interesting social life, let alone speculation about a future assignment of potential national importance.

∽

On 17 March Elaine and an assortment of Belgian nationals were disgorged from the back of a covered army truck. Judging by the length of the journey from their pick-up point in central London, she guessed they were still somewhere in the Home Counties but she wasn't familiar enough with southern England to pick out any landmarks, and in any case they could see little from the back of the truck. Her dozen or so companions were men of all types, from teenagers who looked barely old enough to be in the services to men in their thirties and forties who'd obviously seen action. The young men were excitable; those older and wiser were subdued and serious.

On the journey they'd exchanged cigarettes and first names. No one seemed to know more than she did about what was going to happen over the next four days. Or if they did they weren't telling. There was general agreement though that they faced a test and it was vital not to be found wanting.

It was a relief to get out in the air, and what sweet air it was after the dirt and smoke of the capital. They found themselves delivered to the rear service entrance of a large Queen Anne-style mansion, isolated and surrounded by woodland. Led up the servants' back stairs to the upper floors by an army sergeant, the students were gradually siphoned off to different sleeping quarters. Elaine was pleased to be installed in a small, pleasant room to herself under the eaves.

Dumping her suitcase on the bed, she went straight to the window, pulled back the chintz curtains and threw up the sash. The view made her gasp. The house was on high ground overlooking miles of wooded green countryside and patchwork fields, not flat and featureless like Flanders but rolling and full of budding variety in the early spring sunshine. A glinting sliver of light in the far distance might even be the sea. She tried to visualise the map of the British Isles from her old classroom. From the position of the sun she knew she was looking south over a view that stretched perhaps as far as the English Channel.

Camellias and clumps of waving daffodils dotted grounds that sloped gently away below, grounds so neglected they'd almost returned to the wild. She took in the scene and breathed in the air. This was the English countryside she'd only known before through poetry and picture books. The real thing was so much more beautiful it made her want to cry.

Within an hour of unpacking she was in her training kit with the other students, crawling on her stomach under yards of rope netting whilst an instructor held a stopwatch and yelled at her to hurry up. Then there was a high wall to climb up and jump down to the other side. Elaine stood at the bottom, wondering how she'd ever get her small five-feet-two frame up it, let alone over the other side. The instructor was watching to see how she'd cope. She looked appealingly at the two men coming up behind her and they obliged with a leg-up. She scrambled to the top of the wall and, screwing up her courage, jumped into the abyss, praying that her weak ankles would stand the shock. Really, this was just like their trek with the BEF lads across the flooded fields to Dunkirk, with army sergeants shouting at them instead of Stuka fire. What on earth could this have to do with using her languages and helping the war effort?

At the culmination of the assault course, wobbly from exertion and in some pain, she arrived with the others in a thickly wooded area of the grounds. She felt rather faint – they'd had nothing to eat since arriving in the late morning – but she'd managed with a little help to keep up with the men so far and she wasn't about to give them the advantage now.

The instructor pointed to a platform perched high up in a tree. They were to clamber up a rope ladder and convey themselves to another platform in a nearby tree by any means available. The available means weren't visible from the ground and when she got up there, they weren't very visible from the platform either. She stood there with the instructor, flummoxed for a moment. Then she saw a knotted rope swinging gently from a branch just out of reach.

'You mean …?'

'I'm just an observer. It's you that has to make the decision.'

Steadying herself and her swimming head, she concentrated. This wasn't the most difficult decision she'd ever had to make or even the most dangerous. Someone would surely be there to catch her, unlike when she walked the plank on the Dunkirk mole.

She wasn't prepared to risk making a lunge for the rope so, breaking off a nearby branch, she reached out to hook it towards her and succeeded at the third attempt. The instructor showed her how to get the best grip on the rope with her small hands and off she went, landing heavily on the far platform at the feet of a large man in army fatigues.

'Not bad, Miss Meeus. I've seen plenty of men do worse. Well done. Now, down you go for your dinner.' He winked as he helped her on to the rope ladder. At the bottom she collapsed, crying now – of pain, exhaustion and relief. A fellow student offered her a hand up.

'Come on, you need a drink.'

Yes, she could do with a drink but she needed a bath more. As the only woman on the course, she had the privilege of her own bathroom. The men, she discovered, were sharing up to four in a room, with a bathroom between them all. That bath, albeit in the regulation maximum six inches of lukewarm water, was the most welcome she'd had since stepping off the boat from Dunkirk four years ago. Refreshed but still aching, she came down the handsome main staircase and into the drawing room to join the others for pre-dinner drinks.

There was certainly drink to be had, and in enough quantity and variety to outdo anything she'd seen in any of her family's establishments in peacetime. Deciding she might as well carry on trying new things, she ordered a whisky and joined her fellow students. A surprisingly large measure arrived by her side, with a jug of water. Her father always drank his whisky neat but after trying both she decided the dilute version was for her. The domestic staff, of whom there seemed to be plenty, were all men in army uniform; she hadn't yet seen another woman.

Her fellow students were tired but in good spirits. One or two of the older men were reserved, even taciturn, but an *esprit de corps* was fast developing. They knew little or nothing about the organisation that had brought them together, nor what they would be asked to do in its name, but they all shared the same cause, to free their homeland from the Nazi oppressor. For Elaine, perhaps the only Briton by birth among them, the allegiance to homeland wasn't split, but doubly fierce. She would fight for Belgium's liberation as hard as anyone, but she was fighting for her spiritual home, king, country and Empire, too.

'*Sante.*'

'*Gezondheid.*'

'What shall we drink to?'

'To survival!'

'Yes', said Elaine holding up her glass. 'Survival and success!'

The following morning after a pre-breakfast run, it was a relief to be in a classroom rather than swinging from tree to tree in the grounds, but the 'lessons' didn't give many further clues as to their future role. They started with a battery of written tests and puzzles overseen by an army captain with horn-rimmed specs and a clipboard who came round looking over their shoulders. It was like being back in school. There was a version of something called Kim's Game that she loved from her childhood where you had to remember items on a tray that were removed one by one; they were asked to look for patterns in sequences of numbers, letters and symbols; they watched a piece of film and had to answer questions on it after doing something completely different for an hour or so. Then there was the play-acting where they had to act out situations with a moral dilemma and decide how they should end: one involved having to make a split-second decision about whether to shoot someone. There was no question. Her own life was in danger: it's him or me.

She enjoyed the tasks they were set but couldn't decide whether she'd ended up in a commando school or a psychiatric unit. The day was full of physical and mental challenges, punctuated only by good solid meals and, in the evenings, flowing quantities of alcohol, in which they were joined by their instructors, transformed from shouting tyrants into convivial company. If this was a loony bin, it was a very congenial one.

Succeeding days were as full, with PT before breakfast, medical checks, then more practical and written exercises. They were taken out into the countryside and had to find their way back with only a sketchy map. They were put into small groups to improvise a bridge across a small river – with no abandoned lorries to hand this time – and had to 'tail' a 'suspect' without being detected. It was all very strange and rather fun.

She found that she really enjoyed cracking simple codes and having her first go at sending and receiving Morse code. At the Memorial School she'd always thought it unfair that the boys in Mr Allen's class were taught Morse whilst Mrs Allen took the girls for tedious things like cooking and embroidery: she was hopeless at both. She tapped away on the dummy key, taking to it more readily than the other novices perhaps because of her familiarity with the comptometer at St Helen's and British Relay Wireless.

On the final evening when they could relax at last, her Morse instructor sought her out in the drawing room.

'Ah, Miss Madden, our Morse star!'

A short deliberate pause before she looked up at him.

'I'm sorry, sir. Do you mean me? My name's Meeus, not Madden.'

'Of course. Must have been thinking of someone else. Well, Miss Meeus, how have you enjoyed our little course?'

'Apart from my ankles being shot to pieces, I've enjoyed it very much, thank you, sir. Though I'm still not sure what and who it's all in aid of.'

'That's excellent, because you're not supposed to. What you've been doing here for the past few days isn't training for what you'll be doing in the future. It's designed to see how you react in certain situations. Whether you're prepared to have a go at something that looks difficult. Whether you can work with other people. How you think, solve problems, make judgements, that kind of thing. The kinds of skills you'll need in the field.'

'In the field?' She imagined open stretches of waving corn and poppies.

'Yes. When you're sent *en mission* to occupied Belgium.'

The penny finally dropped. Right at the beginning of all this, Army Man had asked her if she wanted to go back to Belgium. She'd naively assumed he meant after the war was won.

'Of course, sir, yes. I understand.'

'Good girl. Another whisky?'

As they climbed back into the covered truck the following morning, Elaine was somewhat better informed than she had been at the start. She knew where she was going, but when, with whom and for what purpose she knew not. The other students were in a similar state of semi-ignorance. They didn't even know that they'd spent the previous four hectic and perplexing days at Winterfold House, high in the Surrey Hills, also known as Special Training School 7, home to SOE's Student Assessment Board. Those who passed would go on to further training schools in other requisitioned country houses to prepare for their various missions. Those who failed were destined to spend months cooling their heels in even more isolated places on spurious 'training courses' until the memory of what they'd seen and heard at Winterfold was distant enough for them to return safely to their previous lives.

It had been a stretching and fascinating interlude for Elaine. Major Floor was right, she'd enjoyed it. But she had no idea at all whether she'd made the grade, who would decide or what kind of mission she was being judged for.

☙

She didn't have long to wait. A few days later Floor called to ask her to come into the office to see him.

He looked grave.

'Well, Miss Meeus, what do you think? Do you think you've passed?'

She studied his long face for clues. It seemed to spell bad news.

'I've failed, sir?'

His face gave no clues. She couldn't disguise her disappointment.

'I've failed.'

'Unfortunately, you've passed.' The Belgian sense of humour. 'You're in. So now the real work starts for you. Within the next few days you'll be called for Group A training in Scotland – commando school. If you thought they put your through your paces at your SAB, that's nothing to what they'll have in store for you up there. They certainly terrify me, I can tell you. You'll be roughing it with the men, no allowances made.' He scrutinised her petite frame doubtfully. 'Think you can cope?'

'I'll have a go.'

'Good girl.'

'Is there any more you can tell me about what I'll be doing, sir? I know I'll be going into Belgium but that's about it.'

'Every mission is slightly different. I can't say yet what yours will be but we've got a better idea now of what you might be suited for. That's all I can tell you at the moment. You'll do your training, which will last about six weeks in all, and then you wait to be assigned a mission. This could take days, weeks or months, according to operational needs. But let's get your training done before we worry about that. Go home and await instructions. And in the meantime please remember what you've been told about being security minded. Nothing about any of this to anyone, understand? At some stage we'll get you to sign a legal undertaking to that effect but for the moment you're on your honour to keep shtum, OK?'

'Yes, sir. Understood.'

So she took her leave of Major Floor as Miss Meeus, to revert to her former identity once back in the outside world until such time as she was called again.

Floor read through her assessment report again, signed by the president of the SAB, Gavin Brown. *STS.7 20th April 1944. Party number 9. OB. Student number 13.* Lucky for some. So: average for general suitability for service as an agent; well above average intelligence; good passes in mechanical and instructional aptitude and an excellent report for Morse. The assessors' concluding remarks warranted special attention:

> *This girl has a good intelligence, a confident manner, has good imagination and is capable of taking decisive action. She understands fully the nature of the work for which she has volunteered …*

That wasn't the impression she gave this afternoon.

> *… and there is no doubt about her disinterested desire to help the Belgian cause. She is neither a leader nor an organizer, but she is alert, efficient and methodical. At the same time she is not above being helpless and feminine when the chance presents itself. She is sophisticated for her age and quite security minded. Her consciousness of her powers to attract is not likely to interfere with her application to the task in hand.*

> *She is recommended as a quick courier.*

Very good. He knew from colleagues in the French section that the chaps at Winterfold could be unnecessarily hard on the women candidates they put forward; their views sometimes had to be overruled by headquarters. But there seemed little doubt about the suitability of Miss Meeus. Just as well, as there was a lot riding on this. She was the first of T Section's women agents and she might – for a variety of reasons – be the last. He hoped she'd be tough enough to stay the course and do the job.

Their potential agents may have been in blissful semi-ignorance, but no one in Baker Street had any illusions about how difficult and dangerous it could be in the field, or the fate awaiting agents if captured. By this late stage of the war, T Section alone had already lost almost a third of its agents through incompetence, betrayal or plain bad luck. The Dutch had fared worse: their principal circuit had been infiltrated by German Intelligence and, apparently unknown to London, for months agents arrived there to be delivered straight into the hands of the Gestapo. The penalty for capture was torture, imprisonment and probable execution. By a single shot to the head if they were lucky. Otherwise by beheading or a variety of other medieval means. Miss Meeus would need all her strength, wit and charm to survive, let alone succeed.

⌒

She waited at Bayswater Court for the call. And waited. On 7 May – her twenty-first birthday – she had a modest celebration with Susan and some friends. Worldly wise and discreet Susan knew better than anyone to ask questions she knew Elaine would have difficulty answering. Anyone who asked was told that the FANY was sending her on another training course – she still didn't know where or what for, but she felt sure her languages were the main thing they were after. She didn't really care, 'as long as I don't end up stuck behind a typewriter on some godforsaken army base out in the sticks'. Elaine could say that with confidence now, safe in the knowledge that this was the last thing likely to happen.

But she did wonder why she hadn't yet been called for the commando training. It wasn't that she'd been looking forward to it. If it terrified Major Floor, what would it do to her? But she'd be with the same chaps she was with on the assessment course, so they'd be in it together; she just wanted to get on with it.

Shortly after her birthday, Floor telephoned to say that they had decided not to send her up to Scotland with the men.

'We think you're too small, too slight to do the whole course. You might find it too taxing – and your medical report says you've got weak ankles. And anyway, it probably won't be necessary for the work you'll be doing. But you'll still learn some of the essentials, silent killing and so on …'

Silent killing?

'… Instead we're going to rearrange your training. This is arse-about-face, but there's method to it. We're sending you to Group B – our finishing school – next. You'll start there shortly and be away for about three weeks. It's comfortable there but you'll be worked hard. There's a great deal to learn. Any questions?'

Yes, lots, but none she thought he'd be prepared to answer. Floor was today more brusque than his usual laconic self. If he was busy she didn't want to hold him up.

'Alright then, very good. Wait for further instructions, as before.'

It was more a relief than a disappointment. She was sorry not to be joining the men; they'd got on well before and helped each other out. Yes, there'd been a bit of joshing and flirting – on their part rather than hers – but she took the security instructions seriously and kept them all at a friendly distance.

Just as she was about to leave for the 'finishing school', she received a letter via the Red Cross, redirected several times and bearing a date from the previous year. It was from Luc in Belgium, the first she'd heard of him since they parted in Poperinghe. Letters from occupied territories were heavily censored and strictly limited in length so they didn't waste words. He was writing to tell her that he'd married someone else.

Relief and disappointment barely described her response to this news. Though she was never in danger of breaking her old promise to be faithful, she'd never been seriously tempted either, so now she felt any residual burden of obligation lifted from her. Stronger than relief, it felt closer to elation: a profound satisfaction that a good man had found the right woman; and the blessed realisation that she'd now be free at twenty-one to make a wiser choice than she'd made at seventeen. But there was disappointment too. One of her last remaining links with Poperinghe was now severed. She'd cast off Simone. Who knew what had become of her grandparents and aunts and uncles under the occupation? And now, delighted for him as she was, Luc had broken their informal contract to marry. He hoped she wouldn't be too upset and would find her own happiness. No, she wasn't upset and yes, she intended to do just that.

His signet ring was still on her finger, as it had been since the day by the firing post when he put it there: it had brought her luck and, she believed, would continue to do so until she was able to return it. They bore each other no ill will. It was all for the best. At Bayswater Court she finished packing with a renewed sense of purpose: though she had no idea what the future held, the uncertainty and prospect of danger excited her. She was answering her country's call and about to take another step towards her destiny.

On 14 May she waited at the pick-up point, ready to get into another covered truck and travel to another mysterious destination 'somewhere in southern England'.

Back in Baker Street, Hardy Amies, Ides Floor and their T Section colleagues were exceptionally busy. Preparations for the invasion of France under the direction of General Eisenhower's Supreme Headquarters Allied Expeditionary Force (SHAEF) were now at fever pitch. SOE subversion activities in France, Belgium and Holland, in concert with the local Resistance circuits it trained and supplied, would be critical to the liberation of Europe. Its agents needed to be there in greater strength than ever to help secure military success on the Second Front. Recruitment and training of new agents had been frantic for the best part of a year. Though Floor failed to mention this, the most pressing reason for not sending Elaine to Scotland was that there wasn't time: they needed her in the field as soon as possible, even if it meant her training had to be skimped.

New recruit Elaine Madden — a.k.a. Hélène Meeus — would be just one of hundreds of SOE agents infiltrated behind enemy lines, preparing for the Allies' recapture of occupied lands. The invasion plan was only the start. Nazi Germany would soon be in retreat from East and West but the regime would also be desperate, with little left to lose. The aftermath of the Allied landings — and the weeks and months leading up to endgame — would be bloody and chaotic. This was potentially the most perilous time for the agents of the entire war. Survival would depend on good luck - and good training.

৶৹

At first she thought they'd been returned in error to the beautiful place where they did their assessment course. Again they were delivered to the rear of a large and elegant country house on wooded high ground, and escorted to rooms by a back staircase. But this time her fellow passengers were all strangers and the journey was at least an hour longer than before. Another difference: Elaine had a strong feeling that they were close to the sea, or at least near water.

Again, they weren't told where they were or even the name of the house where they would be spending the next three weeks. This time though she had the company of women: one or two trainees and assorted FANYs who appeared from time to time especially in the evenings, though it was never clear to her what their role was. Secretaries perhaps, or drivers. As far as she could see, there were only trainees intended for service in Belgium on the course. Most were Belgian or Anglo-Belgian like her and there were even one or two Americans. All classes would be taken in or from the house where they were also accommodated, though some of the men were billeted in smaller houses nearby. They seemed to be on a large country estate traversed only by dirt roads and dotted with other large discreetly screened houses, all of which were out of bounds to the trainees. As before, they were miles from anywhere.

She changed into work fatigues and, before the introductory session – an address by the commandant – she went downstairs and out on to the south-facing terrace to get her bearings. The accommodation was very comfortable, in the country house style, as Major Floor had promised. Like the previous establishment, the reception-cum-common-room where trainees and staff gathered had a well-stocked bar which she was surprised to note was open all day. Later she was to learn that almost all the staff called the house 'the Pub'.

Outside, it was an ungainly combination of Dutch gables and Edwardian bay windows that managed to be both ugly and impressive at the same time. With an afterthought of a wing to one side, it sat among thick woodland on the brow of a gentle rise, nowhere near as high as the last place. There were no breathtaking views over miles of countryside but the immediate outlook was just as full of interest. On the southern slope immediately below the terrace and its shallow grounds was a surprise – there were rows and rows of vines. She had no idea that wine grapes grew in England. More familiar with hop fields than vineyards, she guessed that these had been neglected over some years. Even in their overgrown state they were an impressive sight, now coming into full leaf and creating untidy lines of lush green, a touch of the exotic in the English countryside. There was an occasional soft hooting noise she couldn't place – certainly not an owl – and large odd-looking birds with long tails scrabbling about on the ground among the lines of green.

Beyond the vineyards, fields and in the near distance a fine stone *chateau* with capped towers in the French manner standing in grounds that still looked immaculately well maintained. In these grounds to the left, what looked like medieval church buildings, some in ruins. An ancient abbey perhaps. And yes, she was sure she could smell the sea.

She was glad to be joined on the terrace by some men from the first course. What had happened to the rest of them, she wondered aloud. Someone mentioned a chap who'd been 'sent to the cooler', though she didn't know what this meant. Another surmised some hadn't survived the rigours of Scotland.

'How was it up there?'

'Terrible. Freezing cold, up to our necks in peat bogs and bloody porridge. The men wear skirts for God's sake. Never saw a real woman in three weeks. But we did learn how to live in inhospitable places. If we can survive there I'm sure we'll be fine on the streets of Brussels. Where the hell were you, by the way?'

'Oh, my weak ankles got me off, apparently! But they've promised to show me something called "silent killing" while I'm here. Sounds frightful. I can hardly wait.'

'You'll need it. Especially a little sprat like you. It's them or us, remember.'

Before she had time to think about this they were summoned to the drawing room to meet their commandant.

Lieutenant-Colonel Stanley Woolrych, an old intelligence officer who cut his teeth in the 1914–18 war, had been recalled to the Military Police in 1939 and was now using his spy-catching and spy-training experience for SOE. He was a committed Christian, a linguist, keen photographer and accomplished pianist, as those at the staff HQ in a neighbouring house could attest, as he practised on the grand piano there for an hour every day before breakfast. Apparently distant, those who knew him better found him a fair and compassionate man and he commanded the respect of his large and disparate staff. Behind his back and not without affection, the FANYs called him Woolybags.

As yet, Elaine and her colleagues knew none of this. They may not even have caught his name. Names were used as little as possible and the usual military compliments to officers – salutes, forms of address – were not required of trainees. Today they saw a punctilious old soldier who was unlikely to suffer fools and who got straight to the point.

Clockwise from above: Harold Lawrence
Madden in 1915, the year he lied about his age
to join the Australian Imperial Force and the
war in Europe. (Neville Madden); Happy family:
Larry, Caroline and baby Elaine, around 1925.
(Neville Madden); Studio portrait inscribed
on the reverse by Larry: '*To Aunty Elaine and
Uncle Jack from Elaine. Poperinghe, Belgium 1927.*'
(Neville Madden)

Elaine (standing behind the headmaster, Mr Allen) loved her time at the British Memorial School, where in 1936 she was chosen as one of this group of school elders (prefects). (Jerry Eaton)

23 Deerhurst Road, Streatham, where Elaine and Simone took refuge after their escape from Dunkirk. (Author's collection)

SHAPELY ANKLES GAVE GIRLS AWAY

TWO girls who "joined" the British Army and carried off the disguise until their shapely legs gave them away were rescued with the British troops and brought to England.

One is English, the other Belgian. They owe their escape to three British soldiers—Knocker, Smudger and Gary.

Knocker and Smudger lent the girls khaki greatcoats, which came down to their feet, and steel helmets. Then the three formed a cordon round the girls so that their disguise would not be penetrated.

It was not until the little party was boarding a trawler at Dunkirk that the two pairs of legs, too neat to be soldiers', were noticed descending the ladder on to the boat. But the captain would not turn the girls away when he heard their story.

Elaine Madden, aged seventeen, whose English father, former gardener for the War Graves Commission at Poperinghe, had joined the British Army, was living with her grandparents, who owned an hotel in the town.

Their Homes Bombed

When the German bombing raids started the household evacuated, but Elaine and her nineteen-year-old aunt, Simone Duponselle, stayed behind to make last-minute arrangements.

They stayed too long. They had to run from their house as the bombs dropped, and the streets were set burning.

They left for shelter in the country. They found it in England.

They walked till they found shelter in a barn. There they were found by the three soldiers. All five then made their way by cars, abandoned lorries, and on foot through the flooded fields.

Elaine, who is now at the home of her aunt, Mrs. Stone, in Deerhurst-road, Streatham, S.W., fingered the gold ring given to her by her soldier fiancé as she told her story.

Ring Brought Luck

"It brought me luck," she whispered. "We might have been burnt to death when we reached Dunkirk. We drove through the burning streets in a lorry.

"We did not know the way to the docks. Suddenly we came upon a stream of soldiers waiting to embark. Our luck had held."

"Gary told us, 'Say you're the Dorsets, if you're challenged.'

"As we climbed down on to the trawler soldiers saw our legs and shouted, 'Look at the lady soldiers.' We thought we were going to be turned back. There was nowhere for us to go; Dunkirk was in flames; the country flooded.

"The captain gave us his cabin when I said I was English."

Both girls have left their soldier fiancés behind. Elaine was to have been married in a week's time.

"But I know I shall see him soon," she said, "when Belgium is free again."

Now Elaine and Simone want to get jobs, so that they can buy clothes.

A story that the *Daily Mirror* seized on with enthusiasm in the dark days of June 1940. (Author's collection)

Girl about town. Taken in London in 1944 before she was recruited by SOE. (Neville Madden)

In the uniform of the First Aid Nursing Yeomanry (FANY), traditional cover for women SOE agents. (Elaine Madden)

The Vineyards, one of many houses on the Beaulieu estate in Hampshire where SOE 'finished' its agents. Elaine lived here in the weeks leading up to D-Day in June 1944. (Author's collection)

The wide open spaces of the Belgian Ardennes around Beauraing where the Imogen team were dropped by parachute on the night of 4–5 August 1944. (Author's collection)

Chateau d'Halloy outside Ciney, where Elaine acted as minder to 'Monsieur Bernard'. (Author's collection)

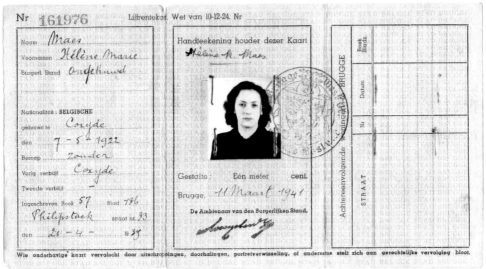

One of Elaine's many false identity papers. (Elaine Madden)

Celebrating the liberation of Brussels, September 1944, with two colleagues. Elaine now has her FANY uniform restored to her, with its precious 'wings'. (Elaine Madden)

Michel Ghislain Blaze from his SOE file, taken in around 1943. (National Archives)

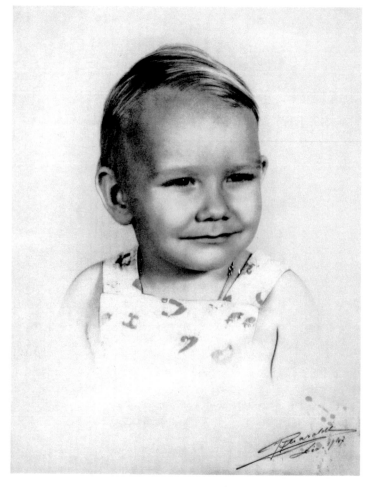

Baby Lawrence Bernard Blaze, born in 1946, before Elaine and Michel moved to Africa. (Neville Madden)

Elaine and her son, inscribed by Elaine on the reverse 'St Sulpice. October 1948'. He was probably already ill by the time this was taken. (Neville Madden)

Valda Barnes, Elaine's Australian cousin. They formed a close bond during Elaine's visit in 1967. (Neville Madden)

Larry Madden returned to Australia after the war and died there, aged sixty-six, in 1965. (Neville Madden)

Elaine at her home in Pont St Esprit, taken in 2008 when she was eighty-five. (Testimony Films)

'Good morning gentlemen – and ladies. Let me first bid you welcome. I hope you will enjoy your course here and will find it useful. Now let's get to work. The purpose of the organisation to which you and I belong is subversion …'

Their training had begun. Over the next three weeks they would learn a great deal about the art and craft of 'irregular warfare' from the motley faculty of instructors who peopled SOE's finishing school. Though she never saw it, Elaine was right about the sea. The ugly house where they were based was called The Vineyards, one of the half dozen or so large private houses requisitioned for the purpose from Lord Montague's estate in the New Forest not far from Southampton on the Solent. Though the crass English pronounce it *byou-lee,* French speakers would recognise it instantly as 'beautiful place' – or Beaulieu.

⁊❧

Colonel Woolrych had been perfectly clear. They were now in the business of subversion, in his view the fourth arm of modern warfare. He took them through its main objects: to damage the enemy's communications and production capacity by sabotage; to strain his human resources by diverting as many men as possible to non-combat activities; to undermine his morale with black and white propaganda; and to raise the morale of the populations of occupied countries in order, as he put it, *'that they may give us vital assistance when the right moment comes'*. Achieving these objects was the job of the SOE agent. Mastery of all manner of dirty tricks by which they would be achieved was what they were there to learn.

During his detailed address, Elaine was interested to note that he used a term she hadn't heard since those walks with her father round the ramparts to the Menin Gate. He called the Germans 'the Boche', so he must be an old soldier, like her dad. But, after he'd briefly summarised the subversion syllabus they were about to undertake in common, she listened most intently to the closing sentences of his long peroration.

'There is only one word of warning I wish to make here. If you follow conscientiously in the field all that we teach you here, we cannot guarantee your safety, but we think that

your chance of being picked up is very small. Remember, the best agents are never caught. But some agents when they get out into the field find it apparently much easier than they expected, and they are inclined to relax their precautions. That is the moment to beware of. Never relax your precautions, and never fool yourself by thinking that the enemy are asleep. They may be watching you all the time, so watch your step.'

The three weeks that followed melded into a strenuous and challenging whole, the course – ridiculously short as it was – designed to prepare students for their new roles as secret agents. The largest and most important part of the syllabus was 'clandestine life': personal security, communications, cover stories, surveillance and counter-espionage. For Elaine, this included some of the most fascinating and bizarre practical work and she wondered again what some of these very irregular skills could possibly be used for. They were taught by a professional burglar how to pick a Yale lock with a piece of wire, make a duplicate key using Plasticine, force an entry with the minimum noise and detection, and open a safe with an ear to the door for the clicks that indicated the right numbers to unlock the mechanism.

But this was a flashy sideshow to the main purpose of teaching the students how to 'pass' for locals in the areas to which they'd be sent. They had to carry out their subversive, illegal and possibly murderous activities without being detected. For this they were schooled in personal cover stories that were close enough to their own lives and backgrounds that they weren't likely to be forgotten in the heat of the moment, but different enough to be plausible at first flush without causing suspicion that might trigger a more thorough investigation. For an ad hoc alibi, Elaine was taught to use what she did yesterday as cover for what she'd actually done that day. They could be stopped at any time by an instructor and interrogated about where they'd just been, what they'd been doing and with whom. They were sent out in pairs on errands and then faced interrogation afterwards for which they had to have an alibi. Because of the gender imbalance on the course she was inevitably paired with a man, which made alibis pretty straightforward: they were a courting couple returning from a lovers' tryst.

In 'passing', she learned, women agents had an advantage over the men. Women were more likely to melt unnoticed into a crowd and could hide a radio, arms or equipment in a pram or shopping basket. They were also less likely to be stopped in snap searches. Conscripted labour in German war factories – the hated STO or *Service du Travail Obligatoire* – meant young men were conspicuous by their presence in towns and villages that by 1944 had been stripped of able-bodied males.

To merge seamlessly and anonymously with their new surroundings they had to be *au fait* with local rationing and curfew rules but also with the customs, eating habits and idiom of the areas where they'd be sent. In France and Belgium for much of the war cafés were only allowed to serve coffee *noir* as milk was reserved for children and pregnant women. Asking for *café au lait* would immediately mark them out as an interloper. They were also warned that using English slang, unfamiliar jargon or references to the latest dance craze in London could easily give them away.

At mealtimes they were reminded that the English habit of leaving a few token remnants and neatly aligned cutlery could be a giveaway in a culture where a crust of bread always mopped up the last morsel. For most, including Elaine, these habits came as second nature. She was fortunate to have learned her table manners from her mother rather than her father, though she recalled these being far from polite and English.

They had great fun with a professional actor in a session on make-up, disguise and tips for getting into and maintaining a character. Most sessions though were deadly serious. They soon learned that the wireless operator had the most lonely and vulnerable job in an agents' cell, so there were strict procedures for scouting safe houses and protecting operators from the dreaded German direction-finding vans that prowled the streets looking for radio signals. She learned about dropping points, reception committees and how to identify landing grounds for pick-ups, and she grappled with the RAF's 'clock ray' system for pinpointing locations.

Less challenging, and altogether less fascinating, were the lectures on Nazi Party organisation and the Wehrmacht ranks, uniforms, arms and equipment that had to be committed to memory for instant recognition. In sessions on political warfare and propaganda she was shocked and amused at the depths to which the British were prepared to stoop to damage German morale, including using *resistant* prostitutes to lace their clients' prophylactics with itching powder.

Learning a cover story and absorbing the many requirements for 'clandestine life' was challenging but essentially rather fun. The classes on codes and ciphers were just plain hard work until she started to get the hang of them, when they became both intriguing and rewarding. She was inducted into the arcane world of secret communication using such mysterious devices as Innocent Letter, Playfair and Double Transposition; she learned about LOPs and MOPs (Letter One-Time Pads and Mental One-Time Pads) and how to use the numbered silk squares the size of a ladies handkerchief in conjunction with a key word – hers was BAYSWATER, her home telephone exchange – to encode and decode messages.

Here she discovered one disadvantage to her British schooling. She was a fluent French speaker, but her written French was scrappy at best. Apart from thank-you letters and those disastrous few weeks at the convent school, she'd had no cause to use it. But many of the messages to and from London she'd be coding would be in French so she needed practice here too. Her instructor, Captain Pip Whittaker, was a patient man but he kept her nose to the grindstone. Coding mistakes could cost lives: one coding error in a message could render it indecipherable and therefore useless to London. And he drummed into her the necessity of destroying all the evidence as soon as possible after use and never to carry coded or decoded material where it could be found in a routine search. It was exhausting work that took intense concentration. She practised until her brain ached and her pencils broke.

Coding was difficult and required a great deal of intellectual effort but no agent cell could survive long behind enemy lines without effective communication with its home station. Building from her initial interest in Morse, she started to think that the role of the wireless operator – though the most technically exacting and potentially dangerous – was the one she'd most like to do in the field.

Combat and weapons instruction was the most physically and mentally challenging element of the course. She was taught how to handle a variety of weapons, especially the Sten gun – crude in construction and operation but cheap to produce and effective at short range. Students learned the 'double tap': two shots fired in quick succession to fatally disable an opponent.

London was true to its promise that she would be taught 'the essentials' of close combat, the art of killing someone as quickly as possible without the benefit of firearms. '*This is WAR*,' the instructor told her. '*Forget the Queensbury rules.*' But there were other kinds of rule to be followed. The instructor showed her how to get out of a hold with the object of killing the assailant without delay, how to fell a sentry with or without a knife, how to break a neck and how to dislocate someone's spine, finishing with '*a quick snap upwards and backwards*'.

She did lethal damage to a number of straw-filled dummies with a double-edged commando knife, designed specially for British and American Special Forces by two former Shanghai policemen. The technique of locking an arm round the opponent's throat and yanking his head back to apply the knife in a single action across his throat was perfected on live subjects – using a dummy knife smeared with red lipstick.

She felt curiously disengaged from the whole gruesome business; it was best not to dwell too much on whether she might have to use these methods and to what effect. Better to think of them as just another set of techniques to be observed, practised and mastered. Fortunately, her mind was already too occupied trying to process a mass of information to let in worries about the possibility of having to kill someone.

Though each session offered new challenges and surprises, the daily pattern was always the same: PT first thing, classroom lectures in the mornings and practical work in the afternoons and often into the evenings. Students were free on Saturday afternoons and Sundays unless required for special exercises or 'schemes', as the instructors called them – though they were encouraged to attend church on Sunday. Meals were regular, at humane hours and surpassed anything Elaine was used to in ration-bound London. For the first time she tasted pheasant and was surprised to learn it was the odd-looking bird she'd seen among the vines and the source of that unfamiliar hooting noise.

The adjutant in charge of The Vineyards was Captain William Clark, who everyone knew as Nobby. Not an officer type at all, it was rumoured that in peacetime he'd been a gamekeeper on the king's Sandringham estate. He taught 'fieldcraft' and survival skills: stalking, making hides and traps, and living rough off the land. Students came back from lengthy sessions with Nobby in the New Forest telling how they'd learned how to survive on baked hedgehog, though they wondered quite how useful a skill this might be to them *en mission*. Elaine was never in a position to find out as his classes weren't part of her timetable, something of a relief as he was known to be antipathetic to women agents.

When sessions and 6.30 p.m. supper were over, staff and students piled into 'the Pub' for a riotous evening's entertainment. Alcohol was cheap and plentiful and no one was discouraged from drinking too much. This was when the FANYs appeared, released from their mysterious daytime labours and in fashionable civvies, to join in the fun. Some, it seemed to Elaine, were on missions of their own to lead the poor boys on to indiscretions of one kind or another. Or perhaps that was the whole idea? They were pretty little decoy birds sent out to test the resolve of the virgin agents. If so, why hadn't they thought to provide her with a handsome hunk of marine to test *her* cover story or push *her* willpower to the limit?

There was little time students could call their own: they were supervised one way or another for much of their waking hours. And possibly outside them too. One chap related how he'd woken one night to discover a man sitting by his bed, notebook in hand, ready he assumed to record any indiscretions revealed in his sleep – or perhaps to note in what language he revealed them.

In what spare time they had, students were free to roam the grounds, the surrounding fields and woods, and the abbey ruins. The fine *chateau*, Palace House, was still occupied by the Montague family and out of bounds, but its grounds and those of the abbey had no physical boundary so in practice these were open to students as well. The pace was so frenetic and the physical and intellectual challenges so intense that finding time for odd snatches of peaceful reflection was essential to many students' sanity.

When she needed to get away from the rabble in 'the Pub' Elaine would wander down through the rows of vines and over the fields to the abbey ruins. In the long, light evenings of double summer time in late May 1944 they seemed to take on an ethereal quality with their wheeling, screaming swifts, bubblegum-scented blossom of blue and white wisteria on the rackety pergola, and the deep red valerian insinuating its way up through the cracks among the stones. She drank in the scents, sounds and secrets of that ancient place, a peaceful counterpoint to the mayhem they were being taught to foment at the house on the hill, balm for all the evils of the world.

On one such evening towards the end of her course, she went in search of solitude in the ruined cloister. Tonight the swifts were drowned out by the cawing of rooks in the yew trees but nothing seemed to disturb the somnambulant peace of the cloister, its four walls and recesses roofless but intact, its grassy quadrangle high with wild flowers.

Settling herself among the flowers, she exhaled and relaxed. She didn't want to think too much about what might lie ahead, but she did need time to reflect a little on what was happening to her *now*, and how suddenly the staid pattern of her life had been shaken up. There was excitement and uncertainty before – there was her war work, the fascinating people who had crossed her path and of course always the possibility of her number coming up in a raid. But nothing like this. This was excitement and uncertainty on an epic scale in which life and death took on new meaning. She would now be responsible for the safety and security of others as well as herself, and for the first time she might have to end a life in order to do so.

Just as she realised this thought was straying into fruitless what-ifs, she became aware of someone watching her. Remembering the class on surveillance and how to 'lose' a tail, she got out her compact as if to check her make-up. In the mirror she caught a glancing shadow in a cloister alcove. Her next move was contrary to everything she'd been taught, but she was intrigued to know who was watching her and why. Her tail couldn't be an instructor: the shadow was too small.

'I know you're there. Please show yourself. I want to talk to you.'

After a few seconds a small, dark figure emerged from the alcove, giggling.

'I made a complete hash of that, didn't I? Good job no instructors are around to mark me down.'

'How long have you been following me?'

'Oh, not long. Only since the pergola.'

It was a shock. She'd had no idea.

'Well, now your cover's blown, at least come and talk to me.'

The young woman, even smaller than her, French and Jewish she guessed, came and sat down on the grass. This was even more intriguing.

'You're not a FANY are you?'

'God, no. I'm a so-called student, like you.'

'But I've never seen you before.'

'That's because they do their best to keep us all apart. There are dozens of us here, all in different houses. Each country has one and never the twain – or whatever the word for half a dozen is – shall meet. I'm with the French section and we're in a house called Boarmans. You're with the Belgians in The Vineyards aren't you? We're not supposed to talk to students from other sections, but blow that. This place is full of stupid rules. I'm getting pretty fed up with it to be honest. Can't wait to get out of here.'

Elaine was genuinely surprised.

'Really? I'm finding it an eye-opener.'

'That's because, my dear girl, you're new to this game. I've already had three years with the Resistance in the Free Zone and there's not much they can teach me here about "clandestine life" or sabotage, I can tell you. In fact I should be teaching them. Some of the stuff they're giving us is out of the Ark.'

'Well, you were pretty good at tailing me. Till just now!'

'Yes, that's never been my forte. I just saw you doing your Greta Garbo bit in the pergola and I thought "she looks interesting", so I followed you here. It's so peaceful, isn't it? I often come. It can get a little oppressive being with the men all the time. What were you thinking about?'

Still unsure whether she was being set up, Elaine declined to volunteer any information about herself. She should be the one asking the questions, a tactic her new friend seemed entirely comfortable with.

'Oh, you know, the usual things. Love, life, death. But tell me what it's really like "in the field".'

'A bit like war itself really. Ninety-five per cent of the time you're bored stiff. The other five per cent you're out of your wits with sheer bloody terror.'

'But if you've already been out there for three years, what are you doing here?'

'London, in their wisdom, thought I needed the benefit of their "training". I suppose it's good to know about the latest explosives and firearms and stuff, but half the course is completely irrelevant to my situation. Cooking hedgehogs and secret inks! Well, really! Boy Scout stuff.'

'Can I ask you … you're Jewish aren't you? Isn't that terribly dangerous for you? I mean the Nazis hate Jews and are always looking to round them up.'

'All the more reason to try and stop the bastards.' She stopped, as if bravado had deserted her. 'People here have absolutely no idea … you haven't got a cigarette I suppose?'

'Only Senior Service I'm afraid. You can't get Gauloises for love or money.'

She shrugged.

'Better than nothing.'

The hand holding the cigarette for Elaine to light was strangely disfigured: all her nails were horribly stunted and deformed. She answered the question before it was asked.

'Yes, they got me once, for the first and I hope the last time. I was very lucky to get out of that alive. And without betraying my *reseau*, my network. I gave them my nails and that's all I was prepared to give. And then it took me seven months to get to England on the escape lines through Spain. I was a marked woman after that and had to get away.'

'And you still want to go back? After all that?'

'Why not? We have to defeat them, don't we? Sitting here on our arses in beautiful English places isn't going to beat the Boche. Actually, I lie. At least the Boche are half-human. The Nazis are something else entirely. Not a shred of humanity. Evil incarnate. Believe me, I've seen the whites of their eyes.'

Elaine believed her.

'You're very brave.'

'Not at all. I do it for France and I do it for humanity. You'll do the same.' The tone lightened. 'But you sound much too English to be Belgian.'

'I am English, but my mother was Flemish.'

'Don't tell me any more. I'm not supposed to know. And you've never met me, OK?'

She stood up, cigarette still in her mouth, looking around the cloister exits as if to check it was safe to leave. Elaine was sorry to see her go. There were so many more questions she wanted to ask.

'Thanks for coming out of the shadows to talk to me. And if I don't see you again before you leave, good luck.'

'You won't. I'm off tomorrow. And you must never say "Good Luck" – it's bad luck! We always say *Merde!* It's like the English actors say "break a leg".'

'OK, thanks for the tip. *Merde!*'

'*Au revoir*, English girl. And *Merde!* to you.'

෨෧

It was almost time for Elaine to leave Beaulieu too. In their final week, they were all assigned a 'scheme', a night-time exercise designed to simulate a real-life situation they might find in the field. After supper one evening Elaine and two fellow students were given a map and rudimentary written instructions: they were to find a particular house on the estate, break in without disturbing the occupants and steal papers hidden in an attic room, accessible only from the roof. So that's what all the burglary lessons were for. And they were expected to put as many of their other newly learned skills into practice as possible, though they weren't warned which ones might come in useful. They were to complete the mission and be back, tucked up in The Vineyards, within the hour.

With a fair bit of giggling to hide their nervousness, at 11 p.m. three novices with sooted-up faces synchronised watches, checked their equipment and set off according to the map into dense woodland, and straight into a series of booby traps set by Nobby Clark. These were harmless but made alarming noises that scattered nesting rooks or marked them with coloured powder. Elaine began to regret missing Nobby's fieldcraft lessons in the New Forest.

They found the house without too much difficulty. Lights were on and music was playing in the drawing room. Somehow they had to get on to the roof of the three-storey building to access a roof light to the rear. There was a kennel, but apparently no dog, barking or otherwise. That was good, as they hadn't thought to bring any poisoned meat. They identified the roof light to be attacked. One of the men scaled a drainpipe to the flat roof of the kitchen and threw down a rope for the others. A handy cat-slide roof took two of them to the third storey and the attic window that was easily jemmied open. Elaine, as the smallest, was deputed to go inside to retrieve the 'secret papers' whilst the men stayed as lookouts on the first floor and on the roof.

Inside the attic room, Elaine had to pick a lock to open a desk drawer, thanking her luck that it wasn't a safe she had to open and, tucking the booty inside her battledress jacket, hauled herself back up through the roof-light with the help of her teammate waiting outside. They made it safely down to the flat roof to join their third member when he signalled frantically to them to lie down below the small parapet. Loud voices below announced the arrival of the occupants.

'I'm sure I heard a noise.'

'No, darling, I think you're imagining it. Look, there's nothing there.'

Elaine bit her lip to stop herself giggling and couldn't look at the others. The voices were so stagey they could all be in an amateur Agatha Christie production.

The actors went back inside, their roles in this regular little charade now over.

The intruders jumped back on to the ground and were thinking about their getaway when a dog started barking furiously nearby.

'Oh bugger! That wasn't in the script. Run like hell.'

They made for the nearest cover and ran, stumbling and laughing, back through the woods to The Vineyards, making the back door with seconds to spare. Nobby was waiting for them.

'You found the traps I see. And you didn't do a proper check for the dog. Got the papers? Jolly good. Bar's still open. Get yourselves a quick nightcap. Well done.'

They collapsed in the bar, mildly hysterical from the release of tension.

'What a performance!'

'... and how did he know about the bloody dog?'

Yes, it was all artificial and slightly hilarious, but they'd learned a lot, about not taking maps for granted, not going the most obvious route, keeping to cover and watching out for bloody dogs. Most of all they learned about teamwork and how adrenalin soon kicks in to replace fear with instinct.

They parted on the first floor landing and Elaine fell exhausted into bed, hardly able to pull her pyjamas on before her eyes closed.

She was dreaming. Uncle Charles was shouting at her in bright sunlight and, unaccountably, in German. The light was so bright it was disturbing and she forced her eyes open to escape the dream. She woke to a large shape standing over her shouting, '*Schnell, schnell!*', and pushing her roughly out of bed. She couldn't see who was behind the voice for the powerful torch blinding her. Stumbling and half-awake, she was frog-marched from her room in her pyjamas by the man in a uniform she recognised from her Nazi rank classes. As she was pushed, more roughly than strictly necessary, down the main staircase she forced herself to come to from semi-sleep and concentrate. More play-acting, but also much more testing than the 'scheme' they'd just performed. She'd heard rumours. This was the closest thing Beaulieu could offer to a genuine Gestapo interrogation.

The room was in darkness except for a large anglepoise on a desk that illuminated only the uniformed torsos of the three men sitting behind it. Knowing they were instructors in costume and she was taking part in a rather unpleasant play didn't help. She had to recall every detail of her cover, think of an alibi and maintain concentration throughout without appearing either nervous or cocky. She was pushed down roughly on to a chair in the centre of a pool of blinding light.

The questioning began along expected lines, with each interrogator taking his prescribed role: the bully, the manipulator and the sympathetic one who extracted information by kindness. She'd been taught strategies for each approach, if only she could remember … keep calm, give closed answers, play for time.

They came and went, changing tactics in turn and doing their best to trick and confuse her into confessions.

'Stand on the chair!'

She obeyed, feeling stupid in her pyjamas. More testing of her alibi. What I was doing last evening, not this …

'Take off your pyjama top!'

Well, this was beyond a joke. What the hell were they playing at? She obeyed, feeling even more ridiculous, standing bare-breasted on a chair. It seemed to go on endlessly and she could feel her calm facade crumbling. Exhausted, confused, and angry now, she barely kept sufficient control to keep answering their interminable stupid questions. But the show must go on …

Just as her knees were turning to jelly and stars danced before her eyes, the bully said sweetly: 'Thank you, Miss Meeus. You can get down now and cover up.'

The blinding anglepoise went off and the lights went up. There was a fluttering noise that got louder. As she adjusted to the light she saw, sitting round the sides of the 'interrogation room', all her fellow students clapping and now whooping approval – of her performance or her semi-naked appearance she couldn't be sure. She was horrified and furious, not with her friends on the course but with the Gestapo impersonators who'd put her through such a humiliating charade. Then she remembered her recent encounter with the Frenchwoman in the cloisters. Humiliation would be the least of her worries if she ever had the misfortune to face the real thing.

༄

Elaine's 'finishing school' ended on Tuesday 6 June. At midday, packed and ready to leave, the Belgian students gathered with their instructors round the radiogram in the drawing room of The Vineyards for the most important bulletin since Neville Chamberlain declared war with Germany in September 1939. Possibly Colonel Woolrych knew, but few others at Beaulieu were aware that within spitting distance of them in the ports and air bases clustered around Southampton for the past few frantic weeks, thousands of men, boats and aeroplanes had been massing, ready to launch Overlord, the largest most critical operation of the war.

> This is the BBC Home Service and here is a special bulletin read by John Snagge.
>
> D-Day has come. Early this morning the Allies began the assault on the north-western face of Hitler's European Fortress … the Allied Commander-in-Chief General Eisenhower has issued an Order of the Day addressed to each individual member of the Allied Expeditionary Force. In it he said: 'Your task will not be an easy one. Your enemy is well-trained, well-equipped and battle-hardened. He will fight savagely. But this is the year 1944. The tide has turned. The free men of the world are marching together to victory.'

And soon, the women too.

NINE

LONDON AND BELGIUM

JUNE–AUGUST 1944

At Baker Street the Head of T Section was due to meet Miss Meeus for the first – and possibly the last – time. Hardy Amies settled with a cigarette to read her passing out report from Beaulieu. She'd had a good SAB but this one, dated 6 June and approved and signed by Stanley Woolrych, seemed more equivocal in its assessment. Ides Floor thought she was up to it but he wanted to be sure his section was making the right decision: about women in general and about Miss Meeus in particular.

She is above the average in intelligence and on occasions has shown that she is able to look after herself. She has a colourless personality …

There was nothing wrong in his book with a colourless personality. In the field it was a positive advantage to disappear in the crowd. Standing out in any way could be fatal. As much as he would have loved to go himself, he had too much self-knowledge to believe he'd make a good agent. He was too large, too loud, too flamboyant – altogether too English – to pass successfully in the field. In his private life and personal habits he was necessarily discreet but even so his preferences would make him a liability. He would never knowingly send another queer behind enemy lines.

… and is inclined to feel she cannot do a thing if it appears at all complicated, without even making an effort.

Beaulieu sometimes got things wrong. They could be infuriatingly incon-
sistent and make misjudgements about students, so it was as well that the
country sections made the final decision about who should go. He knew
Beaulieu: he'd taught there himself in its early days. Not his choice and
certainly not his forte, he winced at the memory of having to teach Nazi
military recognition to bored recruits, keeping barely a couple of pages
ahead of them in the training manual. Thank God Woolrych had got more
of a grip on instructor quality since his own dismal performance. He didn't
envy them their job. The training was impossibly short for the purpose and
some agents didn't even have time to complete that, the need in the field
was so great.

> *Codes: Further practice required. She is unable to write in the French language with any*
> *accuracy.*
>
> *She showed plenty of interest in the course and seems to have absorbed the principles.*
> *She is capable of being a courier but has asked whether it would be possible for her to be*
> *a W/T Operator and seemed to show greater keenness for that than her present intended*
> *role. Provided she has the necessary technical qualifications she should be quite capable*
> *of doing such a job.*

Wireless operators were SOE's most precious asset but they took at least ten
weeks to train from scratch. Being keen and showing an aptitude for Morse
wasn't enough; this was a highly technical job and needed intensive tuition.
He really couldn't spare the time at this stage of the war now Overlord was
behind them, to train her up as a W/T. Like all the European sections, he
was having to pour bods into the occupied countries to ensure the Allied
push continued right through to liberation. If Meeus was judged fit to
be a courier, they'd need her as soon as her basic training was complete.
Hers had been a bit arse-about-face. She'd skipped the commando stuff
at Arisaig and gone straight to Beaulieu. She hadn't yet been to Ringway.
No matter, she'd go now.

If there was one part of an agent's preparation he knew about first-hand
it was the parachute training and he had the badge on his sleeve to prove
it. He believed the least he could do was to share with his agents the vital
and potentially terrifying experience that preceded almost every mission,

so he'd volunteered for the Ringway parachute course in May 1943. It was everything he expected. He was completely bloody terrified sitting waiting for the light in that stripped-down Whitley, but in the event he made respectable descents and survived the course without injury either to his pride or his immaculate person. So he was fully aware of what this latest recruit now faced.

He put out his cigarette and asked his secretary to show her in.

'Miss Meeus, we finally meet.'

'Yes, sir. I usually see Major Floor.'

'He's just returned from an important mission to Belgium, so we're giving him some leave. Do sit.'

The first thing he noticed was that she carried her FANY uniform well; he always looked at a woman's clothes and how they were worn before anything else, even the face. It was part training, part instinct, part preference. But Ides was right: she was small, dark and attractive in a continental way that would make it easy for her to pass as a local. And she had a nice straightforward manner so many simpering English girls lacked. He could quite see how some men might find her irresistible. That could mean trouble ahead, of course. For the moment he was prepared to give her the benefit of the doubt. He remained standing as she sat.

'When shall I be going into Belgium, sir?'

A fair enough question.

'When your training is complete.'

'Oh? I thought Beaulieu was the finishing school.'

'So it is, for the agent training, but you still need to go to Ringway.'

'Ringway?'

'Yes. For the parachute jumping.'

'Parachute jumping?'

The woman was turning into an irritating Little Sir Echo. She also seemed to have gone rather pale. Surely it can't have been a surprise to her.

'Yes, of course. How do you think we get you into Belgium?'

She appeared genuinely shocked.

'I don't know. I didn't think ... maybe a boat? Or a submarine ...'

Either this girl was stupid, or a coward. Either way, she was a liability and rapidly proving his gut feeling to be right: women were temperamentally and intellectually unsuited for this job. He was cross with himself for being talked into the idea against his better judgement.

'What do you think you're doing here? Now you've been through all your training and we can't kick you out, you're telling me you're too bloody scared to jump! What do you think you're up to, wasting all our time like this?'

He expected a cowed silence but she came back at him without hesitation.

'I'm not scared, sir. It's just a bit of a shock, that's all. This is the first time anyone's mentioned parachute jumping.'

'Well you obviously haven't been paying sufficient attention.'

She seemed stung by this.

'But I have, sir. I've worked hard on the courses. I really want to make a contribution. I believe I'm ready, and I know I can do a good job for you.'

'You won't be doing a damn thing for us if you're not prepared to jump out of a plane! In which case, let's not waste any more time. You can leave now.'

He made to move from his desk as if to summarily dismiss her. She rose too but stood her ground. Realising this was her last chance to stay in the game and prove herself, she responded with passion, stamping her foot for emphasis.

'I *will* jump! I *will* jump! I *will* jump!'

So a spirited little Madam then, and obviously not prepared to be browbeaten by him. Alright then, but he wasn't prepared to let her off the hook yet. He sat down, still glowering, poised to sign the paperwork.

'You'd better.' He gave her a penetrating look. 'Or there'll be hell to pay.'

Compared with her first bruising encounter with the top brass at Baker Street, the prospect of going to Manchester to practise jumping out of planes paled somewhat in significance, especially now she was over the initial shock. She got on with most people, but some just rubbed her up the wrong way. Not since Uncle Charles had she felt so rubbed up. She'd behaved rather stupidly and she really should have realised they'd be parachuted in if she'd thought about it, but there was no need for him to have flown into such a filthy temper with her. Now she'd have to work doubly hard to convince him that she wasn't either scared or stupid. At least now her ankles would be up to it after all that pre-breakfast PT at Beaulieu.

No. 1 Parachute Training School at RAF Ringway prepared paratroopers from all the Allied services destined for Europe, including Special Forces people and those who'd just taken part in the D-Day landings. SOE recruits were only a small part of the operation but for security they had instruction and were billeted apart from other trainees. Unlike her previous training courses, Elaine now found herself in a small group of mixed nationalities, all men and all smirking at her as if to say, what's a girl like you doing in a place like this?

A paratrooper, the RAF instructor told them, gets a very thorough training, with a great deal of time spent just on the art of landing correctly and with at least nine practice drops. They, on the other hand, would be lucky to get five days – fewer if the weather was against them – and four drops (Miss Meeus, he said, would be aiming for three, the cue for more knowing looks among the men). But because they would probably only need to jump once or perhaps twice in their operational careers, a crash course would do for them. If they registered the well-worn pun, no one laughed.

The first days were spent learning how to land, relaxed with legs together, knees well up, hands and elbows in front of the chest. First they jumped from modest heights on to coconut matting, then from a trapeze-like swing from a terrifying tower in a hangar on to mattresses and then from the back of a truck moving at a pacey thirty miles per hour on to grass. She was scared, particularly at the top of the tower – it was like being on the high wire in the circus – but she was determined not to let it show. And it comforted her just a little to realise from the joshing bravado of the men that they seemed just as nervous as she was.

To demonstrate the infinite care taken in preparing the parachutes, they went to watch the WAAFs packing them. They practised the difficult job of manhandling the unruly clouds of silk to dispose of them securely after landing. They struggled into the thick canvas jumpsuits and strapped on the round rubber helmets. Then it was off to meet Bessie.

Bessie was one of three barrage balloons tethered in the grounds of nearby Tatton Park, where the drops were practised. If the other two had names, they weren't told them. Four trainees and the instructor climbed into the cradle and sat around the aperture in the centre while Bessie was winched up on its wires to a height of several hundred feet. There they swayed gently beneath the clouds waiting for the order to push themselves through the hole. Here in the eerie silence, Elaine felt sure the others could hear her teeth chatter and her heart pound. She hadn't felt such fear since the mole at Dunkirk, but this was not the time to suppress her feelings by escaping into a second state of mind. She must remain completely alert, conquer her fear, concentrate, listen for the order and then jump.

When the moment came Elaine dropped from the hole and a gut-wrenching sensation ripped the breath from her body, leaving her gasping. Air was screaming all around her, rushing now through her open mouth and nostrils, battering the flesh of her cheeks and piercing the very nerves of her teeth. After only seconds of this high-speed assault, she heard a soft explosion above her as the static line in the balloon opened her parachute and she was gently hoist by the shoulders beneath a billowing silk mushroom. The pain ceased. For an exhilarating thirty seconds she floated over lawns, a lake and flower borders, landing in an ungainly heap but in one piece on open ground.

As she pulled her parachute into the wind to expel the air as they'd been taught, Elaine couldn't believe how ecstatic she felt. It was *wonderful*. More than conquering her fear of the jump, she felt as if she'd conquered the world itself. All she wanted to do now was get back up there and do it all over again.

The next day the weather was good enough for them to do the real thing. Back on the runway they climbed into their waiting Whitley bomber. No wonder crews called them Flying Coffins: their narrow boxy fuselage and inhospitable interior made for a uniquely uncomfortable ride. Inside, they squashed top to toe on the floor of the aircraft, sitting alternately to distribute the weight either side of the aperture as the three engines revved up to a roaring pitch, rattling everything in the fuselage to the point where it seemed the whole superstructure might shake to pieces. They'd had their instructions on the ground, which was just as well as nothing could be heard above the engine noise.

Trainees were numbered in the order in which they were to jump. The red light told them they were in the DZ – the drop zone – the green light told them when to jump through the hole. The main thing to remember with the Whitley was to stay perfectly straight, upright and in the centre, keeping the parachute pack well clear of the aperture, otherwise there was a risk of leaning too far forward, catching your face on the side, knocking your teeth out or breaking your nose.

The silence and airiness of the barrage balloon was far preferable to being cooped up in this cramped, noisy and malodorous space. The nauseating smell of the fire retardant used on the walls of the fuselage was almost overpowering. If she was nervous in the balloon, conditions in the Whitley made her feel physically sick with discomfort and apprehension. The red light went on. A young Pole jumping No. 3 ahead of her reached the hole but took fright and refused to jump, apparently frozen with fear. The dispatcher unhooked his static line and sent him, shivering and humiliated, to the back of the plane to recover his nerve. They were all momentarily unsettled but the instructor briskly waved on No. 4 and jumping soon resumed. Elaine, as No. 5, took her place at the hole as the red light appeared. With the green light she pushed herself forward with all her strength to clear her pack from the aperture and then that familiar, shocking rush of air and adrenalin.

The forward motion of the plane and the slipstream it created meant fewer painful seconds before the blessed relief of the parachute snatching her up from oblivion to send her, euphoric, on a gentle gliding descent to earth. The higher altitude too, meant more precious seconds to enjoy the exhilarating view of the gently oscillating grounds of Tatton Park below. It was more wonderful even than her descent from the balloon. Despite a stiff breeze she made a clean landing, managing to collapse her billowing parachute quickly enough to avoid getting dragged along the ground with it.

Once they were all safely down she went with the others, now joined in common purpose and exultant at their achievement, for notes on their performance from the instructor. No smirking from the men now; she'd proved she was just as good as them and better than some. It was a while before anyone thought to ask what had become of the Polish chap who'd been too scared to jump. He wasn't among them. Perhaps he'd sneaked back to his billet to avoid the ribbing. He wouldn't get away with it that easily. He'd have it coming to him in the morning.

There was no point in a cover-up, so the instructor spoke plainly.

'I'm afraid our Polish colleague has had it. After you'd all jumped – including you, Miss Meeus – he seemed to have some sort of brainstorm. He ran to the hole, yelled some kind of oath and jumped. But the stupid bugger didn't have his 'chute hooked up to the line. So it didn't open. He hit the deck. I'm sorry. Don't let it worry you. We have very few accidents here and this one was entirely preventable.'

It was a chastening reminder not to let pride, panic or bravado overcome common sense. The instructor was right. Ringway's safety record was pretty good considering the dangers involved with novice jumpers. Occasionally parachutes failed to open because of manufacturing or packing faults – the dreaded 'candle' – and there were injuries and some fatalities from bad landings or getting up caught in the lines. There was no point fretting about this one because it could so easily have been avoided. What he omitted to tell them was that accidents were much more likely to happen in the field than in the training grounds of Ringway or Tatton Park.

Elaine had to do one more jump to complete her training, a night descent to simulate operational conditions. For several nights they waited, ready in the hangar for the meteorological reports. Each time they were stood down. In the meantime, she learned how to retrieve and unpack containers of arms and equipment, how to dispose of her parachute by burying it, and how to arrange a reception committee for a container drop or a landing of Lysander aircraft.

The night descent never happened: the weather defeated her. She left Ringway on 17 June to return to London to await instructions, her training incomplete. Nevertheless, Special Training School 51B's report for HQ was positive, if a little patronising:

Was rather nervous during the ground training but tried hard to overcome this. She had no difficulties and was quite fit and cheerful. She made two descents. The first one from the Balloon was quite good though she was very nervous. The second descent was from an aircraft. Her descent was good but she was still a little nervous. It is considered that had she completed the course here her nervousness would have been overcome. She received lectures on containers, disposals and reception committees.
TWO DESCENTS.

Miss Meeus was happy here in spite of natural nervousness and very anxious to return.
She showed no hesitation in the aircraft or balloon when the time came to jump and made
safe landings. The second one being fairly fast. She should return for the night descent.

Elaine never went back to Ringway. A mission for her was already being prepared in Baker Street.

∽

At last, after what seemed like weeks of hanging fire at Bayswater Court with only Captain Whittaker's codes for company, Elaine was relieved finally to receive some instructions. First, she was told to make a will. That was simple: she had nothing to leave and no one to leave it to. Then she was given an address in Knightsbridge where she was to report the following morning.

In a quiet square opposite Harrods and adjacent to its rather ugly Depository she found a group of once smart but now Blitz-weary town-houses. Nearby two high explosive bombs had laid waste to a swathe of Brompton Road almost as far as the Scotch House. Nos 2 and 3 Trevor Square were tucked into a corner by an alleyway. Here she was warmly greeted by a colourful young man wearing make-up.

'Come in, lovey. Get that delightful overall on and we'll make a start on you.'

More intrigued than alarmed, as usual Elaine had no idea what she was in for.

'What will you be doing to me, exactly?'

'We'll be creating someone called Hélène Maes. A.k.a you, my dear. This is Station 15c, the organisation's Make-Up and Photographic Section. Oh, my Lord, I shouldn't be telling you all this. Wash my mouth out …' He walked round her, appraising, touching her hair, 'And what a lovely barnet! We'll have to do something about that!'

A homely woman in her forties guided her to a chair in front of a mirror studded with film star bright lights.

'Do give over, Kevin. Ignore his chatter, dear, he can't help it.'

In fact she found his chatter fascinating, and she learned that the hair and make-up team at Station 15c were all moonlighting from their main jobs in Britain's wartime film industry, churning out heroic B pictures to keep the home front happy. They exchanged gossip about the Hollywood stars she'd met while Kevin and company worked their magic.

Over the next two hours Elaine Madden became Hélène Maes, Belgian citizen resident in Paris and registered with the alien authorities at the Belgian Consulate in Nice, currently unemployed – the character created in her carefully rehearsed cover story at Beaulieu. With her hair rolled up in continental style, a dowdy frock and ageing make-up, she didn't recognise herself.

'Well of course you don't. That's the whole idea, lovey. Now, down to the bowels of the basement with you, so that Tony can take some snaps.'

She would be even more unrecognisable in the austere-looking poses taken for her identity papers, developed on-site and sent on to the group of exiled Poles whose (possibly criminal) expertise in forged documents was without equal in Europe and whose skills were at the disposal of every Allied secret service.

Elaine emerged into the sunlight several hours later, relieved to be herself again and full of excited anticipation that something was finally happening. After all the preparation, the slightly absurd exercises and simulations, she'd soon be on a real mission. She wanted the feeling to last, so instead of going into the Underground at Knightsbridge, she went into Harrods and up the escalator to the first floor ladies' dress department. Just to browse, she told herself, to wander among beautiful, unattainable things and dream of what unimaginable excitements her future might hold…

A few days later she was summoned to a flat in a mansion block off Baker Street where a FANY officer gave her a sheaf of papers in French, mostly typed but with handwritten annotations, the contents of which she was required to read and commit to memory. The Operation Order began:

The name of this operation is IMOGEN and you will be known by this name at the departure point. This name must never be used in the field. Your Head of Mission's operational name is BRABANTIO. The operational name of the wireless operator who will accompany you is DONALBAIN.

She recognised the characters from *Othello* and *Macbeth*, but her own was unfamiliar. Imogen. It sounded very English. She liked it.

But then there were another set of names to be used in the field: she was to be Alice, her *chef de mission* Odette and the W/T Foxtrot. She knew this didn't mean that her organiser was a woman: SOE didn't train women organisers but it wasn't unusual for men to be given women's names for the field.

Her Mission Orders were to act as assistant to Odette and '*under all circumstances*' strictly follow his orders. If anything happened to Odette, she was to transfer her allegiance to a local Resistance leader by the codename Huguette. So many names to remember.

She would be leaving – from where she wasn't told – at some point within the next moon period, between 30 July and 12 August, to be parachuted into an area of the Belgian Ardennes close to Beauraing. This puzzled her. From what she knew of the Ardennes, it was full of thick woods and cavernous river valleys, far from ideal dropping territory. Odette would organise her accommodation and the mission was expected to last at least three months. Before she left she would have a meeting with an evacuation service officer to brief her about the arrangements for her return to England at the end of the mission or in an emergency, whichever came first.

As well as following Odette's instructions, she also had the detailed SHAEF briefing given to all agents infiltrated after D-Day, requiring specific intelligence about launch sites on the Belgian coast for the V1 flying bombs that were now plaguing London and the south-east. She would be issued with 5,000 Belgian francs, with a further 50,000 together with 10,000 French francs concealed in a box of talcum powder. If she needed to prove her bona fides to anyone on the ground, the BBC's Belgian service would broadcast a message ('*We are going to pick blackberries*') at 19.15 hours on certain days.

She'd be paid as a Category 3 agent – £5 a week – to be paid for the duration of her mission and '*for six consecutive months after the official announcement of your death in service*'. Also, in the event of her death, a third of her Category 3 agent's pension would be payable to her beneficiaries. As she didn't have any, she ignored the bit about submitting her instructions in case of death to the British authorities.

The final sheet required her signature. It read:

We must stress that for the sake of your own safety and that of the Organisation it is essential that you keep strictly within the limits of the mission which is hereby assigned to you.
I accept the mission and my operation orders.

Elaine duly signed, as E. Meeus, and dated it London 29 July 1944.

ᕲᕤ

'This isn't just another damned tricky exfiltration job, Ides. Operation Patron-Lysander is Top Priority.'

Amies jabbed in the direction of his colleague with his cigarette for emphasis.

'It's come from the home secretary and chiefs of staff via Gubbins. Belgrave Square want him back here as a matter of urgency to establish the post-liberation order in Brussels *now*, whilst they can still influence events. It's a Lysander job – the codename's the clue – so it's down to us. At least we can count on the full co-operation of the RAF for this one, which will make a refreshing change. He's in hiding, the Gestapo are after him and he can't travel easily – some kind of problem with his legs, apparently. And the moon period is almost upon us. Who've we got available? They have to be first class. We can't afford to take any chances.'

Floor had no hesitation.

'It's got to be Wendelen. And as luck would have it, we've already got a mission lined up for him, going in next moon for sabotage, liaison and the V1 sites. And he'll be carrying Eisenhower's personal message of thanks to the Resistance groups. A little exfiltration job on the side shouldn't tax him too much.'

'Excellent. He's our man.'

Not yet thirty, André Wendelen was without question T Section's star agent. A lawyer by training and a major in the Belgian Army, he'd escaped to London, like Elaine, in May 1940. His potential was spotted from his earliest assessments: his courage, maturity and *'lucid and orderly mind'* were all commented on by senior staff in London and at the training schools. A highly unusual combination of physical, intellectual and organisational strengths made him a gift to SOE as a leader-organiser. He was the man for the job.

'Who's going in with him?'

'Van de Spiegel as W/T. He's worked in Belgium and Holland, knows the terrain. Young, but keen and a very good operator, we've never had a problem deciphering his skeds.'

'Good. And the courier? Ah. Don't tell me, I think I know what you're going to say.'

'Well, why not?'

'I suppose now we've trained her we need to make good use of her. She's had her twenty-first hasn't she? We don't need to chase any relatives for permission?'

'She hasn't done a night drop, but apart from that she's ready and briefed.'

'It's a risk. Do you think she's up to it?'

'I do. Think about it, Hardy. Wendelen's a wanted man. We know there's a reward on his head. He won't be able to move about easily so he'll need someone who can do his bidding without raising suspicion. It's far easier for a woman, out and about, shopping, in cafés, in and out of each other's houses ... and they get stopped in controls far less frequently than the men. It seems obvious to me, but if you're still doubtful ...'

'No, you're right. I'm fussing. But only Wendelen must know Patron's true identity and why we're getting him out. As far as the other two are concerned, it's business as usual – surveillance, sabotage et cetera – with an unexpected Resistance bod to pop on a Lysander for the home run.'

'Of course. Don't worry, Hardy, she'll be fine.'

∞

On 3 August Floor telephoned to tell Elaine she should prepare for departure the following day. She was picked up in the late afternoon by a large Chrysler with curtained windows that were drawn as soon as they left Edgware Road for the A1. So they were going north, but that's all she knew. In the back was the same FANY who'd issued her mission instructions. On the journey she was told, in breathlessly admiring tones, a little about Brabantio/Odette.

'Aren't you the lucky one? Your first time out and with our star agent! I'm so envious. And he really is a sweetie, you'll get on marvellously I'm sure. His English is perfect. But he's been out twice already on sabotage missions and both the Gestapo and the SD – the secret police – are after him. There are wanted posters up everywhere apparently, so he can't show his face anywhere. You're to be his ears, legs and mouth – be his representative in every way he requires. I can't tell you too much about him, but he's a very brave man. Only last month he got the Military Cross, for 'valuable services of a secret nature', though of course he can't be gazetted, which is a shame.'

'Gazetted?' She imagined the king performing some bizarre ceremony on him, possibly involving some kind of incision.

'Yes, you know, have it formally announced in *The London Gazette*. The government publication? So that the world knows how brave you've been.'

What she couldn't tell Elaine, and perhaps didn't know herself, was that Wendelen had already distinguished himself on two extended sabotage missions to the industrial area of Liege in 1942 and 1943, doing considerable damage to German power and communications networks. Here he'd helped build a formidable Resistance organisation, Groupe G, enlisting fellow students and professors he knew and trusted from his time at Brussels University, keeping it busy with SOE-supplied drops of arms and explosives. After both missions he went on the run, making his way back to London the first time via Switzerland over the course of many tortuous months. The second time he got out via Gibraltar using the Resistance-organised *Cométe* escape line – but only after sundry close shaves and being thrown in prison in Pamplona by the Spanish and bluffing his way out as a Canadian.

When he'd finally got back to London for the second time at the end of 1943, he'd kept contact with Groupe G and was now anxious to see further action as the Allies fought their way out of the Normandy *bocage*, making the liberation of Belgium a realistic prospect at last.

'Any questions?'

Too many, and none. Now the moment had come, she felt an unexpected void. It was all rather overwhelming. Nervousness had taken the place of excitement. All that preparation, all those instructions and yet she still felt she'd be jumping into the unknown. But Belgium wasn't unknown, she told herself, it was her adopted country. She thought of the Memorial School. In her head she heard them singing 'I Vow to Thee, My Country' in the Pilgrims' Hall and Mr Allen telling them about their solemn duty to serve others and their British homeland. She reminded herself why she'd volunteered for this in the first place: to do her bit and use the skills and abilities she knew she had to help Britain and Belgium overcome the Nazi oppression of Europe. As her FANY escort chatted away, Elaine had a stern and silent conversation with herself. Soon she was feeling calmer and more confident.

When the curtains were finally pulled back after a couple of hours, the light outside was failing and they were in deep country lanes, somewhere she guessed in the heart of the rural Midlands. She had no idea where as many of the signposts still hadn't been replaced long after the threat of invasion had passed. There was no indication on the solitary sentry box outside the military base but she recognised the guard's uniform as American. All nervousness gone now, she was excited at the thought of meeting her fellow agents. This, she was sure, was the start of her destiny.

༺࿇༻

For the Carpetbaggers based at USAAF 179 Harrington, the 4–5 August was just another busy night. Forty-two drops were rostered, the majority into France, a handful to Belgium. In the operations block, Flight Officer Wright of 850th Squadron, 801st Bomb Group briefed his crew of eight about their assigned sortie.

'OK fellas, tonight on Operation Tybalt One-Five we have three Joes, twelve containers and five packages. A blind drop, no reception committee so we trust Eureka will be in place to get us to pinpoint. This is our route down to Beauraing – out over the Suffolk coast entering enemy territory through Holland, then looping down to the Ardennes. Usual routine: 5,000 feet till the enemy coast, then as low as we dare. We know where the flak areas are by now, but you'll keep a watch out for night fighters.'

Tail gunner May looked up from his magazine and nodded.

'What's the weather, Brinkman?'

'Fine, boss, a few bits of fluffy white stuff. Nothing to bother us. Dangerous moonlight all the way.'

'Is she loaded yet?'

Bombardier Sauer took a look out of the window to the hardstanding and their waiting B-24 Liberator.

'Loading the last containers now, boss.'

'Wagner, everything ready for dispatch?'

'Check.'

'Good. Should be a breeze. Let's go pick up the Joes.'

In the 'dressing huts', chaperoned by her FANY escort, Elaine was being checked over by dressers from the American OSS. English labels had already been carefully removed from her day clothes and replaced by French and Belgian ones. Now they looked for those small giveaways that could so easily betray a novice agent: the used London bus ticket screwed up and forgotten in a coat pocket, the wrong brand of cigarettes, Elizabeth Arden powder in the compact ...

Declared clean of telltale items, she heaved the canvas jumpsuit over her day clothes and coat and was ready to be briefed about her equipment. She took the compass and 'Wonder' pocket torch. The spade with detachable handle for burying her parachute was strapped to her leg for the descent. Then the flashlight, hacksaw and emergency escape kit. And lastly the commando knife. There were binoculars, spirit flasks and pistols there too, but she wasn't offered any of these. As she was being shown the hidden compartments in her jumpsuit for identity papers, ration cards and personal money, an urbane voice with hardly a trace of accent rang across the hut.

'Ah, our Imogen, I presume.'

She looked up from zipping her papers back in the pocket to see a tallish man, perhaps in his early thirties, approach her. He was wearing his jumpsuit with such ease and familiarity he might have been born in it. Smiling, he held out his hand.

'Hello Imogen, Brabantio at your service. And may I introduce our W/T, Donalbain?'

A smaller, younger man following in his impressive wake stepped forward to shake her hand.

The man as yet known to her only as Brabantio/Odette lowered his voice out of earshot of the dressers and spoke in French. 'Don't worry, we'll drop all this Shakespearian stuff as soon as we're off.' Then back to perfectly modulated English: 'I must say, it's very good to meet you at last. How are you feeling? Raring to go?'

She didn't know what she was expecting but whatever her image of a hero, he wasn't it. Even in his jumpsuit, with his carefully barbered hair and beautifully controlled manners he seemed more junior bank manager than dashing saboteur. But the authority in his voice inspired confidence and she recognised warmth in his grey eyes. She felt immediately and unshakeably safe in his presence.

'Raring to go, sir.'

'You don't have to call me "sir". I'm not especially keen on Odette, either. We'll agree something later. Have you got all your kit?'

'I think so.'

The dresser intervened. 'Just the pills to go, sir.'

'Oh yes, the pills. Just the B and K for me, sergeant, the uppers and downers.'

'No L, sir? You're sure?'

'No L, sergeant. But I think Imogen should have one, just in case.'

The dresser showed her the cyanide pill in its rubber coating, concealed in the base of a lipstick. She accepted it without comment and added it to her personal effects.

'And for you, sir, a .38 Browning and fifty rounds, commando knife, torch and flask containing eight ounces of rum.'

'The really essential items. OK then, let's pick up our 'chutes and find our hosts.'

As they walked across the hardstanding to the waiting aeroplane, above the engine noise he said:

'OK, from now on you can call me André. Don't worry, I'll look after you.' At least, that's what she thought he said, it was too noisy to be certain. She hoped she wouldn't need looking after, but there was something wonderfully reassuring about his presence.

The inside of the Liberator was just as basic as the Flying Coffin, but at least it offered the luxury of space and the only unpleasant smell was kerosene. The welcome from Dispatcher Wagner – they'd have no contact with Flight Officer Wright or the rest of his crew – was warm and effusive, especially for Elaine.

'Hey, whad'ya know? Our Joe's a Jane! Welcome to the One Hundred and First, sweetheart. You're riding with the professionals now, fellas, so just take it easy. Cabin service will be right along with the cocktails.'

Since the start of Operation Carpetbagger and the close operational engagement of OSS with SOE earlier that year, Special Forces drops were being shared between the RAF from Tempsford, not too far away in the Bedfordshire countryside, and the USAAF here at Harrington. Rivalries inevitably ensued and performance comparisons made. Elaine had heard gossip, most likely perpetrated by RAF crews, about the Yanks' unreliability, untrustworthiness and general lack of the stuff that made the Brylcreem Boys supreme in the skies. Wendelen and van de Spiegel were in the unusual position of being able to make a proper comparison, as they'd flown with both. RAF crews naturally prided themselves on their pinpoint accuracy and superior experience; the American boys took a more relaxed approach to the job but delivered their 'Joes' more or less intact and with good humour. Both occasionally missed their targets, hit flak or had to abort in atrocious weather. Some never returned to base. All risked their lives dropping their precious cargo in to occupied territory.

According to Wright's log written in the early hours of the following morning, at 23.10 the Liberator, in sequence with the forty-one others on special ops that evening, took off into the night sky.

The agents of Operation Imogen laughed and joked over their late supper of corned beef rolls and snatched odd periods of sleep as the Liberator followed its appointed course, navigating by landmark and moonlight alone, over the North Sea to the Dutch coast. They woke to the sound of flak and Gunner May in action, but the dispatcher reassured them it was nothing much and they'd soon be through it.

Just before 1 a.m. as they approached the drop zone the Liberator dropped to 600 feet and slowed to release the containers and the heavily padded packages containing their radio equipment. The agents prepared themselves and checked that their parachute packs were secure. Elaine insisted she would go No. 1. She wanted to show them she wasn't afraid.

And to make absolutely sure she would jump. If she went first, she'd have to.

The containers, like giant cigars, plopped with their parachutes out into the night sky and the plane picked up speed to circle for its second approach. Red light on. This was it. They hooked their parachutes to the line and Elaine went to her position by the 'Joe hole' as the dispatcher opened the hatch. They were flying so near the ground and the night was so brilliantly moonlit that the shadow of the plane skimming the treetops was clearly visible below. Remembering, Elaine turned to the others and yelled above the engine noise.

'*Merde!*'

'*Merde!* See you in Belgium!'

'OK fellas, we're right on pinpoint.'

Elaine got into the sitting position by the hole ready to jump, with her head up and knees bent as she'd been taught.

She'd barely registered the light turning to green when Dispatcher Wagner picked her up bodily by the straps of her harness, brought her sharply towards him, gave her a wet kiss full on the lips and dropped her, breathless with surprise, through the Joe hole into the Ardennes night.

TEN

BELGIUM

AUGUST–SEPTEMBER 1944

L aid out like a living map in the August moonlight beneath her was a calm and brilliantly lit vista that looked nothing like the Belgian Ardennes. Where there should have been dense forests a broad uncluttered plateau of crop fields stretched apparently for miles, punctuated only by the occasional copse and isolated farmhouse. Instead of spectacular gorges and deep river valleys the gently rolling countryside was scored only by cart tracks. Nature and man together had contrived to make the perfect drop zone.

Floating above the fields in the beautiful summer night, she was so absorbed in the exhilarating moment the passing shadows of her fellow agents barely registered. She was fully awake – her unorthodox exit from the Liberator had seen to that – yet transfixed as if in a wonderful dream. This joyous moment seemed to go on blissfully, endlessly, until she saw the two men, figures in miniature on the ground below, already folding up their parachutes.

With a shock she realised she wasn't descending at all. The warm night air and her full-size parachute were conspiring to keep her suspended in mid-air. No one at Ringway had told her what to do in these unlikely circumstances so she wriggled and jumped up and down in the air, trying to get the parachute to move. When it resisted any attempt to coax it into compliance she pulled down hard on the cords on one side to try to expel the warm air keeping her aloft. After more wriggling, tugging and manoeuvring she was finally caught on a downdraught and within feet of a field of corn.

She let go of the cords to adopt the brace position for landing and a gust of air breathed new life into the parachute and she started floating gently upwards once more. In desperation now, she punched the large disc below her chest to unhitch her harness, shrugged it off and dropped unencumbered the final few feet to the ground whilst her parachute floated momentarily up and away, to die among the sheaves of corn with a sigh of artificial silk.

The euphoria of descent and her last-minute struggles to land meant she was still high on adrenalin. She'd done it! She was on Belgian soil and the adventure had begun. The possibility that the enemy might have heard the plane, spotted her as she floated oblivious on her sky-borne idyll, or that this adventure might finally call her number, didn't cross her mind. She was back in Belgium and with a job to do.

She ran over to André shouting 'I'm down! I'm down!' but the men seemed not even to have noticed that she'd been in difficulty.

'Ssh! Where's your parachute?'

She pointed to the heap of silk. 'Over there.'

'Well go and fold it up. Quickly, we need to bury them!'

Feeling like an errant schoolgirl, she scrabbled to pack her parachute into as small a parcel as possible for the hole where two similar shapes were already stowed, awaiting exhumation and safekeeping by their host for the night.

They made their way to a farm at the crossroads of two dirt tracks at the edge of a wooded ridge. The farmer was a trusted Resistance hand who'd received and sheltered as many as ten agents since 1942. André greeted him warmly, but the formality of exchanging passwords still had to be gone through, absurd as they might sound to a passing eavesdropper.

'*I've come to collect the kilo of coffee wrapped in the towel and I've brought the materials to make a new bridle for the stallion.*'

To which the ridiculous response came back:

'*Tybalt left the coffee there and the farmer still has it.*'

They embraced as a silent cadre of men dispersed to the fields to gather up the containers, load them on to a cart and bring them into the barn ready for the morning. After simple refreshments the agents retired to separate quarters to sleep the few precious remaining hours of a busy night.

They were up with the sunrise to unpack the containers and prepare for their journey to Brussels and their first rendezvous with Huguette. Outside the barn Elaine breathed in the untainted air, so clean and bracing after sooty London. The open countryside and waving wheat reminded her of something, a phrase she'd heard somewhere … Yes, that was it. It stuck in her mind because it was just after the fall of France, soon after their flight from Dunkirk. She was safe but Britain was alone and in grave danger. A speech by Mr Churchill in Parliament was reported on the radio. He'd said that if Britons could defeat Hitler, Europe would be free and all the world could move forward into *broad, sunlit uplands*. Such a striking image. There was nothing like it in low, flat Flanders with its heavy skies. He must have been thinking of the rolling, open countryside of the Home Counties, the Surrey-Sussex border perhaps and that view towards the sea she'd seen from her window at Winterfold. Now here they were in the Belgian Ardennes, these broad sunlit uplands, waiting to be freed. This is what they were fighting for.

Among the unpacked radio equipment, arms and other materiel in the barn Elaine retrieved her suitcase of personal effects, chosen by London. Astonished, from a sheaf of tissue paper she pulled out the most beautiful grey and white tweed costume: a skirt with deep box pleats back and front and matching tailored jacket, nipped in at the waist and with neat reveres. She'd seen something similar in Harrods; it must have cost a fortune – and an entire ration book of clothing coupons. Perhaps Lieutenant-Colonel Amies with his penchant for immaculately tailored uniforms had changed his mind about her and decided to mark her SOE debut with a special present …

To go with it was a pair of stylish shoes with big crepe soles and an expensive black leather handbag. She opened the gold clasp to explore its plush interior.

'Oh no! I don't believe it! Just look at this label. "Made in England" in great gold letters! I thought they checked all this kind of thing.'

André was absorbed with checking a consignment of explosives.

'Damn. They haven't given us nearly enough time pencils. What? You'll just have to cut it out.'

'I can't. It's sewn into the leather. I'll have to try and scratch it out some-how. Sorry. I know you've got a thousand things to do. You shouldn't have to worry about stupid things like handbags. It really is too bad of London.'

He put the box of time pencils down and laughed.

'Handbags are the least of my problems over the coming weeks, I can assure you. Let's have a look. But we don't have much time. After we've checked this lot we still have to have to try and get to Brussels today to meet Huguette.'

As they worked together to expunge the incriminating evidence, Elaine felt at ease, useful. I like this man, she thought. He's practical, prepared to help and he knows how to talk to women. There was something more about him that she couldn't quite identify, but she knew she felt secure in his company. They managed to obliterate the offending letters without it looking too obvious, then returned to the serious business of unpacking and sorting the equipment they'd need from the supplies designed for clandestine onward delivery to local Resistance groups, disguised under cartloads of straw or turnips.

She was only starting to get to know André but she'd spoken barely a few words to the W/T operator. Foxtrot was a contained young man. 'Pianists', as they were dubbed, were a breed apart. With their own distinctive 'hand' they played their Morse machines with as much skill as accomplished piano soloists. Often solitary creatures, they were comfortable with their own company. They had to be, set apart from their team for much of the time and alternating between long periods of inactivity waiting for the next scheduled transmission – perhaps with security scares and several changes of safe house to contend with – and intense bursts with headphones and Morse handset. And then all through the 'sked' there was the ever-present danger of discovery by Direction Finder (DF) vans that could detect a transmitter in operation within a 200-metre radius in less than fifteen minutes.

Jacques van de Spiegel knew the form and got on with it. Whilst in the Ardennes, his safe house would be in Jemelle, a nearby railway town. It was for here that he presently set off by bicycle, in the filthy dark overalls of a rail worker, taking his leave of André and Elaine with a wave. For the moment he was without much of his radio equipment. They'd been issued with two transmitter-receivers, each contained in an innocent-looking suitcase, one more powerful and up to date than the other, which would be used as a standby. Jacques wasn't due a scheduled transmission to London for another few days and it had been agreed that it would be safer day-to-day for Elaine to carry the small suitcase containing the main set.

Women were far less likely to be stopped in routine controls and snap searches whereas young men were invariably targets, especially in big towns. Here in the countryside it was easier to pass as an essential worker on the land or, as Jacques' cover story would claim, as a railway worker. But they would all need to move between the Ardennes and Brussels as circumstances demanded, so for security Elaine was in charge of the radio. This was no mean task: it weighed over six kilos – but this was still considerably lighter than the earlier Marconi model used by SOE for much of the war. And there was always the risk of discovery. No matter; it was their lifeline to London and she was being entrusted with it.

So, carrying the radio suitcase and dressed in her dashing new outfit, Elaine followed André after a discreet interval to the station at Beauraing. They knew from their training never to travel or be seen together in public if this could be avoided. Beauraing wasn't the nearest station, but they'd been warned off the local halt at Martouzin-Neuville by London: the station master there was a known Rexist and almost certainly a Nazi collaborator. She remembered her childhood encounter with Degrelle and his Rexists in Poperinghe; nascent Nazis, they were violent then and even more dangerous now.

When she got to the station after a dusty walk of several miles, she found André in the deserted booking hall.

'We're not going to get to Brussels today, I'm afraid. With connections and some of the line out with sabotage …' he smiled as if he knew exactly who was responsible, '… it can't be done. We'll go into Ciney instead. I know the local Resistance leader there. It's a picturesque trip beside the Meuse – it's going to take more than hour but there's a train due in fifteen minutes. When you get there, go to the Central Café in the north-west corner of the square and ask for Delphine. Say you're meeting me. Use field names, obviously. You go first. I'll be right behind you. You don't know me till we're in secure company.'

'Understood.'

Ciney was obviously once a prosperous country town, now brought low by four years of occupation and austerity, the fruits of its land and people diverted to feed the insatiable German war machine. On her way from the station on the outskirts to the wide town square Elaine instinctively looked among the Wanted posters for André's photograph. There were several on the rue de Commerce, the main road into town, alone. She was struck by the signs everywhere in German, the swastikas fluttering from the grand Hotel de Ville and the fine Post Office, and the conspicuous lack of young men. The streets didn't need to be full of grey-green uniforms to subjugate this town. Like all of occupied Belgium, it had an air of weary compliance. And yet beneath the surface, in back rooms, barns and cellars plans were being made, guerrilla groups prepared. Resistance was alive and kicking, ramping up for its most important role of the war.

In the centre of the square a charming Art Nouveau bandstand stood empty and peeling. The church to one side had half its spire missing as if someone – the Devil perhaps – had come along with a giant pair of scissors and snipped it off in spite. It was market day and the square and the bars ranged around it were crowded. The goods on offer on the stalls were poor things in these straitened times and few were buying, but market day was the traditional excuse for old men to gather in bars and womenfolk to gossip in the square, so why should the occupation make any difference? There were few German uniforms in evidence. She hadn't been stopped, though she had attracted plenty of looks, and not just from the men. Catching sight of herself in a shop window she realised with a shock that she must stick out like a sore thumb in her smart city outfit – slightly travel tarnished but unmistakably a mannequin among the rustic aprons, scarves and shawls.

The Central Café was easy enough to find. Glad of sanctuary from the stares and relieved to sit down after a tiring journey with her heavy load, she went to an empty table and put the suitcase carefully under it.

'Yes Madame?'

'Coffee please.'

The young waitress looked at her for several seconds, apparently appraising her outfit and judging whether to ask the next question.

'Real or ersatz?'

She had no hesitation.

'Real.'

Ersatz coffee was disgusting, she'd had enough of that in London. She'd been looking forward to proper continental coffee and she had plenty of francs in her purse to pay for it. She felt she deserved it.

When the tiny phial arrived containing barely a mouthful of the thick black liquid, accompanied by an outrageous bill, she realised she'd made her first mistake. How stupid of her, and how ignorant of wartime shopping those men at Beaulieu were. Of course coffee was a precious commodity. It was available on the open market but only in minute quantities and at exorbitant cost. She tried to look nonchalant, as if she ordered it all the time.

'Thank you. I'm looking for Delphine. Is she here?'

The waitress nodded and disappeared behind the bar. In time an older woman emerged from the kitchen wiping her hands on her apron and approached her. Elaine spoke first.

'Hello. I'm Alice and I'm due to meet Odette here.'

The woman looked her up and down just as the waitress had done, then led her to a back room and told her to wait. Within five minutes she could hear André's voice the other side of the door, talking to the woman about getting a message to someone called Willy Gerard. And then from Delphine a clearly articulated plea.

'And by the way, comrade, your friend! She looks as if she's just stepped off the boat! For her sake and ours, you can't let her walk about like that. She *smells* English! We haven't seen shoes like that in the past four years. And that suit …! If she goes around looking like that, she'll be picked up in no time.'

She heard André sigh. He appeared at the door, smiling and apologetic.

'Sorry Alice, after all that trouble we went to, the handbag's got to go.'

After the attentions of Delphine Elaine left the Central Café alone later that afternoon looking less like a Harrods model and much more like her Belgian doppelganger Hélène Marie Maes, the gorgeous grey and white tweed suit, crepe-soled shoes and beautiful English handbag consigned to a dark corner where they could no longer incriminate her. She'd been in Belgium barely twenty-four hours but she'd learned her first painful lessons about 'passing' in the field. It would be funny if it wasn't so potentially serious. She said nothing to André but a worry niggled away at her. If Amies *had* had a hand in the choice of her outfit, then he was doing her no favours at all. Was it a mistake? Some kind of test? Or was the man who'd already rubbed her up the wrong way at Baker Street deliberately setting out to make life more difficult for her?

∽

Within thirty-six hours she was installed with André in a smart flat off Brussels' Avenue Louise, a main thoroughfare into the city lined with expensive shops and apartment blocks. Less comfortably, the Gestapo was headquartered in a plush Art Deco building at number 347, minutes away around the corner from their new billet.

Their surprisingly sumptuous accommodation – Elaine had her own small suite of rooms – had been arranged for them by Wendelen's well-connected Resistance contact Walter de Selys Longchamps, the head of Groupe G in the Ardennes and scion of a noble line steeped in Belgian public life. His heroic cousin Jean had escaped to Britain in 1940 and joined the RAF. In 1943 he'd flown his Typhoon into those same Gestapo headquarters in a daring and totally unauthorised airstrike for which he got both a severe reprimand and the Distinguished Flying Cross for bravery. He was killed only months later when his plane crashed in Kent. Elaine knew nothing of all this, she would know Walter only by his alias, Willy Gerard.

Brussels was very different from the Ardennes, as she'd expected. What she hadn't appreciated was quite how different it would be from London. Apart from the Nazi flags and banners and the uniforms everywhere on the streets, the city looked untouched by war. Allied bombing raids were being concentrated on communications networks, ports and war production centres – and now on suspected V1 launch sites on the coast. For the poor and law abiding, life was still no doubt very difficult in the capital: strict rationing was in force and she noticed that butchers' shop windows displayed pictures of meat instead of the real thing. But for the wealthy and influential *Bruxellois*, life seemed to carry on much as before. Their womenfolk dressed in the latest Paris fashions (Elaine thought longingly of that lovely tweed costume hidden away in Ciney) and their dinner tables were lavishly provided for with black market luxuries. They didn't go without.

Willy Gerard had provided well-connected contacts to add to André's established network of friends and colleagues and they were not short of dinner invitations in houses in upmarket areas of the city unlikely to be subject to Gestapo raids. Among them was a Madame Lippens, a society lady of a certain age, well known for her good works, less well known for her invaluable facility for moving with equal ease between the great and good of the city, its German occupiers and its underground Resistance movement.

Since arriving André had been busy making contact with the prime movers of this dedicated but disparate movement. Or rather his 'ears, mouth and legs' had on his behalf. Their mission brief was to ensure that the individual groups received the arms, explosives and cash supplied by London, that their sabotage targets were carefully selected and co-ordinated, and that they were properly briefed about preparations for the longed-for liberation. Along the way, they were also meant to gather intelligence for London on troop movements and the supply and position of mobile launch sites on the Belgian coast for the V1 flying bombs. It was already a packed mission and Elaine still had no idea about the sensitive exfiltration job so recently added to their brief.

To fulfil her contact tasks, she used the good offices of a number of café-bars sympathetic to the cause. The Coq d'Or in a rather disreputable street close to their apartment was one of these. The eponymous cock sat atop a painted plinth in the window facing one of two directions: if to the left it was safe to enter and do business; if to the right it was better to pass swiftly by. She met people face-to-face but more often she would leave – or collect – coded messages inside a newspaper or package to be picked up almost immediately without direct contact.

It didn't take her long to appreciate that André was plugged in, not only to his own creation, Groupe G, but with principals from all the major Resistance movements operating in post D-Day Belgium. They all had different political agendas and priorities, and they all shared a profound distrust of each other. This meant an active reluctance to co-ordinate sabotage activities among themselves to avoid duplication or disaster – despite the existence of a central *Commitée de Co-ordination* and the best diplomatic efforts of André Wendelen.

Though she wasn't involved in the detail of their transactions, Elaine soon learned to identify and distinguish between the different groups: the Partisans, established groups Nola and the Communist FIL, the relatively new Milice Patriotique, the MNB (Movement National Belge) and the Secret Army who, grown bored with mere sabotage, now itched for full guerrilla warfare. Through the muddle of disparate aims, specialisms and foibles there was a common respect for Agent Odette as a patriot and proven saboteur. He was their vital source of materiel and conduit for information to and from the exiled Belgian government and its security service, the Sûreté de l'État. More important to the smooth execution of pre-liberation strategy, he was their main contact with SHAEF HQ in London. Because they trusted him, they had no choice – despite an initial *froideur* in dealing with a young woman barely into her age of majority – but to trust his courier. It helped that one of the first messages she brought them was a personal note of congratulation from the Supreme Allied Commander himself, General Eisenhower, for their valuable sabotage work.

In practice, because of the weight of the mission brief, much of Wendelen's day-to-day liaison work with the groups would be delegated to two trusted local agents, Huguette and Nelly. It was better to have a ridiculous codename than risk betrayal by loose talk or through torture. Huguette had excellent contacts and good diplomatic skills; Nelly was particularly 'in' with the Secret Army but because of some mysterious and intractable grudge, Groupe G would have nothing to do with him.

Herding cats, André confided, would be easier than keeping this lot together and focussed on SHAEF's plan for the liberation of their country.

In the meantime he had secret business of his own with a Jean de Landsheere and a Baron Goffinet, which he shared with Elaine only when it was complete some days later.

One of the most important contacts Elaine made in her first week in Brussels was with a young woman called Denise Leplat, an experienced local fixer based in Liege, who would help her find safe houses for Foxtrot to transmit from and recruit people to man his 'close protection service' – the early warning system out on the street designed to alert him to the presence in the area of the horribly efficient German DF vans. The meeting went well: Leplat was both efficient and friendly. She already had an established network of safe houses dotted around the city and beyond, and a rota of trusted helpers she could call on, most of them women. Elaine was relieved not to have to work hard to overcome the initial suspicion she'd encountered from the men and they parted on excellent terms with an agreed plan for Foxtrot while in Brussels.

She felt confident that everything was going well. They'd been in the country almost a week and all was going to plan, good contacts had been made and she'd had no trouble from controls despite often carrying the radio or small arms, sometimes both. Her false papers had barely been looked at. But Woolrych's warning at Beaulieu had registered: undue confidence could be fatal. André had also warned her that though the Germans were on the brink of defeat, no one knew how long this would take. As a result of this heightened tension, Hitler's high command were more paranoid than ever and desperate to salvage his vision of the Third Reich. The Gestapo and the SD – the *Sicherheitsdienst*, the Nazi Party's own secret police – were everywhere, troops were trigger-happy and everyone was a suspect. Round-ups and revenge shootings had become a horrific feature of everyday life. Resistance workers and the foreign agents who supported them were more at risk now than at any time in the war.

It was on her return from another rendezvous that she had her first real security scare. Walking through the quiet suburban streets, she became conscious of a 'follower', a textbook Gestapo goon in standard-issue mac and Homburg despite the heat. He wasn't doing a very good job of disguising his intentions – he stood out a mile – but that was merely a professional observation, he still posed a threat. At least she wasn't carrying the radio but there was a pistol underneath vegetables in her shopping bag that she'd been unable to pass to a contact earlier in the day. A half-thorough search would find it. Perhaps her rendezvous had been under surveillance and her contact was already blown. She needed to confirm that she really was the one he was interested in and then try to lose him. Her Beaulieu training would now be put to the test.

It was much too obvious to stop to tie a shoelace. In any case she wasn't wearing lace-up shoes: it was high summer and only old ladies wore lace-ups in summer. Another tactic apparently designed without women in mind. There was safety in numbers so it would be sensible to get to some-where she could disappear in a crowd. She hopped on the nearest tram, changing to another at the last minute. Her shadow stuck doggedly behind her. It was definitely her he was after.

She alighted as soon as she saw a large parade of shops. It wasn't as crowded as she'd have liked, but it would have to do. Her pace slowed to a meander as she mingled with shoppers, pausing to look in several windows before stopping for a good look at her reflection – and that of her follower, now loitering rather obviously in a doorway several shops away. Escape tactics now came into play.

She weighed up the options. There was no café-bar where she could go, as if to the lavatory, and then look for a back way out. She could probably outrun him but she'd been taught *'walk, never run, never show fear'*. There was a lingerie shop with several women browsing and at the counter inside. He wouldn't have the nerve to follow her in there: he'd have to wait for her to leave from a discreet distance across the road.

In she went and starting browsing among the negligees, picking out two and waiting until Madame was busy with a customer to slip into an empty changing cubicle unnoticed. With the curtain pulled tightly across she set about her modest disguise. She didn't have much time but it was amaz-ing how the addition of a headscarf and the subtraction of a jacket could transform one's appearance. She quickly wiped off her make-up, tied up her hair in a turban with the scarf and tucked the bag of vegetables and the gun with it, under a chair. This was a loss they could ill afford but it meant it could no longer incriminate her. She hated wasting the vegetables too but it couldn't be helped.

The 'resting' actor at Beaulieu had shown them that mere disguise was hardly ever sufficient to convince: they had to alter their bodily stance, their gait, their demeanour in some way too. She stuffed tissue paper from the negligee into the toes of her shoes. This was uncomfortable, but it would force her to walk with shorter, more mincing steps and so hold her body in a different way. She took off her stockings and stuffed them into her brassiere, giving her a more matronly décolleté. It would have to do. Finally, she furrowed her brow and experimented in the mirror with a variety of worried expressions. She might just get away with it.

With her clutch purse and jacket under her arm and holding a small parcel from the discarded shopping bag, she emerged a different, older woman. If Madame had noticed the transformation, she made no sign of it, acknowledging the return of the garments to the counter with a nod. She followed two women out of the shop, as if she was with them. Yes, there he was, conspicuous as ever in a shop doorway opposite.

She walked purposefully to one of the last shops in the parade before she dared glance in a window to see whether her disguise had worked or whether he was still in pursuit. Oh joy, he was still waiting in the doorway, eyes fixed on the door of the lingerie shop. She didn't wait to see if he would finally catch on but hurried as quickly as her crippling shoes would carry her to the nearest tram stop and from there down into the Metro.

It had all taken much longer than she thought. When she got back to the apartment, still buzzing from her successful escape but now walking without impediment and her hair free, André was waiting for her.

'I was getting worried. I thought you were meeting Lapoivre this afternoon? It's gone ten. And ...' he looked suspiciously in the direction of her breasts, '... you look a bit ... unusual. Are you alright?'

She looked down at her artificially enlarged chest and laughed with relief. She'd almost forgotten about the stockings. She hadn't felt frightened at all this evening but now she was back she realised how good it was to be in a safe haven with someone calm and sympathetic to talk to about it all.

'Oh, I'm fine. I just had to lose a follower, that's all. Gestapo I think. I stuffed my stockings up there and I could hardly take them out on the Metro! Luckily, he was pretty useless and didn't see through my pathetic disguise. But you would have been proud of me.'

'I'm sure. God, the things they teach you at Beaulieu these days. Amazing. But well done, it's not easy to lose a tail. And I rather like the new *embonpoint*. Perhaps you could leave the stockings in?'

It was so obviously a joke but she blushed and he hastened to apologise.

'I'm sorry, that was quite uncalled for. Go and get yourself tidied up, then come and have a drink. You can tell me all about your trials with the Gestapo and then I need to brief you on something important.'

Elaine spent more time in her bathroom than she intended, removing the stockings and having a strip-down wash, but also taking time to look at her breasts in a new light. They were perfectly alright, she thought. Neat, not big but not small either. She'd always taken pride in her appearance, but for the first time she realised that she cared very much about how she might look to others. Perhaps to one in particular.

Restored to her usual self, she relayed the adventure to André over a glass of wine. He laughed at her ingenuity and congratulated her once again as he lit her cigarette.

'Well done, you've come through your first real test. Now, here's another. We've got a new job, and it has to be done whilst we've still got the moon.'

'A pickup?'

'Yes. Our passenger needs to get away to London urgently. The Gestapo have got their sights on him. They think he runs the Secret Army. He doesn't, but he's still important to us. I can't tell you much more. We've got to recce landing sites for a Lysander. I've got the perfect one in mind at Sovet but it'll still be tricky convincing the RAF. They're such fussy buggers. And I'm warning you, the clock ray descriptions they insist on having are a damned nuisance to code.'

This was all news to Elaine, but at least she'd heard of clock ray descriptions. They were based on a clock face but weren't nearly as simple as they sounded. None of this was in the mission brief, but then she'd made a solemn pledge to follow Odette's orders under all circumstances. An exfiltration exercise would test more of the skills learned in training and would make a change from running courier errands and dodging goons.

'I'll do my best. When do we start?'

'First thing tomorrow. I need you to take the radio to Foxtrot in Jemelle. I'll be right behind you but I have to go back to Sovet, do the clock ray routine for you to code for London. Good luck with that, by the way. Then there's a special job for you. Our pickup is being moved from his safe house tonight, down to Willy Gerard's place outside Halloy – it's close to the landing field. You're to go on to Willy's where our man will be holed up till we can get him away. You'll be his warder-cum-nursemaid for the duration. Take good care of him. We need him.'

'Alright.' She looked doubtful. Babysitting a semi-prisoner, perhaps a reluctant one, alone in some isolated farmhouse in the Ardennes countryside didn't sound such a fascinating assignment. He caught the look, misread it as apprehension, and smiled at her reassuringly.

'Don't worry. He can't run far. Apparently he's a cripple. So, *Merde!*'

They touched glasses and looked each other in the eye as continental custom dictated. He held her gaze.

'You know my name, now I think it's time I knew yours.'

'Imogen. Alice. Hélène. Take your pick. They're all me.'

'Really? I doubt that. What's your real name?'

'Isn't that against the rules?'

'Certainly. But I've told you mine, and who's going to know if we only use them between ourselves? You don't need to tell me anything else about yourself. But I don't feel I can get to know you properly till I know your name.'

She was being seduced into revealing something she shouldn't, but it didn't matter. She trusted him absolutely.

'My name's Elaine. Elaine Madden.'

He touched her glass again.

'Well then, Miss Elaine Madden. I'm very glad to know you. Now you'd better drink up and get your beauty sleep. We've got a busy time ahead.'

Awake and restless, Elaine went over and over the day's events. What if her rendezvous with Lapoivre had been observed? And supposing her tail hadn't been fooled by her disguise? Could she have evaded him? She rehearsed alternative scenarios and escape strategies. A visceral excitement was holding back sleep. Not just about the work. She knew she loved that. This was something else, something new and uncontainable.

ᖇ

Jemelle had a distinctly industrial feel, its many-platformed station and vast marshalling yards full of wagons of war materiel out of character for this agricultural area and out of scale for a small country town. Even more down-at-heel than Ciney, it had no fine public buildings and carried the depressed air of a poor suburb of Brussels or Charleroi. But Elaine could see why the top-floor rooms in the shabby building in the rue du Congo were chosen: it was handy for the station, elevated enough for good radio reception, yet totally anonymous.

She lugged the suitcase up six flights of stairs and knocked on the numbered door.

Foxtrot was pleased to see her and even more pleased to see the radio. He'd had little contact with anyone for days; his sympathetic landlady kept him supplied him with food and his co-tenant – a gruff rail worker who like many of his kind aided the Resistance – appeared briefly between shifts but that was all. No matter, he'd used the time profitably to test the bits of equipment he'd brought with him and experiment with the long aerial, which needed to be strung in zigzag fashion across the ceiling and out through the window which, by luck or design, faced into a central void.

He obviously loved his work and he explained it all as he plugged the set into the central light socket and carefully ran a wire from the earth terminal to a cold water pipe running along the skirting board. Elaine was glad on reflection that her request to train as a W/T hadn't been followed up. She felt quite at home on the Morse handset, but she wasn't sure she could cope with everything else that had to be done before the tap-tapping could begin.

Like all operators, though Foxtrot gave every appearance of being dedicated to his work, he did like to grumble about his equipment, its unreliability, lack of spare parts and general inability to live up to the exacting task expected of it. And with some reason. It was hardly surprising that equipment got damaged in transit in the field, much less by being dropped from the sky. Because sets had to be compact, they were also crude. The technology, too, was unsophisticated, though the boffins at SOE's research and development base, outside Welwyn in Hertfordshire had made significant advances during the course of the war. But the fact remained that communications with London – beset by technical or reception problems, and overlaid by the additional barrier of being transmitted in cipher that could be miscoded or misread by the operator, resulting in an 'indecipherable' – were never a straightforward affair.

Elaine was about to discover just how problematic they could be. Over the next couple of days, she and André broke protocol by meeting together in the open at the landing site in Sovet to calculate the clock ray description for the RAF. The field was known to have been used in the past by the Germans so André was confident there would be no problem for the small Lysander.

'A medium-range bomber could land there with no difficulty', he assured Elaine, but it wasn't her he needed to convince.

Their problem was that they couldn't risk being seen stomping about open fields taking measurements, so the calculations had to be made from the nearest convenient point with cover – a cart track shielded by trees. Not ideal, but they would have to do. Even so, the calculations were time consuming to make and for Elaine to note down. And when it came to coding them, they were not only tricky, she realised they were so extensive they'd take Foxtrot more than one sked to send to London. It was danger-ous to stay on the air for more than fifteen minutes as it gave the DF vans time to pick up the signal and, anyway, operators usually had set transmis-sion schedules – hence the 'sked'. This long message would need at least two and probably three skeds, she calculated. They just didn't have enough time to transmit the whole thing and get replies back from London before the end of the moon period. She was apologetic, but André took the news in his stride.

'Bugger. We'll just have to chance a summary description and hope the boys in blue will be content with that.'

Though coding the summary was delightfully straightforward by com-parison, poor Foxtrot had so many technical problems with the set that the message had finally to be sent instead through Huguette's W/T operator. All the time, the moon was on the wane.

As they waited for London to reply with the RAF's response and the go ahead for the pickup, Elaine went to meet her new charge.

André was obviously having some fun at her expense. 'Willy's place' turned out not to be some ramshackle farmhouse in the middle of nowhere, but the Chateau d'Halloy, a gracious grey pile a couple of kilometres to the north-west of Ciney, set in extensive grounds and forming part of a fine quadrangle of stables and outbuildings behind large gates. Unlike French chateaux, Halloy was unpretentious, its modest embellishments just two small onion domes on each end of the roofline and ornamental railings on a central balcony and on steps up to the main entrance directly below.

As she pulled on the bell ring, she envied Willy Gerard his comfortable country home and hoped the man she was about to meet would be half as agreeable.

Harbouring an image of a hobbling old man with bad teeth and worse manners, she was taken to a high-ceilinged room and into the presence of a gymnast. Here was a fit-looking man, perhaps in his late thirties, doing strenuous physical exercises on a mat on the floor. He didn't seem at all embarrassed to be interrupted. He stopped, paused for breath and rose to greet her.

'Ah, my new keeper. Welcome Mademoiselle Maes.'

He took her hand and, instead of shaking it, swept it to his lips in a glancing kiss.

'*Enchanté*. May I call you Hélène?'

Caught off guard by this unexpected display of charm, and wondering why on earth André had described him as a cripple, she hesitated. She realised André had only used his codename, Patron. She couldn't call him 'Boss', it was far too informal.

'Of course, sir. I'm sorry … how should I address you?'

'I answer to a variety of names, but you can call me Monsieur Bernard.'

She pointed to the mat.

'Are you an acrobat, Monsieur Bernard?'

He smiled.

'No, I'm not an acrobat. I have sciatica. It affects my legs. It's tiresome but I have to do these exercises twice a day, otherwise I seize up completely.'

She had the chance to look at him closely now. Not particularly attractive, his features were rather sharp, but he had a certain appeal. Casually dressed in clothes that wouldn't be out of place on the Cote d'Azur, he glowed with the combination of perspiration and a light tan. Reassuringly upright of bearing and with perfect dentistry, he couldn't have been more different from the hobbled old man of her imaginings.

'Let's have some tea so that we can get to know each other a little better. We'll be spending many hours together in close proximity. It'll help if we get along.'

They sat down and he invited her to pour.

'I do hope this isn't going to be too tedious for you. We'll try and make it bearable.'

She wondered who the 'we' were. Though the house was obviously staffed, there was no sign of Willy Gerard.

'Where are you staying?'

'I'm in a small hotel in Ciney.'

'All the hotels are small in Ciney. And no doubt flea bitten. You must stay here. There's plenty of room. Bring your things tomorrow.'

It sounded more like a command than an invitation.

∞

In confident expectation of the go-ahead from London, André arranged with the farmer at Sovet to have the crops removed and the field rolled. He then returned to Brussels to resume his liaison duties. Foxtrot meanwhile made contact with Denise Leplat and established himself in a safe house in a quiet suburb there, ready to receive London's reply but again leaving the radio in Elaine's custody.

At Chateau d'Halloy she and Monsieur Bernard whiled away the time agreeably waiting for confirmation of the pickup. He really was the most pleasant prisoner. Confined within the boundaries of the estate, in between his exercise regime they filled the long days with walks through the grounds and games of cards and ping-pong. Whenever they were alone together, which was much of the time, they spoke English at his request.

'It's funny. French is my mother tongue of course. But English is somehow more relaxed, don't you think?

She knew better than to enquire who he was or what London wanted him for, but she was intrigued nonetheless. His English was perfect, almost unaccented: he must surely have been educated in England. Or perhaps, like her, at an English school abroad? And he was the most charming company, cultured and intelligent, apparently widely travelled and he obviously knew London well. She supposed he must be some top Resistance leader. If not of the Secret Army, then what? But it was difficult to imagine him leading a rabble of gung-ho *resistants*. It was difficult to imagine him roughing it. He seemed perfectly attuned to a life of luxury and pleasure.

On their walks through the grounds they'd stop for a cigarette. Conversation between them soon became easy. They talked about

179

the war, the Blitz and the mood in Britain. Elaine heard herself say that now the tide had turned, and especially since the landings in Normandy, people were looking forward more confidently. They could see 'the beginning of the end' at last. They were dog-tired of course, fed up with rationing and the daily hardships on the home front – the V1s were making things worse again now. Even so, people were more determined than ever to see it through. She knew she sounded like a Ministry of Information script but she also felt it to be true. She'd seen it, heard it all, over the past four years. She'd observed every shift and nuance of feeling around her, so she felt qualified to express an opinion on the matter.

He seemed especially interested in how things were in London.

'Tell me, where are the smart people going these days? Clubs and dinner places I mean. Are the Grosvenor Room and the Café Royal still open? I used to love going to see Snakehips Johnson at the Café de Paris when I was there. That's before Jerry got his filthy hands on it of course.'

So he *was* well informed.

'I was in the West End with some friends that night. We saw those poor people taken out of the wreckage. Do you know, some of them were completely untouched? Had the life sucked out of them by the blast. And poor Johnson had his head blown off. I hate the bloody Boche!'

She was surprised at her vehemence, and more surprised to be using that word from childhood learned from her father. So he was still with her, part of her, whether she wanted him there or not.

'Me too, Hélène. That's why we're here', said Monsieur Bernard.

He enjoyed gossip, and the more scurrilous the better so, her tongue loosened by whisky, in the long evenings she shared her stories about the Hollywood stars she'd met and her glancing encounters with naughty Prince Bernhard of the Netherlands and the Duke of Luxembourg at the ARP station.

'"*I danced with a man who danced with a girl who danced with the Prince of Wales*"… My dear, you *have* been mixing with demi-monde. But tell me, what are people in London saying about the Royal Family.'

'Oh we love them!'

'Really?' He seemed quite taken aback.

'Of course. The queen's adorable. He's a bit of a stuffed shirt, but he tries his best, and everyone's behind him. They never left London, you know, all through the Blitz. Well, they might have gone to Windsor, but that's not very far away. And the Princesses Elizabeth and Margaret Rose are really ...'

'I mean the Belgian Royal Family.'

'Oh, sorry. Well. That's different. People think King Leopold is a traitor for surrendering without much of a fight, and I tend to agree with them. I was still in Belgium in May 1940 and I know the Belgian Army did their best against all the odds, but *him* ... all the Belgians I know in London have no time for him. And that business of his secret marriage while he was supposedly a prisoner-of-war, that didn't help. He's let Belgium down. And where's his no-good brother when he could be doing something useful? He seems to have disappeared off the face of the earth, the coward. He's supposed to be a big drinker and womaniser, isn't he, so he's probably lying drunk outside some brothel somewhere even as we speak ...'

She stopped dead. She'd probably gone too far, but he seemed tickled by the idea of the king's younger brother, Prince Charles, lying in a gutter.

'Yes, a most disreputable character. You're probably right!'

They can't have been together for more than a few days but it seemed longer, the time stretching out luxuriously as if on a holiday – like those sunny days at La Panne so many summers ago with Maman. The hours in comfortable seclusion at Halloy passed in a procession of laughter and entertainment. It was just like being on the most delightful all-expenses-paid *vacance*. He encouraged her chatter and she tolerated his cheating at cards. He even tried to cheat at ping-pong but it only made her collapse with laughter. He was completely incorrigible and the most charming man she'd ever met.

The holiday mood was broken by a message from André with an urgent request for the radio. The reply from London was imminent and she needed to get back to Brussels.

She took her leave of Monsieur Bernard, who seemed disappointed to see her go. Taking the radio, she hurried into Ciney. At the station anxious-looking passengers were going nowhere: the line to Brussels had suffered a major sabotage attack overnight and would take some time to repair. Not sure what to do, Elaine returned to the small hotel where she'd first stayed in the town. At worst, she might need a room overnight so she could leave first thing in the morning. At the desk she enquired about a room and explained the delay to her journey.

'I'd really like to get to Brussels today. My parents are expecting me and they'll be most anxious if I don't turn up. But the line's been blown up again, it's too bad.'

The woman at reception wanted to be helpful.

'I don't have a room I'm afraid, but I have a suggestion. See the officer over there? I happen to know he's going to Brussels this morning. He might be able to give you a lift. I'll ask him if you like.'

She turned to look at the uniform standing by the door waiting for his car. She couldn't see his face but, thank God, it wasn't the black and silver of the feared SS, but the grey-green of the Wehrmacht. It could be worse. She didn't have time to weigh up the risks. It was a solution and the best one on offer.

'Oh, please. Would you? I'd be so grateful.'

His French was reasonable, his manners impeccable.

'At your service, Mademoiselle. My car is here. Is this all your luggage?'

He looked at her suitcase and went to take it from her. She had no choice but to relinquish it without hesitation.

'It's very heavy. What have you got in there?'

She looked at him coquettishly, as if in confidence.

'Well … a small ham. Some cheese, butter …'

He winked at her.

'Ah, *marche noir*?'

She feigned mild affront.

'Oh, no. Just for my family, you understand.'

He handed the suitcase to his driver and opened the car door for her.

'After you, Mademoiselle.'

The radio was safely stowed in the boot. Everything now depended on her ability to stay cool, remember her cover story and parley it convincingly.

The German's good manners prevented their conversation straying into controversial subjects like the progress of the war. Their intercourse, such as it was, stayed light, polite. She'd been visiting relatives in the Ardennes – hence the gifts of food – and was returning to her parents in Brussels.

His lack of fluency in French meant, mercifully, that there were *longeurs* of silence on the two-hour journey, but they weren't awkward. He read his newspaper; she looked out of the window. She gave him no cause for suspicion and, anyway, it would have been impolite of him to ask to see her papers.

As they approached Brussels he asked for her parents' address. Betraying no surprise or panic, she quickly worked through her options.

'I don't want to take you out of your way. If you drop me at the top of Avenue Louise, I can walk from there, it's no distance.'

'But I insist. My driver knows the city well. He can find it.'

She couldn't have the car drop her anywhere near their apartment. She sifted her memory for the names of the streets she'd passed on the way to the Coq d'Or.

'That's very kind, but it's really not necessary. It's hours away from curfew. I shall be perfectly alright.'

'I insist.'

Further remonstration might arouse suspicion so she said the first street that came into her head.

'Rue van Eyckstraat, then. Thank you.'

She didn't give a number because she had no idea how the street was numbered. She'd just have to play it by ear when they arrived.

'Yes. Just off here. You can stop halfway down. It's just a couple of doors away.'

They stopped in a quiet residential street where the large town houses opened straight on to the pavement. The driver got out to retrieve her suitcase. With her hand on the door handle, she turned to the officer.

'Thank you. You've been very kind.'

'The pleasure was all mine, Mademoiselle. Please convey my respects to your parents.'

'I will. Thank you.'

The driver opened the door for her and handed her the heavy suitcase. She thanked him and walked slowly down the road, fumbling in her shoulder bag as if for keys. She expected the car to roar back into life and pass her. Instead it sat, engine idling, at the kerbside. Oh God, he was waiting for her to go in. She hesitated outside a house, with more fumbling to play for time.

Perhaps a wave would encourage him to leave? The wave was returned but the car didn't move. She had no option but to step into the shallow porch of the nearest house. She had no idea who lived there, or whether anyone was in. She fervently hoped not as she went through the charade of trying to fit her key into the lock, her hands shaking now. What next? *Never run.* How would she explain her failure to get into her own family's home?

She leant out of the porch to give what she hoped would be a final smile and wave and heard, with great relief, the engine pick up as the car moved smoothly away. She waited there, pressed into the porch, until she judged it safe to venture back out on to the streets then picked up the suitcase and made to the apartment as nonchalantly as her frayed nerves would allow.

When she arrived, trembling slightly, she was surprised at André's casual greeting.

'Oh, hallo. I wasn't expecting you for ages yet.'

She plonked the suitcase down with some irritation. After her travails and so many days absence, she'd hoped for a warmer welcome.

'Oh? Why not?'

'Well, the line's out, isn't it? How did you manage to get here so quickly?'

Now she was rather annoyed. And she'd thought they needed the radio urgently.

'Oh, it was quite simple really. I got a lift from an *Oberstleutnant* in the Armoured Corps. He was perfectly charming.'

That made him sit up.

'You *what*?'

'Seriously. I got a lift with a German officer. All the way. Well, not to here, obviously. I made him drop me off a couple of streets away. I had a nasty moment at the end though …'

She didn't manage to finish her story because André was laughing so much he spilled his drink over the arm of the chair. He leapt up and opened his arms wide.

'You clever, clever girl. Come here. Let me give you a fraternal embrace. I've missed you, Elaine Madden.'

෴

The news from London, when it came, was a crushing disappointment for all concerned. The RAF had rejected the summary description, claiming it depicted a rutted wasteland with a horrendous slope and insufficient runway. André's calm facade finally cracked.

'Imbeciles. They've deliberately misread it. The field's perfectly fine. The bloody Luftwaffe used it in 1940 for Christ's sake. Now we've wasted a whole moon, and we'll have to do those damn clock ray thingies all over again.'

Within thirty-six hours of arriving in Brussels, Elaine was dispatched back to Halloy to break the news. She found Monsieur Bernard at his exercises in the library.

'Dear Hélène! You've come back to me. Does this mean we're finally off to London?'

'I'm afraid not. I'm so sorry to have wasted your time, but we're having trouble getting London to agree the pickup site. Now we've missed the moon and we'll have to wait till next month. Everyone's fed up about it.'

'What a pity. And I was looking forward to visiting all those London clubs we talked about … Oh dear, so it's back to Spa with those rough Resistance types for me, I suppose, till I get further instructions. And just as I was getting used to more conducive company. But you don't have to rush off just yet, surely?'

'I do, I'm needed back in Brussels. I'm so sorry. We could have sent you a message but I wanted to tell you in person.'

'How thoughtful.' He took her hand as he had done days before when they'd first met. 'Well, my dear Hélène, let's hope this is merely *au revoir* and we'll have the chance to continue our delightful acquaintanceship in September.'

'I do hope so, Monsieur Bernard. I've so enjoyed our chats about London.'

He kissed her hand.

'Until we meet again.'

ରେ

The remaining weeks of August were frenetic with activity as British, Canadian and American troops continued their advance north and east out of Normandy towards Belgium. Elaine's courier duties – carrying cash, messages and arms to Resistance groups in readiness for liberation – escalated. But it had taken three months of bloody fighting for the Allies to break through from Normandy: that longed-for and much prepared-for day when Belgians would be free was still thought some way off.

Much of her time and effort was spent organising the protection service for Foxtrot, concentrated on his safe house in a middle-class area on high ground fifteen minutes from the city. Here local knowledge and contacts came into play and Elaine was soon introduced to Denise Leplat's Resistance colleague Jean Smets and the sisters Lucy and Jeanne Rouffingnon who allowed the attic of their tall house in rue Chant d'Oiseaux to be used for the dangerous business of transmitting coded messages to London. They knew the risk they were taking: if discovered they were likely to disappear without trace into the 'night and fog': *Nacht und Nebel*, Hitler's special fate for those caught aiding the Resistance.

Elaine would go in first to deliver the radio, leaving Denise, Jean or two of their associates outside in the street to patrol the block on the lookout for DF vans. These were often disguised as bread delivery vans so the scouts had to be especially vigilant. Elaine would stay close to the house, from where she could hear the warning signal and race to help Foxtrot hide his equipment and himself before the van arrived.

In this quiet street of unexceptional bourgeois houses, the city – and the war – seemed far away. Though she was always on her guard during skeds, and it was an anxious time, it was still a relief to be away from the flags, the uniforms, the controls that made the city so unpleasant. Here in this well-named street, apart from the occasional passing vehicle and residents minding their own business, there was only beautiful, natural birdsong.

Either side of transmissions there was coding to do. Such was the volume of traffic between Belgium and London at this point that timetabled skeds were abandoned and messages were sent and received whenever necessary. André had resumed the thankless task of trying to persuade the RAF that the Sovet field was suitable for landing a Lysander and was attacking his clock ray descriptions with renewed determination. Elaine wasn't looking forward to having to code them.

But perhaps she wouldn't have to. On 20 August André received a message from Spa that stopped Operation Patron in its tracks. It seemed Monsieur Bernard was having second thoughts about his exfiltration. André was sufficiently concerned to put these doubts to London for their advice. Coding his message, Elaine wondered why her charming charge had suddenly got cold feet. He'd seemed so enthusiastic, so co-operative when she was there less than a week ago. Was his sciatica playing up? Reading between the lines of the message, it was something to do with the liberation and whether it was worth leaving Belgium. She didn't understand this. They all believed liberation was still some way off and if the Gestapo was after him, surely he'd want to get away to safety at the earliest opportunity? André would probably know more but she knew better than to ask: the less he shared with her about operational matters the better for both of them.

Before they could receive London's response another message arrived from Spa. Their exfiltration subject had made the decision to stay put: Operation Patron was off. Elaine tried to hide her disappointment. She wouldn't see the charming Monsieur Bernard again, and she hadn't even said a proper goodbye.

Despite the hectic times, her heavy responsibilities and the disappointing news from Spa, it wasn't Monsieur Bernard who was invading her thoughts at every unguarded moment. Since André's return from Ciney they'd had more close contact than at any time since the start of the mission. Without the distraction of Patron and clock ray descriptions, he was able to concentrate on co-ordinating sabotage operations and gathering intelligence about V1 launch sites and production of the vicious new Vengeance missile, the V2. A network of sources supplied a mass of reports daily on V1 launch sites – not all of them accurate or useful. It was more straightforward to discover which railway lines were being used to transport them to the coast and to galvanise Groupe G saboteurs into action.

Using a substantial sum from the bounty they'd brought with them from London he bribed a well-placed German worker to supply information about V2 production sites and missile movements. By the end of August, the flow of information was fast and furious. Over many cigarettes and late-night whisky, they worked together to translate this into transmittable form that London could use to best effect.

Every discovery, sabotage attack – planned, successful or aborted – each item of intelligence on troop and equipment movements, had to be precised in the least possible number of words but include every essential fact. They would then be encoded for onward transmission, ideally within the advised ten minutes. Any longer and the wireless operator would be in danger of detection.

By this late stage of the war, codes and ciphers had become sophisticated and complex to master. Even some of the coding systems she'd been taught at Beaulieu were now obsolete. From the beginning, every agent had a poem code to use as a standby. The more original or obscure the better: an over-used ditty, once cracked by the enemy, would reveal every message sent and received by every agent using it. But *in extremis* a poem code was better than nothing. Elaine's was based on random extracts from a long narrative poem about the Dorset countryside, *Lewesdon Hill*, written in 1788, from the anthology she'd brought with her on her trek to Dunkirk. This was certainly obscure enough, but she hoped she'd never have to use it – she had a more fail-safe system, designed by SOE's cipher genius Leo Marks.

Elaine got through sheets and sheets from her Mental One-Time Pad, the only constant being her key, BAYSWATER. To decode a message she would lay the transparent silk square over the encoded message so that both sets of letters showed. She would then transpose the letters in such a way that her key word appeared and from there she could work out the code. Each transmission over, with relief she would put a match to the silk square and watch as the columns of random letters curled up and collapsed into fine grey ash.

How far away and long ago Susan and Bayswater Court seemed now. Those late August days in Brussels were long and everything about them was intense: the pace, the work, the excitement, the fear of discovery. Above all, her feelings about André. However hard she tried, she could no longer ignore, deny or disguise the truth. She no longer liked this man. She loved him.

෧෨

In the last dry days of August Brussels was alive with rumour, denial and counter rumour. The Germans had surrendered Paris on the 25th and things were moving fast, but how fast? They heard that the Allies had crossed the Belgian border and were on their way. Impossible: this was propaganda designed to raise false hopes. The Third Reich was impregnable and would last forever. But the underground communication networks knew better, and all the signs were that the occupiers were rattled and on the run, whatever their official sources might say.

One evening in this febrile atmosphere of preparation and anticipation, Elaine was returning to the apartment much later than she intended, after working with Foxtrot on an extended exchange of communications with London. A set of vital messages took much longer to decode than usual and her journey home was delayed. To be out on the streets after the eight o'clock curfew was asking for trouble. Here she was on the Avenue Louise a little after eight, the wide streets almost empty. She planned to dodge into the maze of side roads well before she got to No. 347 but a smoky mirage in the vicinity of the Gestapo headquarters drew her closer. Were those flames? A little further on, the avenue was blocked by guards. The area had been sealed off around the headquarters. She felt a tremor of fear. Every instinct told her to make herself scarce but curiosity overcame sense. Something unexpected, significant, was going on. A block nearer and she could make out a series of fires on the grass strip that separated the avenue's carriageways and a procession of uniformed functionaries feeding them with boxes and boxes of paper. Other boxes were being loaded into lorries. The Gestapo were burning their records and preparing to decamp! Then the rumours must be true: the Allies were closer than anyone had dared hope. She stood, transfixed by the sight of the fires and everything they signified.

'*Fraulein! Wo gehen Sie hin?*'

In her fascination with the fires she'd been completely oblivious to danger, easy prey for any German soldier on patrol. Now she was in real trouble. Not only was she out after curfew, a punishable offence, but in her handbag – quite contrary to everything she'd been taught – were her decoded messages from London. She was so late finishing she'd just stuffed them in her bag. She'd not even bothered to use the false compartment to conceal them from a cursory inspection. It was bad luck, rotten timing, and she had no one to blame but herself. In her haste to see André she had endangered their security and potentially that of dozens of others. The joyous sight of the Gestapo preparing to quit their notorious HQ didn't make her any safer; if caught, she'd be taken elsewhere to be tortured for information and then executed.

She knew a little German but feigned an innocent fluster in stuttering French about being lost. It had no effect. He wasn't going to let her off lightly. '*Papieren, bitte!*'

She offered up her false identity card. Of all the dozens of times she could have been stopped and searched in the past three weeks, it had to be now, so close to deliverance and with her death warrant in her handbag. He studied the pass under the failing light. She watched his face for any sign that he might somehow see it for what it really was: a forgery created in London by clever Poles. He was perhaps only a little older than herself, but old enough to be her nemesis.

'*Sie kommen aus Koksijde?*'

The question was unexpected but they'd been taught at Beaulieu that the unexpected was surprisingly common and the most likely thing in the world to trip them up. Yes, she said. Indeed, 'Hélène Maes' purportedly originated from the West Flanders town of Coxyde just along the coast from Dunkirk. Elaine knew it well.

Then you speak Flemish, he said, and she could do little but agree. Her nemesis was a Flemish boy in French-speaking Brussels, probably conscripted, perhaps lonely and a little scared for his future, apparently now desperate for a friendly exchange in his native language. Or more likely this was a test to uncover whether she was who she claimed to be.

Apart from her brief exchange with Ides Floor at her SOE interview, Elaine hadn't spoken Flemish in almost five years, not since leaving Flanders for the last time in 1940. Now her life depended on it. He launched into a guttural flood, expecting her to respond in kind. She was surprised to find it came out of her mouth as naturally as it had on the streets of Ypres and Poperinghe another lifetime ago. For the first time in years the memory of Simone came into her head. If she had one thing to thank her for, it was insisting they speak Flemish together when they were girls.

But what was she doing here, he wanted to know. She hastened to explain that she was on holiday, staying with her aunt.

'I got off the bus at Avenue de Charleroi but then I lost my bearings and couldn't find my way home. I've been wandering about for ages. I know it's around here somewhere …'

'But it's curfew.'

'I know, I'm sorry. But I have to get home. I can't sleep out on the streets, and they'll be so worried about me.'

The boy in uniform gave her a hesitant smile.

'Alright then. For a girl from Koksijde, I'll walk you some of the way.'

She could afford to show relief and return his smile. For the next 300 yards or so she had a military escort up the Avenue Louise. He might have been a conscript from a poor farming family in a familiar landscape, but his presence in German uniform and with a German rifle slung over his shoulder was still oppressive. He represented the enemy and the danger had far from passed. Please God, don't let him decide to look in my handbag …

He stopped just short of the cordon of guards and pointed to the other side of the Avenue.

'It's just up there, turn left. But you'll have to hurry. You don't want to be stopped again.'

That was true enough.

'Oh yes, of course. I know where I am now, thank you.'

And then she was on her way. It was a scary moment and she didn't dare think what might have happened if she hadn't been able to summon up the long-forgotten language of her childhood. A thorough search would inevitably follow. But she'd come through. And the handbag, held tight in the hand that still bore another Flemish boy's ring, kept its secret. Her number wasn't up yet.

∽

Five years to the day since Britain declared war on Germany, and barely a month after the Imogen team's arrival in Belgium, on 3 September 1944 tanks from the Guards Armoured Division thundered into Brussels from the south-west after a day-long dash from the border. By late evening the commotion of tooting horns in the streets could be heard from the apartment. André leapt to the window and leaned over the balcony, though there wasn't much to see in the dark.

'They're here! Could be the Yanks or the British. Let's go and find out!'

The temporary tenants of 347 Avenue Louise may have quit Brussels in a hurry but the city still harboured pockets of Nazi resistance, now holed up, desperate and preparing to fight to the last. In this uncertain interregnum dancing in the streets would be precipitate and venturing out unarmed foolhardy. Tucking pistols into their jackets, André and Elaine followed the noise south.

There was a weird, wild air on the streets. The pavements were empty – residents were wisely staying inside until their liberation was confirmed – but the roads were strangely busy. Petrol was scarce and much non-military traffic was gas-powered, but all manner of vehicles were out, crammed with young men, horns blaring and ammunition firing into the air, a combination of relief, release and long-suppressed revenge.

At the top of Avenue Louise they found what they were looking for. At the wide entrance to the Bois de la Cambre, the charming wooded park that gives on to the vast expanse of the Forêt de Soignes, stood tanks bearing British markings, stationary but with engines grumbling. The two agents in civilian clothes approached the lead tank and found the commanding officer slumped, exhausted, by its side. André gave a salute as the figure in battle fatigues stubbed out his cigarette and got wearily to his feet.

'Good evening, sir. Welcome to Brussels! I don't need to tell you how pleased we are to see you. Major André Wendelen and Cadet Ensign Madden at your service. We've been here since August on orders from Special Forces HQ in London. Can we be of help?'

'Well I'm blowed! Since you ask, major, you can. I want to check on my men and get them into a billet over there for the night. We've been on the road since before dawn. Seventy-five miles non-stop in one of these beauties is no joyride, we're all jiggered. My battle orders and other sensitive stuff are inside, they shouldn't be left unattended. Been in a tank before?'

'Once or twice. Don't worry, sir, we'll look after her. You go and see to your men.'

Being inside a tank with another person is a uniquely intimate experience. Elaine found herself physically closer to André than she had been at any time since that first embrace after her unexpected return from Ciney with the German officer. As they talked, animated by the evening's events and keyed up for what might follow, it was time for official confidences finally to be broken.

'Did you recognise Monsieur Bernard?'

'What do you mean?'

'Well, who did you think he was?'

'Some big Resistance man, obviously, who needed to get out of the country. Something to do with Groupe G perhaps?'

André laughed at her lack of guile.

'God, no! We wouldn't let him within a mile of Groupe G. Didn't you guess? Your Monsieur Bernard was Prince Charles, Leopold's younger brother. He's going to be very important here from now on, he's about to become prince regent.'

Elaine put her hand to her mouth in shock, knocking her elbow in the confined space.

'Ow!' The pain in her elbow was nothing to the discomfort of her embarrassment. 'But you don't know the terrible things I said to him!'

André was still laughing: 'So tell me.'

She relived with horror their walks round the grounds and the late night whisky-fuelled chats when she gave her unguarded views on the perfidious king and the cowardly behaviour of his useless drunk of a brother. He threw his head back and roared with laughter, using up what little air remained in the stuffy interior.

'Dear Elaine, you're just perfect!'

He took her hand, still attached to her mouth, removed it to her lap and kissed her.

'Happy Liberation Day, Miss Madden.'

Elaine felt light-headed from lack of air and the rapturous imprint left by André's kiss. And again she was submerged in an airless sea of bliss, to resurface only with the sound of boots running on cobbles and sporadic gunfire outside in the darkness. André broke away to reach into his jacket.

'Sit tight. I'm going to see what's going on.'

She heard him fire shots, then he called to her.

'A rabble, NCOs mostly, running for their lives, but armed. About a dozen of them making for the Bois de la Cambre. And more coming by the look of it. See if you can get the gun going, we'll try and head them off from trying to escape into the woods.'

Firing a tank gun was one skill unaccountably missing from the SOE training syllabus but she got up into the turret. After struggling with the controls and finding she could range the gun to the right but only a little to left, she ventured an experimental shot in the general direction of the escaping figures as André continued firing. The tank recoiled with a jolt that nearly knocked her off her perch.

'Have I hit anything?'

'Nothing worth mentioning. But there's a monument over there with a nasty new hole in it. Come on, let's go and see if we've hit anyone. Then I think we should go after them.'

'What about the papers?'

'They'll be alright, no one's going to steal a tank. Just stick close to me.'

He helped her down and they quickly surveyed the immediate area for dead or injured. There were none. With midnight approaching and with the sound of sporadic gunfire still around them, she followed André into the dark embrace of the Bois de la Cambre.

Once clear of open ground and into the woods of the Forêt de Soignes, it was increasingly difficult to keep up with André in the thick night. After less than an hour Elaine realised that she'd lost sight of him altogether. She was alone in the rustling forest with only night-sounds and distant shots. Far from the nearest road even the blaring horns had stopped, muffled out of existence by the blanket of trees. She pressed on uncertainly, still clutching her pistol, ears attuned for any unnatural sound yet conscious that she betrayed her own presence with every stumbling step. For the first time she was afraid. This was different from her previous escapades with the follower or when she'd been stopped by the Flemish soldier. Then, she could think or talk her way out of her predicament. Here, her wits were numbed. She was shivering with the cold and shaking with exhausted emotion. The warmth of that kiss and the proximity of André's body next to hers seemed so far away as to be lost forever. The dark was disorientating, the woods potentially alive with armed and desperate men. She'd lost her protector and she had, for the first time she could remember since that hellish night at Dunkirk, lost confidence in her own ability to survive. With her back to a tree she stood watchful and waiting, but vulnerable, uncertain and fearful of what might happen next.

Unsure how long she'd been there, or even if she'd fallen into a dreamless doze, she was brought sharply to her senses by the sounds of human presence nearby. She readied the Webley for the double tap as she'd been taught: the first shot disabling, the second fatal. As she was about to shoot at the figure emerging from the shadows she heard André's voice.

'There you are! Have you seen anything?'

She let the gun go limp in her hand with relief, her head fell back on the bark of the tree. Professional wits regained, she couldn't admit to him that she'd been frozen to the spot in fear for who knows how long.

'No, nothing. You?'

'Nothing. But they're still around here somewhere. We should get back to the tank and warn the Brits that Jerry hasn't cleared out quite yet.'

By the time they got to the temporary billet by the entrance to the Bois de la Cambre, the sky was beginning to lighten. The tank commander didn't seem very interested in their news. Surviving pockets of German resistance were the least of his worries. Other Allied forces were close behind and would secure the city and deal with outliers; as the liberating vanguard he and his men now had to press on north-eastward towards the Dutch border after only a few snatched hours rest.

In the quiet streets of the post-liberation dawn, past the vacant block at 347 that only days ago had housed evil men and witnessed unspeakable torture, Elaine and André too were feeling the effects of lack of sleep. Returning to the apartment exhausted but elated, their mission now overtaken by events, nothing seemed more natural than to celebrate deliverance as men and women have always done in the exigencies of wartime.

‹∞›

Elaine had never been so happy as in the joyous blur of days and nights that followed. The day after liberation Ides Floor came out from London to join them, full of congratulations and solicitous as to their needs. Would they like to go back to the UK and have a bit of time off? A nice holiday perhaps? Elaine knew exactly what she wanted: she wanted her uniform.

All residual resistance in the city had been overcome and Brussels was now thronging with the liberators and their adoring crowds, but here they were still anonymous in their civvies. She wanted to be recognised as an official player in the capital's liberation. A couple of days later the familiar FANY uniform arrived and she was delighted to see that it now bore the coveted 'wings' that proved she was a bona fide parachutist. She could at last break cover and take her place out in the packed streets with the other uniforms and all their Resistance friends.

What an extraordinary time that was. There were parties and parades, dinners and long nights of carousing. In the daytime she was stopped in the street:

'Are you English?'

'Yes!'

'And are you really a parachutist?'

'Yes, I am!'

She didn't tell them she'd landed weeks before liberation; it wouldn't have made any difference, they were proud of her and she was a celebrity. The nurses and WAAFs and ATS girls hadn't yet arrived and she was the only British girl in uniform in Brussels. She was an exception, the object of attention, admiration and, yes, desire, kissed by complete strangers, hoisted on men's shoulders and paraded with cries of 'Regardez la Parachutiste!' She was plied with champagne and proposed to more times than she could count. She'd never been so fêted nor felt so loved. Best of all, there beside her was André. Her own hero. The war wasn't over but in prospect she could see only a perfect future with the wonderful man she knew to be the love of her life.

Towards the end of that magical time, they were summoned to Ciney for a celebratory dinner with Willy Gerard and the Ardennes Resistance people. When they arrived, she was mortified to see the man she now knew to be Prince Charles, informally dressed but the centre of attention, talking to an aide. She made a face at André but he just laughed.

'Of course. Didn't you realise he'd be here?'

There was no hiding place: they had to be introduced to the guest of honour. Quite apart from her hideous faux pas, there was a question of protocol. Now he was regent and effectively the head of state, would she have to curtsey, or what?

'Major Wendelen and Miss Madden, Special Forces.'

He greeted André warmly, then fixed her with a disapproving look.

'Ah, yes. Miss Maes. My keeper at Halloy.'

'Good evening, sir. Sorry, I don't know the correct form of address. What should I call you? Your Majesty? Your Highness?'

Then that familiar twinkle:

'Just call me Bernard as usual. Come and have a drink.'

Like the charmer she'd got to know over those few languid days at Chateau d'Halloy, he seemed to find her slanderous behaviour highly amusing. The hours, fuelled by joy, relief and alcohol, passed easily between them. That evening of laughter and companionship in Ciney among comrades, and with her adored and attentive lover at her side, Elaine could not have been happier.

ELEVEN

BELGIUM AND GERMANY

OCTOBER 1944–APRIL 1945

But the war wasn't over. SOE and Elaine still had work to do. The Allies had overrun Brussels sooner than expected and by the end of November the Canadian First Army had secured the vital port of Antwerp, but the east of the country remained in German hands and much of the Netherlands was still occupied, its people starving through the 'Hunger Winter' of 1944–45. From Dutch launch sites V1 and V2 rockets bombarded Antwerp and terrorised south-east England, and in the Ardennes the German counter-attack was about to turn into the long and bloody Battle of the Bulge. Victory in Europe was still many months off.

After the euphoria of those post-liberation weeks of partying and love-making, reality dawned for Elaine. There was now a new forward special operations unit in Brussels run by Hardy Amies. Its job in Belgium and Holland was to co-ordinate with Allied forces, Resistance groups and the security services of governments now returning from exile. The Belgian SOE agents could expect new instructions at any moment. It was quite possible she and André would be assigned different missions. The thought of separation was painful but little else blighted her happiness. Nothing now could keep them apart. Surely the end of the war was in sight and then they would be a proper couple, man and wife. Living together was blissful, but marriage would be even better. He hadn't proposed yet but she had no doubt that a wedding would follow: she'd given herself to him completely, they loved each other and he was a wonderful, honourable man. Her future happiness and security was assured.

On 30 October Elaine's Brussels idyll ended. She was to be one of two women assigned to the Verstrepen Group and dispatched to Antwerp as a 'Coder-Secretary'. She would be a Class 4 agent paid £30 a month in Belgian francs and would retain her rank as a FANY Cadet Ensign. Unlike the Imogen/Patron mission that summer, she wasn't given any alias or codenames but she'd be known by the French version of her name, Hélène.

Verstrepen was a specialist communications unit and included some of T Section's best W/T operators – Foxtrot was one of them – and others recruited from Resistance groups. Led by Flemish radio expert René Verstrepen, following D-Day it handled coded communications between the Secret Army and its five operational zones in Belgium. Now they'd be doing more dangerous work with Dutch Resistance groups providing tactical intelligence for the Canadian First Army as it pushed into the occupied western Netherlands. One of Verstrepen's tasks that winter was 'infiltrating W/T ops through enemy lines'. Even this close to the end of the war in Europe, the mission was typical of SOE: audacious, perilous, possibly foolhardy. Elaine was briefed only on the barest details but she was by now familiar enough with SOE and its methods to know that, despite her cosy-sounding job title, it would be no picnic. There was no question of refusing. The job was there to be done and she'd been trained to do it.

André had been busy in Brussels meeting people in the weeks since liberation and seemed preoccupied, but he hadn't been assigned another SOE mission. This surprised her, given the speed of events at this critical late stage of the war. Something else important and exciting was going on, she could see that, but André would only put his finger to his lips and smile when she asked what is was. 'Early days', was all he'd say. She didn't worry too much. He was clever and well connected, their war work would soon come to an end and he'd be in demand. Whatever and wherever, she would be with him: his future was hers also.

∞

In charge of Verstrepen's Antwerp home station was a twenty-four-year-old Belgian W/T operator who'd already distinguished himself handling W/T traffic for the head of the Secret Army in one of its most vital zones

– a mission that later earned him a military MBE. He'd already seen action in the Belgian Army, been captured, escaped, got recaptured, served an enforced six months in the Foreign Legion in North Africa (the alternative was a concentration camp) and finally escaped to England in 1943 where he was quickly recruited by SOE.

In February 1944 an SOE request for a security assessment of this candidate addressed to Kim Philby at MI6 resulted in a lengthy and glowing report. It concluded: '*Makes an exceedingly good impression … very obvious integrity … eminently suitable for Special Duties.*'

His Student Assessment Board admired his '*intelligence … guts and self-confidence*' and picked up his early aptitude for Morse, which quickly developed over the course of his training. His high morale, winning charm and good sense of humour ('*he is now one of the most amusing members of the party*') also impressed his instructors. But the long training for wireless operators was frustrating for a man itching to see action in the field. Cracks started to show as his training progressed: '*a decided tendency to resent criticism*'; '*inclined to sulk if he doesn't get his own way*'; '*something of a playboy … takes life too easily and lacks self-discipline*'. As with all SOE trainees, his instructors monitored his off-duty behaviour for signs of any weakness that could be a liability in the field. His principal assessor noted: '*I believe he is rather partial to women but is not the type to have a regular "girlfriend" and rather prefers the casual acquaintance. He is, I must say, a very good-looking fellow and is looking forward to a good time in London in the near future.*'

At the end of his ten-month training, he emerged from the Group B finishing school with a rather less than unequivocal report: '*Can make a good W/T operator provided he can overcome the temptations of the world, the flesh and the devil and remain inconspicuous. In this respect his good looks and social gifts may not prove an advantage …*'

Elaine was about to meet Michel Ghislain Blaze.

೧೦

Antwerp was very different from Brussels, the capital left largely untouched by the depredations of war. Belgium's second city, already battered by Allied bombing, was now under attack from German V2s: Antwerp's medieval heart, its strategically vital port and its people were all suffering. There was little gaiety or joyous celebration of liberation here. The enemy was still too close and too active for comfort. Elaine settled into her billet, a large private house arranged for her, like the rest of the Verstrepen team, by the Canadians. Then she got to work.

Blaze was one of the first people she met at Verstrepen's temporary HQ. He was one of the most striking men she'd ever seen: tall and imposing, he had near jet-black hair immaculately waved and brilliantined, and green eyes deep-set under heavy brows. He turned on the charm as soon as he saw her, holding out both hands to greet her.

'Miss Madden. *Enchanté.* Welcome to our humble home station. Michel Blaze. I shall call you Hélène. With my finger work and your transposition techniques, we shall make beautiful music together.'

Here was a first-class flirt. He couldn't be more different from the quiet, studious Foxtrot. Or indeed from her own dear André – so solid, so confidence-inspiring. She was immediately on her guard.

'That's why I'm here.'

She knew the type. He was most attractive and amusing, and knew it. He could be dangerous. She intended to keep a professional distance until she got the measure of him.

There were other operators to code for, but she saw nothing of Foxtrot, who was one of a handful of valued W/Ts already sent behind enemy lines. Though they were under constant threat from the deadly V2 rockets, they were safer here in Antwerp than wherever Foxtrot was. Elaine was often paired on skeds with Michel Blaze and she soon got to know him better. He was an excellent W/T operator and great fun to be with. Transmission and coding sessions were never a hardship in his company. He was also an accomplished womaniser. Any attractive woman who passed through their station was fair game, and Elaine saw more of him than any other. Away from André and the familiar comforts of their Brussels apartment, she found his attentions flattering, though she was punctilious about not encouraging them. Attractive as he might be, he wasn't the man she loved.

The relative calm of their professional intercourse was about to be broken. They were technically on loan as Special Forces support to the

Canadian First Army and they soon had separate instructions to leave the dubious security of Antwerp for less comfortable work in the field. Blaze was to go behind enemy lines into the occupied western provinces of the Netherlands to support the Resistance there. Elaine was on a much shorter operation to rendezvous with a Dutch Resistance contact in an area where sporadic fighting was still going on and be taken into enemy-occupied Holland – a potentially hazardous mission. 'But don't worry', she was told, 'you'll have an American escort to look after you'. This was meant as reassurance but she felt rather patronised. Hadn't she been trained to look after herself?

On the day of the operation as she put on her gloves on the way to meet her military escort she realised she wasn't wearing Luc's signet ring on her middle finger as usual. Annoyed with herself, she pictured it on the bathroom shelf where she must have left it that morning. She was already a little late so there was no time to go back for it. She wasn't superstitious but she did believe in luck. This was the first time she'd been without it since May 1940. No matter. If the rendezvous went as planned, it should all be straightforward and she'd be back by the evening. She'd get it then.

The mission, straightforward as it sounded, was a shambles. Nothing went right. The truck taking them from the army base to the front line got lost; her escort was a young lieutenant of about her own age, but new to theatre, unsure of the terrain and rather too self-consciously gung-ho for her to be confident in his company. As he talked non-stop at her on the bumpy ride in the back of the truck, she wondered which of them was in most need of an escort ...

The truck dropped them in the flat countryside some way from the rendezvous point. There was distant muffled gunfire, but the immediate area seemed quiet enough. They were making their way across the edge of a ploughed field when a nearby copse suddenly exploded in machine-gun fire. Rapid return fire followed from a ditch further down the field. Without thinking, Elaine threw herself to the ground and covered her head with her hands. They'd walked straight into crossfire. Beside her there was a scrabbling noise and furious swearing. She turned her head to look at the crouching figure beside her, silhouetted against the sky and a fine target for stray bullets in an open field.

'What the hell are you doing?'

He was digging at the clay earth with his bare hands.

'We have to dig a foxhole for cover!'

She grabbed at his shoulder.

'Don't be ridiculous! Stay flat!'

He pulled away, affronted to be given orders by what he assumed to be a subordinate, and a woman at that. But a screaming bullet too close for comfort persuaded him otherwise and he threw himself down.

'Now stay down and follow me.' She hissed the words out and started crawling to the sanctuary of a hollow, where they sheltered, prone to the earth, till the crossfire and sounds of movement suggested the action had moved elsewhere.

'Come on, we'll chance it now – we're late already. Just stick close to me and do what I do.'

He followed her, glowering, his confidence shaken and his pride dented.

That wasn't the end of their troubles. By now the Dutch contact had given up waiting and had gone. A wasted journey and a broken link. In no man's land and dressed in civilian clothes, Elaine and her American escort were deliberately unidentifiable but they were still very much in danger. In the chaotic interregnum between occupation and liberation, this part of north-west Europe was awash with amateur informers, double agents, spies. Any stray civilian caught in a conflict zone was immediately suspected – by both sides.

Returning frustrated and muddy from their abortive mission they were picked up by US Military Police and taken to an army base for interrogation. This was the second humiliation of the day for the young lieutenant and none of his outraged protests would convince his comrades-in-arms that he was not a German plant. Elaine was more sanguine: she had no identifying papers but explained calmly that she was part of a British Special Forces detachment and that a call to Lieutenant-Colonel de Rome of the Canadian First Army would soon establish her bona fides. She'd met Maurice de Rome and they'd got on well; he came from the Francophone Royal 22nd Regiment, the 'Van Doos', and they'd been at home conversing in both French and English. There were few enough women mixing at that level in Allied military circles. She prayed that he'd remember her.

It was some hours before the colonel could be reached. From the side of the telephone conversation they overheard, it seemed he recalled her only too clearly.

'We've got a young woman here, sir, claiming to be Special Forces, Hélène Madden … Er, yeah, sir, small frame, lots of dark brown wavy hair …' A short, dirty laugh. 'Well yeah, kinda pretty … OK, sir. Thank you, sir.' The MP held out the receiver and gestured to her to come to the phone. She was reassured to hear de Rome's voice.

'Miss Madden. What *have* you been up to, getting yourself arrested? How careless of you.'

'I'm sorry, sir. I take full responsibility. We had some bad luck on the op and then we were picked up. It was all a bit of a misunderstanding. No harm done, I hope. My escort seems to have survived the ordeal.' She looked across at him sitting in the corner, sheepish, dirty and deflated. 'Yes, sir. Of course. Thank you, sir. I'm sorry to have troubled you.'

By the time they'd been delivered back to the Antwerp base, she'd taken her leave of her chastened American on less than friendly terms and got back to the billet, it was nearly midnight. It had been a frustrating and fruitless day. It was only when she went to the bathroom to wash, exhausted and still flecked with mud from the field, that she remembered the missing ring.

Enquiries of the woman who owned the house and her cleaner the following morning drew a blank. They hadn't seen a signet ring engraved with initials. There were no other residents to ask. More in hope than expectation she searched through her few belongings and scoured the floor in her room. She remembered taking the ring off to wash the previous morning, as she usually did, but she didn't recall putting it back on. She was certain she'd left it there, on the shelf. Now it was gone. Worse, it wasn't hers to lose. She'd always intended to return it, one day, to Luc. Now she'd let him down and it added to her sense that, bit by bit, she was losing her hold on luck.

After yesterday's misadventures she now had to face her superiors and explain why the rendezvous had failed and why she'd ended up in the custody of the Americans and having to call on the time of a busy senior officer to bail her out. Now this. Perhaps she wasn't as competent – or as favoured by good fortune – as she thought. She wasn't used to failure and felt her habitual armour of self-confidence melting away. For the first time feeling alone and vulnerable, she longed for André's loving words and reassuring embrace.

In the few weeks she'd been away from Brussels, they'd managed only a few snatched telephone calls. Neither had the time or inclination for letters and anyway the wartime post was unreliable. He'd been so busy. There was the prospect of a major new assignment, he said, though he couldn't say more until it was confirmed. She understood, of course. Was it another special op? Well, no, but certainly something of national importance, especially in the peace they all longed for. Intrigued, she wanted to get back and learn more about the wonderful post-war life in prospect for them both. Until that happy day, she'd just have to carry on with her duties here, without André, without Luc's lucky ring, and with only the flirtatious Adjutant Blaze to distract her.

In early December she finally got a weekend pass and returned, happy and expectant, to Brussels to see André and hear more about his plans for their future. She'd hardly got her coat and hat off when she started firing questions at him.

'Is it confirmed? What's the job? Tell me everything – I'm dying to know!'

She was like an excited child. He caught her hand, kissed her and told her to sit down. He poured them both a drink.

'I'm to be Belgium's Ambassador in Vienna. It'll be confirmed as soon as the war is over.'

She didn't know what she expected but it wasn't this.

'Well, that is a surprise! What marvellous news! Congratulations, my darling, you deserve it. Well done!'

She went to embrace him. There was the smallest hesitation in his response as he drew back from her.

'There are … implications.'

'Well, yes. We'll have to move to Vienna, obviously! The winters are pretty dreadful but it's supposed to be such a lovely city … museums and art galleries, and the music …'

'Elaine, my sweetest, dearest love …'

He was so serious, as if about to tell her something terrible, but surely this was the best news they could wish for?

'… This is going to be the biggest change in my life. A really important job for the country.'

'Of course. I realise that. And you'll do it brilliantly.'

'Before I can take it up, certain conditions have to be met.'

'But you're more than qualified with your law degree and everything. And your war service … the Military Cross. Where would they find someone better? They're lucky to have you.'

'This isn't about my experience or qualifications. Being a war hero isn't enough. There are financial conditions, social ones too. In the diplomatic world one has to maintain a certain standard of living, move in certain circles … To do the job I need an independent income and a social position. At the moment I have neither. My father's a military man but there's no money in the family, and I don't have any of my own.'

'What are you saying? That I'm not good enough to be an ambassador's wife?'

'I wanted to tell you myself before you see it in the newspapers tomorrow. I'm engaged to be married.'

For a fleeting moment she almost laughed with relief. But you haven't even proposed to me yet, she thought! She stopped herself. The engagement wasn't hers. Of course the engagement wasn't hers. A chill went through her. She held her lips together in a tight purse to stop … what? Tears? Questions? Accusations? The shock had sucked all sense out of her. André filled the void, answering the question that hadn't yet formed in her head.

'She's someone I've known for quite a while off and on, the daughter of a prominent family with money and influence. Call it a marriage of convenience if you like, but she comes as part of the deal. I can't take the job without her. I'm sorry, Elaine.'

'Do you love her?'

'I respect her. We'll make it work.'

'You said you loved me.' It sounded petulant, pathetic. She felt so stupid.

'And I meant it. Still mean it. But I'm not able to marry you. Can you understand that?'

'No' she said, 'I can't.'

ൟ

The following hours would have been agony if she had felt anything other than numb. She couldn't stay in the apartment a moment longer than she had to. Packing her few things, she reported back for duty in Antwerp a day earlier than expected. Michel was there, suave as ever, headset round his neck, cigarette in his hand, feet on the desk between skeds. He pushed the cigarette packet towards her.

'You're back early. Change of plan?'

'Yes.' Something was obviously wrong. Vivacious Hélène didn't usually look this distant, this distracted.

'Boyfriend trouble?'

'Do we have to talk about it? I'd rather be getting on with some work.'

'Of course. None of my business.' He swung his feet off the desk and nodded in the direction of the intray. 'New batch just logged in. They're all yours.'

They carried on in silence. She knew she was making mistakes; at the fourth attempt at one message she threw down her pencil.

'Oh for God's sake, this is completely hopeless! I'm going out for some air.'

In the freezing courtyard, she hugged herself and lit another cigarette. After five minutes Michel came out with her coat.

'Come on, you'll need this. Or perhaps you'd forgotten it's December?'

How could she forget? Only days ago she was looking forward to her perfect, sunny future, only weeks ago she was joking with Monsieur Bernard at Ciney with André close by her side in the late September warmth. Now it was suddenly midwinter.

'Thanks. That was thoughtful of you.'

He put the coat gently round her shoulders.

'He must be some kind of bastard to be causing you this much unhappiness.' The words were quiet, purposeful, uncharacteristically sincere for such a practised flatterer. She gave a bitter half-laugh.

'No, not a bastard. Just a very practical man. Apparently I didn't fit in with his plans.'

There. She'd said it, summed up his betrayal in a sentence.

'Practical perhaps. Foolish certainly. I can't imagine any man not wanting you … as part of his plans.'

At any other time, she might have found his attentions irritating or irrelevant. Now, in her despair, she found them a strange comfort. André had made her feel so young and naive. How could she ever have believed that she could hold on to such a man beyond the unreal excitements of a casual wartime affair? She'd seen enough of them during her four years in London. Thrown together by danger and circumstance, it was easy enough for lovers to mistake transient passion for something more substantial. In the post-liberation light of day the landscape looked very different. He was thirty and on the threshold of a brilliant diplomatic career. She was a girl, a nobody from small-town Flanders with no prospects at all after SOE had finished with her. It was never going to work.

The coat, the cigarette, the warmth of another human being beside her started to thaw the chill. Chill turned to heat; hurt to anger. Abandonment and betrayal had dogged her childhood and youth; now they threatened to haunt her young womanhood. Well, she wouldn't let them. She'd railed against the injustice of it in the past and she wasn't going to accept her fate meekly now. This handsome man so solicitous by her side reminded her that she was somebody after all. Hadn't she done courageous things for her country? Wasn't she still attractive? André's cruel rejection wouldn't mark her. She wouldn't just be cast aside, she'd come out fighting, as she always had. She turned to him and laughed.

'Oh, Michel. Do you *ever* stop?'

'Not while there's still a chance of winning the fair lady.'

'Fair lady?'

He moved much closer to her. His green eyes really were quite beguiling.

'You, Hélène. Couldn't you tell? I'm mad about you. I was from the moment I saw you. A hopeless cliché I know, but I'm afraid it's true.'

Another affair on the back of such a vertiginous rebound was, at the least, ill advised. She knew as much, but she was in no state to be stern or sensible with herself. She was fighting mad with her former lover and determined to show that, if he didn't want her, someone else just as attractive did. She was thrilled and alarmed at the helter-skelter pace of the developing affair; it was slipping, relentlessly, ecstatically, beyond her control and she didn't care. By Christmas she'd accepted his proposal of marriage.

෬

As 1945 began Allied victory was edging nearer. By the end of January the long and costly Battle of the Bulge had been won and Nazi Germany was fighting desperately on all fronts to retain its shrinking Reich. With liberation exiled governments were returning to reassert control in lands left in chaos: relations between European allies started to fracture. Common cause had kept them close despite their many differences. The prospect of peace meant reversion to national agendas and jockeying for the spoils of war.

Relations between T Section and the Sûreté, the Belgian security service, though always delicate, had been largely cordial and co-operative thanks to the effective liaison efforts of Ides Floor and the smooth diplomatic skills of Hardy Amies (though he later described it as *'a trial in diplomacy'*). SOE relied on Belgian and Anglo-Belgian manpower in the field and the Sûreté's local contacts. In turn it relied on SOE resources and know-how. They needed each other. But the cracks were starting to show.

On 17 February 1945, Floor sent a furious memo, marked 'Top Secret, Strictly Personal and Confidential', to Amies.

> *I have just learned that an official visit was made to the Verstrepen Group by Brigadier Mockler-Ferryman [SOE Director of Operations, North-West Europe] accompanied by Colonel Rowlandson. I have also learned that during this visit decisions were taken to make changes to staff ...*
>
> *I feel that it was completely out of order that this should take place without any instructions from my Service. We have complete responsibility for this group which is on loan to a Canadian unit through your Special Force missions. I cannot therefore allow decisions to be made which affect the staff of this mission without having previously given my agreement.*
>
> *In view of the good relations of the past three years I prefer to believe that this is an oversight rather than a deliberate lack of courtesy. Nevertheless, I would ask you to ensure that a similar situation does not reoccur.*

On the same date in Antwerp the 'withdrawal' of Michel Blaze, Hélène Madden and two others from the Verstrepen Group was confirmed. They were to be replaced by new people, one of whom would be Denise Leplat, described as *'en qualité de Codeuse'*, the Resistance woman in Brussels Elaine had worked so closely with on the Imogen mission.

The changes were obviously controversial but Elaine wasn't told why she was being replaced. She'd carried out her coding duties conscientiously, sometimes under difficult conditions, and done everything else asked of her. It wasn't her fault that the Dutch rendezvous operation went so badly awry. Had the American lieutenant perhaps made a complaint against her? But on what grounds? She'd probably saved his stupid life. So it must be about her and Michel.

Their proposed marriage was, strictly speaking, prohibited under Routine Order 32 which barred the union of active SOE agents as a possible security risk. To get round this, Elaine was prepared to make the sacrifice women were usually expected to make: she would resign from the service. But there was another impediment. Being British by birth, Elaine couldn't marry a foreign national – even one from a friendly nation – without special dispensation. But she played it by the book, applying to Special Forces HQ in Brussels, her request ending up with T Section's administrative officer in Baker Street and then going up to the highest level. Correspondence on her personal file and that of Michel Blaze tracks the arcane internal discussion that took place on the young couple's future.

Reconciled to having to leave SOE, Elaine didn't intend to give up altogether the clandestine work she'd been trained for, enjoyed and was rather good at. '*She intends to apply to OSS and thinks it likely they will employ her. I think so too,*' noted a senior officer on her file. This presented another difficulty. They might now work for different organisations – and powers – but there was a distinct possibility they might be posted to the same place and would meet, by accident or design, posing a new and even more sensitive security risk.

The question of Elaine's impending nuptials appeared to go as far as Air Commodore Boyle, a member of SOE's controlling council. SOE in its bureaucratic wisdom decided that it was better that they continued, married, in SOE employment so that they could be kept on separate operations: '*Far more secure if we employ both of them … but note that Security Section be consulted before either is employed in the field so we can ensure they are employed in such a way as they are not likely to endanger the people they work with,*' Air Commodore Boyle noted on Blaze's file. That matter settled, Boyle approved an exception to Routine Order 32 '*in the exceptional circumstances of this case*'.

With the marriage now approved in principle, Elaine and Michel flew back to London, arriving at Croydon Airport on 10 March. Their wedding plans could now go ahead, and the sooner the better.

Susan Heath welcomed her back to 24 Bayswater Court. Elaine was anxious to catch up on all the news.

'Is the club still going? How are all the boys? What about Army Man? Is that still going strong? I heard about the doodle-bugs and the V2s – we got a taste of those where ... By the way, thanks so much for packing up my uniform so they could send it over to me. It meant so much to have it.'

She stopped herself. There was nothing more she could tell Susan about her work or where she'd been for the past six months. Her flatmate understood.

'Don't worry, I'm not going to interrogate you on what you've been doing so mysteriously with the FANYs all this time. Yes, Army Man is still on the scene, though not for much longer. He's about to be posted, so no more Yankee hospitality for us, worse luck ...'

Their golden evening at the Criterion and the start of her enchanted time seemed so long ago, though it had been little more than a year. She felt much older now.

'... But you look well, Elaine, and happy. Are you back in London for good? There must be *something* you can tell me!'

'Well, yes, there is *something*.' She laughed. 'I have a little job for you if you'd be prepared to do it for me. I'd like you to be a witness at my wedding in a couple of weeks' time. Quick and quiet, down the road at the Registry Office. Nothing special.'

Susan clapped her hands.

'I knew it! I thought you looked pleased with yourself! Congratulations! I'd love to! Who's the lucky man?'

'His name's Michel. He's Belgian. I met him through work. I've got a photo somewhere ... here it is, only a tiny Polyphoto but it gives you an idea.'

'Oh yes! Very dashing and continental. How long have you known him?'

'Not long, a few months.'

She handed the photo back.

'So, a whirlwind romance then, how thrilling!'

'Something like that.'

'Will you live in London?'

'Not sure. It depends what happens with the war. I expect we'll get new postings soon. Everything's happened rather quickly and we haven't had time to plan ahead.'

'Who has these days? I don't think we dare imagine what peace might be like until we're actually celebrating it. It can't be far off now, can it? Then we can all start living normally again.'

⌒⌒

Elaine had some problems on her return to London. When she'd requested her uniform to be sent to her in Brussels the previous September, she asked Susan to put her British identity card in with it, but when the uniform arrived the card was mysteriously missing, presumed stolen in transit. She needed to replace it urgently: she had any number of false documents, issued for her foreign missions, but without her real one she couldn't register with any shops to buy food and she was obliged to produce it for inspection at any time. Most pressing, she couldn't get married without it.

This caused some irritation in Baker Street, though none of it was Elaine's fault. Apparently she hadn't been properly registered as a FANY when she was first recruited by SOE, and FANY HQ, with no record of her on their books, were now refusing to issue a new identity card for her. Fractious memos showed that SOE Headquarters staff clearly believed they had better things to do:

'*This girl is wandering around London without any document whatsoever, at a time when she is particularly in need of one, as she proposes to get married within the week, or so ... She is also in possession of a ration book, which has never been used, nor is she registered with any shopkeepers ...*'

Hardy Amies, took up the theme in a separate memo of 16 March:

'*Madden [has] frankly been a bloody nuisance ever since the liberation. She did some quite good work when she was first with the Verstrepen Group, but caused trouble later on, which ended in both she and Blaze being sacked. However, one must not forget that [she] jumped into Belgium and we must do what we can to fix [her] up in the FANYs regularly. I do not recommend [she] be used on any further SOE work.'*

Completely unaware that she and Blaze had been 'sacked' or that she was under any kind of cloud, Elaine was surprised at the reception she got from Amies when they next met at a T Section luncheon to mark the end of SOE operations in Belgium.

She arrived to find Michel already in animated conversation with the T Section boss. Susan was right. How dashing he looked in his dress uniform. And Lieutenant-Colonel Amies was his usual immaculately presented self. They made an imposing pair, laughing and joking together in the crowded room. They seemed surprisingly relaxed in each other's company. Even though SOE staff didn't follow usual military protocol and relations between ranks were less formal than in the regular services, it was still common courtesy to defer to officers of higher rank. Yet here they were, the humble adjutant and the lieutenant-colonel chatting away like old friends, even gripping each other occasionally on the arm for emphasis. She hesitated to interrupt so intimate an exchange, but Michel saw her hovering.

'Darling. You're late. Hardy, let me introduce my lovely fiancée, Hélène Madden.'

Amies' smile dissolved as he turned to face her.

'Yes. We've met.' His forced formality was chilling. This wasn't how she'd seen him seconds earlier with Michel.

'Sir.' The embarrassing interview before she went to Ringway came flooding back. Now she felt under interrogation all over again. He looked her up and down, making her feel distinctly uncomfortable. It was as if he was looking at something loathsome. She needed to get out of his eyeline. She squeezed Michel on the arm, aware that she was being deliberately proprietorial.

'Excuse me, I'll just go and get myself a drink.'

Amies still fixed her with a look of disgust.

'Yes, do.' But what he said next, though delivered sotto voce, she was also clearly meant to hear as she moved away through the crowd towards the bar.

'Really, Blaze. Don't tell me you're going to marry that stupid girl?'

She was disturbed more than hurt. She knew she wasn't stupid, so what did Amies have against her? And why did he seem so intimate with Michel and then act like a jealous lover when she turned up? When they were alone again later, she didn't expect to get answers, but he might give her some clues.

'You seem very pally with our boss.'

'Why not? I got to know him in training. He's jolly good company off duty.'

'He wasn't good company with me at lunch. Why was he being so horrible?'

'Was he? I didn't notice. I think you're being over-sensitive, darling. Not everyone in the world can adore you quite as much as I do.'

He was laughing but there was an edge to his voice. She seemed to have touched a raw nerve; it was Michel who was being sensitive. It wasn't worth pursuing; she left it with a shrug.

ℂ℁

They would have an Easter wedding on the Saturday between Good Friday and Easter Sunday. It was to be a very simple affair: just their two witnesses – Susan and a friend of Michel's – and a few others, then on to a local restaurant. Hardly a 'wedding breakfast', it would be whatever was available on the day within the five shilling limit. She'd heard of newly-weds having the choice of sardines on toast or beans on toast for their celebration meal – and then being told the sardines were off! He would wear his Belgian Army uniform, she'd wear a plain suit with a smart hat of Susan's ('You *must* have something borrowed'). There would be no bouquet but she'd managed to order a corsage of fresh flowers to brighten the suit.

There would be no honeymoon either: from 14 March Michel was to be transferred to SOE's X Section and was awaiting further orders. This was the German Directorate tasked with securing the successful occupation and subjugation of Nazi Germany, so he was very likely to be posted abroad. Elaine, too, expected a new assignment at any time. For the time being they were obliged to stay in London.

Unaware of Amies' recommendation to terminate her SOE employment, Elaine also didn't know that, in any case, T Section's work was winding up.

Amies himself would soon be given early release from the organisation, much to his relief. He'd had enough of diplomacy and subversion and was anxious to get back to his first love, fashion. Elsewhere, plans were afoot for redeployment of a rather different kind for SOE's agents.

Hundreds had been recruited and trained in the past eighteen months and now the war in Europe was fast approaching its endgame such large numbers would no longer be needed. Agents were in the main male paramilitaries, schooled in the arts of death and deception, a potentially dangerous workforce to be summarily turned on to the open market in a volatile post-war world. A Top Secret document of 21 February discussed options for their future employment. One of three options mooted in the document was '*in teams of two to drop into POW camps after a state of collapse inside Germany has arisen*'. There were no further details about the purpose of this operation, nor a codename for it. Neither was there yet any official sanction from SHAEF. But there soon would be.

At Bayswater Court on the eve of her wedding, with Susan out on a farewell date with Army Man, Elaine had a quiet time alone to gather her thoughts and take stock of the hectic times over the past months, something she realised she'd been putting off for too long. It had been far too easy to be swept along on the tide of events without much thought, when more serious consideration might have given her pause. They'd been back in London barely three weeks; she'd known Michel properly for little more than three months. Now she was about to marry him. This wasn't at all unusual, she reasoned. Wartime weddings happened like that. You had to take your chance, find your happiness when and where you could. The end was in sight but the war wasn't over; Hitler was on the skids but the Nazis weren't defeated yet. Who knew what could still happen or when it would finally finish? Being the wife of a junior army officer about to be demobbed wasn't the dream future she'd fondly imagined, but she'd been naive then and this was now. Michel was good-looking, amusing and popular. If she could only keep his roving eye concentrated on her, then they would be just fine.

She was still thinking about this when the telephone rang. She wasn't expecting Michel to call; they'd parted that afternoon for a final chaste night apart. Who might be ringing at this late hour?

'Bayswater 0011.'

'Elaine?'

She didn't immediately recognise the voice.

'Yes?'

'It's André.'

It was even later by the time she arrived at his hotel. He met her in the lobby, coming forward to kiss her on both cheeks.

'You're cold. Come over here and have a drink. It's marvellous to see you.'

'You're in London?'

Of course he was, what a silly thing to say, but she was still in a daze of confusion and barely concealed excitement. This was the man she'd walked out on, the man who'd betrayed her, broken her heart. So what on earth was she doing here?

'Yes, I've been assigned to another special op.'

'You're not married yet, then?'

'No, I'm not married.'

'And the job …?'

'I haven't finished with special ops yet. But yes, all going to plan. Which is why I wanted to see you.'

Her heart leapt. Perhaps the engagement was off? They settled in a quiet corner of the bar and he got straight to the point.

'Elaine. When it's all fixed, hopefully by the end of the year, I want you to come to Vienna. I can find you a job at the embassy and a little flat …'

She realised what he was saying.

'… as your mistress, you mean.'

'We can be together, that's the main thing. Not all the time of course, but …'

'As your mistress.'

'That's a hard word for it.'

'Is there a nicer one?'

She'd been called a whore once, a long time ago, at the Palace Hotel. 'Mistress' might be two steps up from the gutter but it wasn't that much better. He took her hand.

'I love you, Elaine. I was distraught when you left. You can't marry that man Blaze. He's not the one for you, believe me. If you knew what I know about his …'

This was too much.

'Stop it! It's too late. It's tomorrow. If you really loved me that much, you could have married me!'

'I couldn't. I can't. You know why.'

'Yes. You explained. But I didn't accept your explanation.'

People were now looking in the direction of the lovers' tiff apparently in progress in the corner. André got up.

'We can't talk properly here. We'll have to go to my room.'

This was the point at which she knew she should say goodbye and just walk away.

∞

On the morning of Saturday, 31 March 1945, her wedding day, Elaine woke late in unfamiliar surroundings. André was sitting on the bed, dressed and ready to leave. He kissed her.

'Good morning, my darling. I didn't want to wake you. I've got to go. But let me ask you one more time, are you sure? It's not too late, even now. You don't have to marry Blaze. Come to Vienna instead. I can arrange it all. You only have to say the word.'

She was barely awake but nothing that had happened over the past few hours had changed her mind.

'Absolutely sure. You're to be married. I'm to be married. I can't see me living with you as your mistress and having to hide all the time. I couldn't stand that. You go. I'll be OK. Good luck with everything.'

'I'm sorry. Goodbye then. I wish you all the luck in the world.'

Then he left. She followed shortly after, back to Bayswater Court.

Later that day at Paddington Registry Office Elaine Marie Madden married Michel Ghislain Blaze, who gave his profession as 'Lieutenant Belgian Army (Student of Law)'. The ceremony was witnessed by Susan Heath and Jules Monnickendan. The fathers' professions were given, respectively, as 'Professor of Languages' and 'Investigation Officer, War Graves Commission'.

∞

Two days later on 2 April, Easter Monday, Elaine was formally transferred from the employment of SOE to a new special operations outfit to be known as the Special Allied Airborne Reconnaissance Force. This was such a mouthful to say that it was universally known by the people involved as SAARF. '*Somewhat larger than that of an Infantry Division*', it had been set up at breakneck speed over a fortnight the previous month under orders from SHAEF.

The new joint Anglo-American force was tasked with mounting a special operation into Germany in the dangerous vacuum created by its imminent collapse. The country was now in a state of chaos with Allied forces encroaching from west and east and Hitler holed up in his Berlin bunker, his mood increasingly manic, his command crumbling. Intelligence was sketchy but on the ground many areas had already descended into law-lessness: German troops were deserting and on the run, advancing Russian troops behaving like savages among local populations, and civilians taking up arms and on the rampage. Against this chaotic background, Operation Eclipse – the covert race against Russia to secure Berlin for the Western Powers – was also being played out. Operating in these '*Eclipse conditions*' meant danger, not only from the last desperate strongholds of Nazi power, but from an increasingly belligerent Soviet Union.

SAARF's original brief, as intimated in the Top Secret note of 21 February, was to parachute agents behind enemy lines into or near German prisoner-of-war and concentration camps in advance of liberation by advancing Allied forces. In up to 120 teams of three on the SOE model – two agents and a W/T operator – they would recce camp conditions, establish radio communications with Allied forces and if possible negotiate with camp commanders for the safe conduct of prisoners during this volatile interreg-num. Conditions in the camps were suspected to be poor but at that stage no one knew for certain quite how bad they would be. Neither did the senior command at SHAEF have any idea how the final desperate stages of the war in Europe would play out. Hostage taking or wholesale murder of prisoners was a possibility. There were already reports of camps in the east being evacuated en masse in the face of the Russian advance. Thousands of POWs were being forced on to exhausting marches in punishing condi-tions and at great cost to human life. The SAARF operation was in essence a humanitarian effort to stop the forced marches and secure the safe and speedy evacuation of prisoners, ideally in advance of the liberating forces. But it had another agenda. There were a large number of particularly valuable or important political prisoners in the camps – including captured SOE agents – who needed special protection and speedy repatriation. SAARF needed to get them away from danger as a priority.

Like all special operations that demanded absolute secrecy, it used codenames. The total SAARF mission into the camps was codenamed VICARAGE. Continuing the innocent theme, its operations into different areas were named after flowers: VIOLET, BLUEBELL, DAISY and POPPY. Individual teams were codenamed, somewhat bizarrely, after items of stationery: PENNIB, BRIEFCASE, PENCIL, ERASER, ESCRITOIRE and STAMP among them. There was a further piece of subterfuge. It was suggested that anyone inquisitive enough to ask what the initials SAARF stood for should be told: 'Salvation Army Auxiliary Relief Force'. It wasn't so far off the mark.

This was a classic SOE-type operation so large numbers of former SOE agents like Elaine were being redeployed, together with regular Special Forces personnel and American OSS agents – altogether 120 French, ninety-six British, ninety-six American, thirty Belgian and eighteen Polish, each operating in separate detachments. Training was to be done jointly by OSS and SOE.

Elaine was given the briefest outline of the task ahead and the opportunity to decline if she wished – SAARF was effectively recruiting volunteers for a potentially dangerous operation. There was no question but that she would accept: her intention was to carry on fighting the Nazi oppressor until the job was done. There was still work to do and she'd been trained to do it. So, as one of a small number of women former SOE agents, she was assigned to the Belgian team and began her training almost immediately.

Also in training with her at the Old Clubhouse, Wentworth, the famous Surrey golf course, were the two men in her life: Michel and André. This was potentially very awkward for her but she could do nothing about it. That was the trouble with operating in such a small and secretive world. She resolved to behave entirely professionally with her husband, and to keep her distance from André as far as possible. Fortunately, he appeared to be assigned to the British detachment so there was no likelihood of them being on the same team, though officers of all nationalities messed together and had the opportunity to use Wentworth's rather splendid recreational facilities. But the training time was short, the days packed, and Michel was as attentive as ever, so it was easy enough for André and Elaine to stay at a polite distance.

The plan to parachute teams in before the liberating forces arrived was controversial from the start. No one had any idea what they'd find or the reception they'd get. Apart from anything else, they'd be airborne targets, easily picked off from the ground. At their first detailed briefing, the new teams expressed their reservations in no uncertain terms. Elaine was one of them.

'What? Parachute in uniform in broad daylight? Close to a concentration camp? We'd be dead before we even arrived! We'd be shot on sight!'

The staff thought they were exaggerating but those who'd operated behind enemy lines knew better.

'They'll listen to force, but they won't listen to a negotiator!'

Ides Floor, speaking for the Sûreté who were funding the Belgian detachment, had operated in the field himself and had no doubts about the risks his agents would be running. He refused permission for any Belgians to be parachuted: '*I could not reconcile this method with my conscience or give any justification to my authorities.*'

These fears were realised with the fate of the first airborne operation, VIOLET. All six teams of British, French and American agents had problems retrieving their equipment and with making contact with HQ, and were all eventually captured. The French team had a particularly unpleasant time: they landed wide of the intended drop zone and were captured by the Russians and interrogated as dangerous counter-revolutionaries. They didn't manage to escape back to American lines until early June. Local conditions were reported to be chaotic, with armed civilians '*going haywire*'. They were all fortunate not to have been shot – by the Germans, by the Russians, by renegade civilians or by the rampant Nazi national militia, the *Volkssturm*. From then on, the plan to parachute SAARF personnel into the camps was abandoned in favour of land transport, but VICARAGE continued undaunted.

On 21 April as she sat strapped in the back of the transporter plane grinding its way to Brussels for the onward journey into Germany by truck and jeep, she was calm. There was none of the nervous excitement of her last outward flight from Harrington. It was daytime now, there was no flak to dodge and no parachute pack on her back. She wouldn't be steeling herself to jump this time, but that wasn't it. She felt altogether different now. Older. Certainly wiser. A great deal had happened during those last nine months. Her enchanted time, but also her betrayal and the loss of the love of her life. She wasn't the same open, trusting girl who'd first embarked on this adventure a little over a year ago.

Hard to credit that it was almost five years since the invasion of Belgium and the start of their trek to Dunkirk and the hell they found there. She and Simone really were girls then. She thought of Simone and hoped she'd finally settled and found happiness in London. She remembered Knocker, Gary and Smudger and the lasting debt they owed these brave lads who'd rescued them and delivered them safely to the Dunkirk dockside. She didn't know their full names and they hadn't even had the chance to say thank you. She fervently hoped they'd survived the war.

But what about the family she'd left behind in Poperinghe? Where were they? She prayed they were safe. And her father? Where was he now? The thought that she might never see any of them again pained her. Once she wouldn't have cared but time had helped soften past hurts. She understood more about life now. But had she ever doubted that she would survive? After Dunkirk, not ever, not even now that she was flying back into enemy territory, into she knew not what. There had been stories about the camps, certainly, some of them so extreme they were unbelievable. But concentration camps were nothing new; the British had invented them years ago in South Africa. Her training had been short but thorough; she was well prepared, ready to face the latest challenge.

She felt quite confident about her mission. She was to be part of Operation BLUEBELL. Going into Forward Areas where British and American army groups were operating, three of the BLUEBELL teams would start in the Weimar region entering concentration camps at or shortly after liberation, to '*obtain particulars of certain important personnel*'. One of their main tasks would be to identify Belgian SOE agents and prioritise their evacuation. All she knew about the camps or what they would find there was the name of the first: Buchenwald.

She'd been buffeted by life in the past months but had survived the turbulence. She was calm, nothing much could shake her now.

∞

The secret report of SAARF's operations, its lessons and achievements, was written up by commanding officer Brigadier J.S. Nichols on 10 July. The tone is brisk and upbeat: Operation VIOLET is judged a success despite the difficulties encountered. Elaine's BLUEBELL teams achieved their objectives: they '*collected and despatched valuable information about Belgian and other Allied personnel found in the camps … and [assisted] in the evacuations of DPs* [displaced persons] *and internees*'. The multi-national teams were singled out for praise: '*All Operational Personnel in the Force were volunteers and showed remarkable powers of initiative*'. Lessons learned referred to technical recommendations about equipment and communications. Though the names of several camps were mentioned, the conditions found in them by the teams were not.

Operation VICARAGE was over. All teams were back at Wentworth by 20 June where they were treated to a Farewell Dance on the 22nd and a Final Parade and Inspection on the 23rd, followed by a Garden Party to which 550 external guests, including members of the Belgian Sûreté, were invited. SAARF was formally disbanded on 2 July 1945, an intense and short-lived secret operation about to slip into post-war obscurity.

TWELVE

GERMANY, NORTH-WEST ENGLAND AND BRUSSELS

JUNE 1945–APRIL 1946

The child, he must have been about five, was scrabbling around in the dirt barefoot, barely dressed in odd scraps. She held out a dry biscuit to him. He approached warily then snatched it from her and put it, whole, into his mouth. It stuck out of cheeks not fleshly pink and glowing but a desiccated yellow. She asked his name in French, Flemish and German. He just looked at her in silence from hollow eyes. A voice rose slowly, deliberately, from a group of people sitting, barely moving, nearby.

'He doesn't speak. No one knows who he is. Probably born here. Mother's dead. We try and look after him but he doesn't speak any language. Doesn't speak at all.'

The boy came closer, now holding out his hand. She pulled another biscuit from her skirt pocket. It soon joined the half-eaten one already in his mouth. He hadn't taken his eyes off her the whole time. In this most unsettling of places, this disturbed her more than anything. She made to move on. There was so much to do, she'd been distracted. But the child, seeming to recognise something in her that was too precious to let go, lunged at her and wrapped his bony arms tightly round her leg. There was a shuffling noise from the group nearby. It was a kind of mirthless laughter.

'Ha! You're his mother now.'

She gently prised his little arms away but they left an indelible impression. Even as she walked away, she felt this small child, filthy and starving, still clinging to her.

She walked on in a world of the dead and barely living, among scenes of such human desecration she wondered whether she was in the real world at all. The people who'd been incarcerated there, if that's what they'd once been, were now so reduced as to have lost any semblance of humanity. Many were barely distinguishable from the naked and half-clothed corpses already being loaded on to trucks by former guards, now guarded themselves by armed servicemen, on their way to mass graves.

She listened as the half-starved man, a scion of the Michelin tyre family, told them how he'd been castrated with a rolled-up table napkin by his laughing captors. She saw the lampshade they said had been made of human skin by the guard, Ilse Koch. She believed it. And the bodies still hanging from their gallows, among them a pregnant woman, with a gaping gun-shot wound to her belly and the mutilated form of her almost full-term foetus clearly visible inside…

She walked on roads made from crematoria cinders and saw the piles of wasted naked bodies, dead from typhus, overwork, starvation, perverted experimentation, waiting to be burned. And those still left in the gas chambers. Even those still living looked dead, lying listless and with their hollow eyes and fleshless faces. The inescapable smell of death and excrement …

Every night Elaine walked among it all and woke sweating, gasping, still breathing in that stink of blood and shit.

She wasn't sure how long she'd been having these nightmares. Time had hung heavily since their return from Germany and – day or night – she couldn't erase the images of what she'd seen. But the job had been done. They found two Belgian agents, one in Buchenwald – a wireless operator, André Fonck, who'd been there since 1942. He was alive, thank God, and they'd handed him straight over to the Red Cross to get him out. They all came back, relieved to get away from those terrible sights, at the end of June. Everyone at SAARF HQ was very grateful and it was all rather hazy now. There was a party, she must have been there with Michel, but she barely remembered it. Was it outside? Then they were paid and thanked, and that was it. Finished. She was demobilised, her war was over.

They'd missed the riotous Victory in Europe Day celebrations all over Britain on 8 May. Hitler was dead, Germany had surrendered, Operation Eclipse ended in an uneasy draw in a ruined Berlin. They'd gone into the camps almost immediately after the liberating British or American forces and were there altogether little more than three weeks. Yet, even now so close to the event, she couldn't quite recall the names. Yes, Buchenwald was the first, she remembered that because of Fonck. Flossenbürg was the last, that's where she'd seen the hanged woman and her baby. And there were one – or was it two? – in between. Dachau was one. Was Bergen-Belsen the other? The horror of those camps now merged into one recurring nightmare. The names no longer mattered, only what she'd witnessed there.

The teams had been asked to take photographs and she'd kept some. If there hadn't been photographs, no one would have believed what they saw. As compelling and corrosive as pornography, the black and white images of those pitiful sights drew her in again and again. She stared at them for hours trying to make sense, for her own sanity, of the evil they represented. But she couldn't bring herself to describe what she'd experienced to anyone who wasn't there. They wouldn't have believed her, or understood. And those who were there only wanted to try and forget.

Michel was there. He understood, but she'd seen hardly anything of him since getting back to Britain. Now SOE and SAARF had finished with him, he still had to be demobbed from his substantive rank in the Belgian Army. While he was in Brussels negotiating his release and scouting for peacetime jobs, she was left unemployed and homeless in London. Susan invited her back to Bayswater Court but this didn't feel right. Susan had been a good friend but she needed a complete change of scene. She was strangely tearful – so unlike her – and she didn't feel herself.

One of her Duponselle aunts, Josephine, was now living in the north-west. She asked if she could stay with her up in Bolton until Michel came back to London or sent for her. It would be a rest, a recuperation from all that she'd seen and done since leaving Poperinghe in May 1940. She was physically and mentally exhausted. That's when the nightmares must have started.

∞

'Where are those photographs of the camps I brought with me? They were in my bedside drawer. Have you moved them?'

Her aunt looked unapologetic.

'I've burnt them, I'm sorry.'

'But they're evidence. They'll be needed. Why on earth did you do that?'

'I had to. You've been here for six weeks now and every night you've woken up shouting. I can hear you pacing the floor. It's those photos. You shouldn't be looking at them. They're disgusting and they're giving you nightmares … I just couldn't bear the thought of you looking at them again and having it all come back, so I destroyed them. They're no longer here to remind you so just forget about it now. It's done with. The war's over and we all have to try and get back to normal.'

Normal. She'd never known normal, not other people's normal anyway, and there was absolutely no chance of her just forgetting.

'Thank you for your concern, but you really shouldn't have done that. I'll be fine, I just need a bit of time to adjust.'

Time went on but the nightmares didn't stop. She still felt strangely disconnected from the world as if she was no longer part of it. Everyday life in the northern mill town carried on around her, the bombsites and factory hooters, the women workers in their overalls and turbans, children playing in the streets, screeching with delight and calling to each other as they raced their rackety homemade trolleys. She watched this unreal, unfamiliar normality like a sleeper who knows they're dreaming and yearns to wake up.

She existed in this listless half-life for much of the summer, until Aunt Josephine confronted her.

'Do you think you might be pregnant?'

'I shouldn't think so. I'm just a bit run-down, that's all.'

'Well, you weren't at all well when you first got here. And you haven't been eating properly. Why not go to the doctor and make sure? If you are, then you really should start taking better care of yourself. And what better news to cheer us all up than a honeymoon baby? That'll soon make you forget all this war business, give you something lovely and positive to put your mind to! And won't Michel be thrilled!'

She wasn't sure. She'd been putting off the confirmation but she knew it was true even before her aunt's suspicions. It explained such a lot. It wasn't that she didn't want to have a baby – they hadn't taken any precautions so perhaps it was inevitable and now they were married it was perfectly acceptable. She would have the settled home and family life she'd been denied as a child and had always yearned for. But it was a far from ideal time to bring a child into the world. The war in Europe was barely over and there was still fighting in the Far East. Everything was still in flux. They didn't know where they would be living or what work Michel would be doing. Jobs might be plentiful but housing everywhere was a big problem, so many people had been made homeless by the bombing. Michel would probably want them to settle back in Belgium and they might have to live with his parents for a while. It would be strange to go back there to live again. She had always felt far more British than Belgian and the war had only made that sense of belonging more solid. Belgium was her adopted home but Britain was her country. She would have liked to have stayed.

Soon it was confirmed. Yes, she was pregnant, probably at least four months. She felt better once she knew for sure. On the telephone to Brussels Michel seemed delighted.

'That's great news, darling! You must come over straight away – we've got so much to celebrate!'

It was true, they had. By the middle of August the war was finally over in the Far East. Dropping the atomic bomb on Hiroshima and Nagasaki had forced the Japanese to surrender. At last they could start to look forward to a more settled life. Demobilisation would take a while but there was the prospect of a good peacetime job for Michel in Belgium – or perhaps abroad – with Unilever. Elaine wasn't troubling to look for work; she had a husband and would soon have a baby to look after. Her future was set. André Wendelen's marriage was announced in the Brussels press at the start of the month and he was on course to take up his new diplomatic career. She couldn't afford to waste time thinking what might have been, her sights were on her future with Michel and their child.

After the war came official recognition for those who'd served in Special Forces on covert operations. On 1 October Elaine was awarded a Mention in Despatches by the British for her SOE mission. Michel would later be appointed MBE for his wireless work. The Belgian government, too, was anxious to show its appreciation for services rendered. Together with many former comrades from T Section and the Resistance organisations, they were invited to the Royal Palace in Brussels to receive their battle honours from Prince Charles, the prince regent – Elaine's old friend, Monsieur Bernard.

She hadn't seen him since Ciney. After her initial embarrassment, they'd had a wonderful informal evening full of laughter and good company. This would be a very different occasion, a formal investiture with hundreds of people watching. She was to receive the *Croix de Guerre avec Palme* for bravery in the face of the enemy and she wasn't looking forward to it. Now the war was properly over, she was proud of her small part in it. There had been risks and she'd been prepared to take them. She was lucky never to have been in mortal danger – or to have been obliged to kill anyone – but much was demanded of her and she'd given everything she had. She didn't need a medal on her chest to prove it. Everyone who needed to know knew what she'd done. As for medals and award ceremonies, well, it was all for show and unimportant. On this, Michel disagreed.

'You're being ridiculous. It's a huge honour. All our friends will be there. Why not enjoy it? I intend to. It'll be fun – and something to tell our grandchildren.'

She somehow doubted they'd be interested.

'By the time they come along we'll be ancient history and no one will want to know what we did in this old war.'

'Well, we'll tell them whether they want to know or not! Come on, you know you'll be the best-looking woman there. I want to show you off.'

If she was honest, she knew she'd be embarrassed all over again to meet Prince Charles in such a formal setting. In the regal surroundings of the palace she wouldn't be able to stop thinking about all those awful unguarded things she'd said to him at Chateau d'Halloy about the shortcomings of his family. But a royal invitation wasn't something one could easily refuse, and anyway, Michel wouldn't have countenanced it. He was as proud of her as anyone and as he was receiving his own award, he wanted her there to be as proud of him.

The day arrived. The afternoon ceremony would continue with a reception into the early evening. She dressed carefully: she wanted to live up to

Michel's expectations but anything too glamorous would be crass. Though she was one of few women award recipients, she didn't want to stand out too much. A well-cut costume concealed her growing bump and a smart picture hat balanced her blossoming shape. She looked in the mirror and was content. Michel, too, approved. She would do.

Nevertheless, when it came to it and her name and citation were called, she approached the podium full of nerves and was unable to look the prince in the eye. She saw him pick up the medal but the brim of her hat obscured his face. The hand approached her right breast. She kept her head down. Then she gasped, a sharp unexpected pain where his hand lingered: he'd deliberately pricked her with the clasp of the medal to get her attention. Her head came up sharply and caught his eye. He gave her the most conspicuous stage wink. All nerves now gone with the shock of the pain and the incongruity of their situation, she couldn't help but smile as she reversed carefully backwards down the podium steps. Her medal now in place, she turned to face the audience and returned to her seat to warm applause.

'There. That wasn't so bad, was it?'

'Apart from him stabbing me in the chest ... thank God it's over and we can go and have a drink.'

At the reception afterwards, she was regaling a group of comrades with the story of her previous encounters with Monsieur Bernard when a discreet civilian appeared at her side and introduced himself as the prince's private secretary.

'Madam Blaze, the prince wonders if you would be kind enough to join him in his office. I'll take you there now.'

The others exchanged knowing glances and Michel looked irritated.

'Well, don't be long. You know we're meeting the others later at the Coq.'

'I won't. If I'm not out in half an hour, send a search party!'

They all laughed but she knew her embarrassment wasn't quite over yet.

'Ah, Miss Meeus. Come in.'

It was little more than a year since their time at Halloy, yet the cares of state had weighed heavily on the prince regent. No longer the suntanned playboy, he was older, greyer, less frivolous. He'd been a drinker before and judging by the open whisky bottle on the table beside him, little had changed. He signalled for her to sit down. On the chair lay a newspaper folded open at a picture of his brother, the now disgraced and exiled King Leopold III. She went to remove it so that she could sit down.

'No', he commanded. 'Sit on it.' He was making a point about his brother and enjoying her discomfort. 'Now then, if I remember rightly, whisky is your drink.'

He hadn't and it wasn't but she wasn't in any position to demur. He poured her a tumbler of whisky, filling it to the brim. She'd started drinking whisky at Winterfold but she always took it with water, never neat, and never in this quantity. She baulked as she took it from him. He poured himself an equally large glass, draining the bottle.

'Cheers! And many congratulations. On the Croix and, by the look of it, on your other little acquisition.' He nodded at her bump.

She blushed and took a gulp of whisky.

'Well, I'm married now of course.'

'Ah yes, to the dashing Adjutant Blaze I understand. Now drink up, I want to hear all about it.'

Just as at Halloy, the whisky lightened her mood and loosened her tongue. They were soon laughing and chatting like old friends. He really hadn't changed that much – still the charming, wicked companion, engaged and engaging, interested in everything she'd been doing and how everything was in London. She was selective: she told him the story of the green American escort and how she'd met Michel, but nothing about Wendelen or the camps. Both were too painful, in their different ways, to be shared, even under the influence of alcohol.

Two hours in his company passed more quickly than she could have imagined, by which time Elaine realised she was so drunk that even getting out of the chair would be difficult. She managed to rise unsteadily to her feet, leaving King Leopold a crumpled mess on the seat. She wagged her finger at the prince.

'You're very, very naughty. My husband is going to be very cross with me for spending so much time with you. You shouldn't have given me all that whisky … how on earth am I going to get where I'm supposed to be …?' She looked, horrified, at her watch. '*Was* supposed to be, hours ago?'

He waved away her concerns as he picked up the telephone and spoke briefly into it.

'Don't worry about that. My chauffeur will drive you. Just tell him where you want to go. But this has been such fun, hasn't it? Just like old times – without the ping-pong! I miss those days, you know. Life's pretty dull here. I do hope our paths cross again sometime, my dear Hélène.'

He took her hand and kissed it. She kissed him on the cheek just as the private secretary appeared in the doorway.

'The car, sir.'

It was kind of the prince to organise her transport but her problems weren't over. In the back of the royal limousine she was hardly able to keep her eyes open and feeling horribly sick. She needed the driver to drop her at the bar where Michel had arranged to meet his Resistance pals to carry on celebrating. The Coq d'Or was in a notorious street. What would the prince's driver make of the situation if she asked to be dropped in a known red light district? It could rebound horribly on the prince. But at this late hour and in her state, she had neither the energy to explain her innocence nor the wit to think of an alternative strategy. When the German officer gave her a lift into the city a year ago, discovery could have ended in disaster. Now the worst that could happen was embarrassment for her and the prince. She'd just have to hope the chauffeur wasn't as much of a gossip as his boss.

They arrived outside the Coq and she alighted, still unsteady, into a blast of night air which sobered her up enough to make her way into the packed and noisy bar without mishap. Michel was easy to spot. He was taller than most and one of the few carousers still upright.

He came towards her, unsmiling.

'Where the hell have you been? And look at the state of you! You're drunk!'

Inebriated as she was, she knew this was grossly unfair. Though he was relatively sober, everyone around him was much drunker than she was, slumped and hanging on to each other, singing slurred and incomprehensible songs, some passed out altogether. But she looked at him, contrite.

'I know. Sorry. It was *his* fault. And now I just want to lie down … Can we go now?'

He took her sharply by the elbow and pushed her through the swaying crowd to the door.

'This was going to be such a special day for me', he hissed, 'and you've completely ruined it. You and your bloody prince.'

'He's not my bloody prince. But I'm sorry if you feel that way.'

Though she wasn't as sorry as she thought he wanted her to be.

∞

He hadn't forgotten in the morning. The recriminations started over their breakfast coffee, but Elaine was feeling wretched.

'Please. I've got a splitting head. If we're going to row, can we do it when I feel a bit better?'

'You let me down. You should have been with me. But no, you're off with your precious Monsieur Bernard. What's going on between you two?'

'Oh for God's sake Michel, nothing. He's lonely and wanted a drinking companion. I happened to be there.'

'Hmm. Too much of a bloody coincidence.'

'What was I going to say? "Sorry, Your Highness, I can't come. My husband would be jealous"?'

'There's something about that time in Ciney you're keeping from me.'

'There's nothing to keep. It was my mission to be with him. It was entirely proper. But we did have fun. He's good company.'

'I bet.'

'You're being unreasonable about this. Nothing happened. Then or last night. He got me drunk, and I'm sorry about that. But where's the harm? All your friends were so sloshed they can't have noticed.'

'I noticed. I seem to have married a slut.'

'What?'

'I can't trust you, Hélène.'

Her head was about to burst but she couldn't let this go.

'*You* can't trust *me*? That's rich. I could ask you about all the other women you flirt so outrageously with. Come to that, I could ask you about that pansy Amies.'

'Don't call him that! He's a friend.'

'Yes. So I saw the other day at that lunch. He was all over you like a rash. You talk about me! How do I know there's nothing going on between you two?'

'Now you're being disgusting. I think you'd better stop.'

They stopped and made up after a fashion, but it was an uneasy truce. She was still angry but it wasn't Michel she felt she'd let down, it was herself. The hammering hangover and the unexpected rush of new emotions caused by her pregnancy made her feel especially vulnerable and tearful. She felt ashamed as she finally faced up to some unwelcome truths. She'd married out of spite and revenge. Michel turned heads and hearts wherever he went but she had always known that these were dubious qualities for a husband and father. Worst of all, she'd always known that she didn't love him. Now she knew she never could. But she was expecting a child and about to take responsibility for another human being. This was all entirely of her own making. There was no question of divorce and no one else to blame for the situation she now found herself in. She'd made her bed.

∾

Elaine's son, Lawrence Bernard Blaze, was born the following year, a beautiful boy with blue eyes and white-gold hair. His parents were besotted. The family's life, however, was about to face a major upheaval. Michel was to take up a post abroad with Unilever and they were making preparations to move to Leopoldville, the capital of the Belgian Congo. Though their new life would, on the face of it, be more comfortable than in Brussels, with a company house and servants, Elaine was nervous about moving to Africa with a young child. He looked bonny enough but he hadn't been the easiest baby and seemed to pick up the smallest infection. She worried about the climate and whether there would be good medical facilities.

'Don't worry', Michel had said. 'The company will look after us.'

Before they left Brussels, Elaine had a duty to perform. She had been thinking about Luc and feeling guilty about his ring. She didn't even know if he had survived the war. The last she'd heard was the Red Cross letter from him breaking off their engagement. This might be her last opportunity to try and find him and explain why she hadn't been able to return it. Through his father in Poperinghe, she got his address and went to see him. He greeted her warmly and when she launched on her prepared apology was surprised to learn that he'd forgotten all about the ring and was only anxious that his new wife shouldn't find out about this previous engagement. She was relieved.

'I'm so pleased you're settled and happy, Luc. You deserve it. It was a good job we didn't get married in 1940. We were far too young. We've had to grow up since then, haven't we? Things have a way of working out.'

'And they seem to have worked out pretty well for you, too. Starting your family and looking forward to an exciting future in a new country.'

'Yes', she said, not entirely convincing herself, 'I'm very lucky'.

⌒⌒

She was surrounded by packing cases and newspaper and trying to keep the baby happy when the doorbell rang. Taking off her housecoat on the way up the hall, she was irritated at the interruption. She wasn't expecting anyone. There on the doorstep was an elderly man in an ill-fitting demob suit. He took off his hat. She was so surprised she didn't know what to say.

'Aren't you going to ask your old dad in?'

Was it possible that the pathetic-looking figure nervously fidgeting with his trilby on the doorstep was really the father who'd caused her so much anguish?

'Dad? I'm sorry, I didn't recognise you, it's been so long.'

'Getting on for eight years. It's good to see you, Elaine. You're looking well.'

'I'm just surprised to see you. What are you doing back in Belgium? The last I heard you'd gone to England to join the army.'

'Make me a cuppa and I'll tell you.'

She led him into the reception room strewn with packing cases and half-wrapped china.

'Have you eaten? I can make something. Sorry about the mess, we're packing up to go to the Congo.'

'So I hear.'

Larry saw the high chair, where baby Lawrence was gurgling happily.

'And who's this little fella, then?'

'This is your grandson, Dad. His name's Lawrence.'

Larry's face lit up.

'Really? What a lovely looking lad. Proper Madden colouring. And what a fine name! He looks just like a lovely little girl I used to know …'

He turned to her.

'How are you Elaine? What have you been up to? You didn't forget all about me, did you?'

'Of course not. How could I?' She hadn't forgotten, but she didn't want to admit to how little he'd been in her thoughts these past years. 'Keep the baby amused and I'll make some tea.'

Still the same old charmer, she thought, but he was looking so much older, battered by life. Was it the war, the drink or what, she wondered as she waited for the kettle. She could hear him baby-talking Lawrence in the next room. She smiled. He'd always been good with her as a young child. It only got difficult later when he started drinking.

'Here we are. So, what brings you back to Belgium?'

'You know, visiting the old haunts, paying my dues. I've been to visit your mother's grave. Poperinghe's just the same, not damaged too much in the war.'

'What about the Palace? And Mémère and Pépère? Did they manage to get back alright?'

'The Palace is still standing and Charles is still lording it, but I'm afraid your Gran and Granpa are no longer with us. I'm told Marie died not long after the invasion and Egide went in '44. I'm sorry, love, I know you were fond of them.' Then he chuckled. 'Your aunts and uncles are having a fine old time squabbling over his estate. You can imagine! Though I wouldn't be surprised if he'd left you something. Caroline was always his favourite.'

'I *was* fond of them. Pépère especially, but I doubt he's left me anything. Anyway, I don't want anything. I left that family a long time ago. Why go there now, after all this time and all that's happened between you and Charles?'

'Stuff I needed to do before I go back.'

'To England?'

'Nah. I'm going back to Australia. Got a repatriation passage after doing my bit for the old country. Pioneers. Thought I'd try my luck back home. I expect it's changed a bit. I was sixteen when I left. Land of opportunity now, so they say. People from all over Europe are flocking there. I'm going to live with your Aunty Elaine in Sydney for a bit till I get settled, find a job. Maybe the Graves Commission will take me back on, I've still got a few years work left in me. I'm sailing next week. But I wanted to see you first. Took a bit of detective work. I found out you got married and I got your address through your husband's office. That's how I knew you were going overseas. Thought I'd better catch you before it was too late.'

'I'm glad you did.'

'So am I. A week later and both of us would have been on boats to foreign parts. So tell me, where were you in the war? Not here under the Boche I hope?'

'Oh God, no. I got away at Dunkirk. Long story, but I spent most of the war in London.'

'I was there in '40, '41. Blitz clearance. Dirty work it was. You weren't in the services at all, then?'

'I was in the FANYs at the end of the war.'

'Fannies? What's that?'

'A bit like the ATS. Transport, stuff like that.'

'Interesting work?'

'Nothing special', she said, realising what a very deliberate lie it was.

'Never mind. We answered our country's call, that's the important thing.'

'Yes. We did.'

'And now let's hope we're both going on to something better.'

He put his teacup down.

'Do you think we can put the past behind us, start again, Elaine? I've made my mistakes, God knows. I lost your mother, and then I lost you. Everything I ever loved. All my own fault. But don't lose sight of your old dad, now, will you? Perhaps you'll even come out and see me in Australia one day, eh? Bring the boy. Meet the family. Your Aunty Elaine would love to meet her namesake. And you've so many cousins you've never seen. Me neither, as it happens. My brother Jack's girl Valda is about your age. Quite a glamour puss from the pictures I've seen. I'm sure you'd get along great. Just remember, you've got a big family waiting for you over there, any time you want to make the trip.'

Australia sounded a very long way away. She'd only just come to terms with going to Africa. But she didn't want to discourage him.

'You never know, I might.'

They chatted on until the tea was finished, then Larry wrote out an address on a scrap of paper in his fine copperplate handwriting and went to pick up his hat.

'That's Aunty Elaine's address. If I'm not staying with her, she'll know where to find me. Now I'll let you get on. You must have a lot to do.'

'Yes. But I'm glad you came, Dad. Thank you for taking the trouble to find me. I *will* try and stay in touch, I promise.'

'I can't tell you how much I'd like that, love. Write to me from Africa. Send me some snaps of my grandson as he grows up.'

'I will.'

They embraced.

'Bon voyage, love.'

'And to you. And ... good luck in Australia, Dad.'

She stood in the doorway with Lawrence in her arms, waving his little hand at Larry as he went off down the street.

'Shall we wave goodbye to Grandpa? Goodbye Grandpa. Goodbye.'

THIRTEEN

<u>**LETTERS**</u>

1967

Bujumbura, Burundi
22 May 1967

My dear Valda,

Thank you so much for your wonderful long letter. I was so happy to hear from you. I should have written to you too, Aunty Elaine asked me to in each letter, but you know we Maddens don't seem to like writing and I too kept thinking, tomorrow will do.

Jenny and I are both so excited about our trip to Australia, another six weeks and we're on our way. To think that we shall arrive in Sydney, probably on the 4 July … I'm certainly looking forward to meeting you and Neville and intend to visit you in Tasmania and to hell with the expense, after paying our ship to Australia the little extra won't make that much difference. I have been working hard for a great number of years and have not spent much on myself, and feel that, now that I have also turned 44 (on 7 May) I deserve a splurge and have decided to spare no expense even if it means working in Africa another few years to make up.

We are looking forward to being in a civilised country as Africa gets very dull, no concerts or theatres, just some very old movies, hardly any shops and since Independence hardly any goods for Europeans. I make most of our clothes and it's even difficult to get decent materials, so this time we have ordered some clothes for our trip in Belgium, which also adds to our excitement. It's such a luxury for me to go to a beauty parlour, a hairdresser or have my nails manicured, never mind looking at shop windows. We are nearly in the bush here and have nothing.

Jenny celebrated her 15th birthday last Saturday (the 20th), she had a wonderful party and danced till almost midnight. The noise was terrific but she was so happy. It's a pity she speaks no English but I do hope she'll make an effort and pick it up quickly. She's a big tall girl for her age, taller than I am and two sizes larger. She has her father's green eyes and I find her most attractive. Between ourselves, I would so much like her to love Australia as she doesn't like Europe and Africa is certainly out as far as youngsters are concerned. There's no future for them at all out here, and I would like to think that she might like to settle in Australia. She is terribly lazy at school, it seems to be the same with most teenagers here in Africa, and it's a pity because her teachers say she's clever and intelligent but there's nothing much I can do as she's at a very awkward age. I hope this trip of ours will interest her enough and make her realise that she will have to make an effort if she wants to get on in life.

I'm lucky I have Jennifer, for after my son died I was desperate and thought I couldn't have any more children. It took almost three years and an operation to have her but it was worth it and although financially it has sometimes been difficult for me, she's a great consolation.

I'm happy to hear that Aunty Elaine is still so active, attractive and elegant. Jenny and I spend hours talking about you all and since reading your letter. Reading about balls and dinner parties, she says you must lead the same kind of life I do, as here in Bujumbura we have lots of dinner parties and cocktails, but there again there is no other entertainment at all. She was a little upset at learning that Aunty Elaine lives such a long way out of town but I presume there are train and bus facilities. I don't know why but Jenny imagines that Australia must be very backward, something like Bujumbura, rough and uncivilized and bush country. Living here, we forget that other countries have trains, buses etc. We have about one plane a day but only two per week out of the country. Air mail arrives once per week only. There's very little traffic and it's very quiet, a large village or a very small town.

Don't expect me to write to you again before I go to Australia. Time flies and I still … [page missing, presumed lost or destroyed] *… very lonely, but now at last I'm looking forward to being part of you all, <u>my</u> family, as I never did feel part of my mother's family. I didn't get on well with my Belgian relatives. You know it's sometimes quite difficult to be a dual nationality. I was in school in England and was there right through the war and often feel more English than Belgian and yet when* [obscured] *… recently felt quite a …* [obscured] *It's all very complicated. My reactions are never typically English or Belgian, maybe I shall find myself at last and turn out to be pure Australian!*

Well Valda my dear, goodbye for now. We shall be meeting very soon, isn't it wonderful? My love to you both from both of us.

Elaine

Surfers Paradise, Queensland, Australia
Thursday 10 p.m.

Valda honey,

Just a few lines in haste to say how happy I am to have come to Australia to meet you all, especially you, and my only regret is that we didn't have more time together and that part of the time we did have was wasted through us not being able to spend more time alone. Still, we have met, and we know each other better now, and I shall feel more at ease when writing to you, knowing that I can say just anything and will be understood as we feel the same way. I can't find the right words to tell you exactly how I feel, but you'll understand if I say that I love you and am very happy you are my cousin. I love Neville too, you're both so perfect and so much as I wanted you to be, thanks honey. Knowing you both has made our trip out here worthwhile. Jenny feels about you both just as I do so we're freshly proud and happy about our family ...

... So honey I'm leaving you all for now and I certainly hope it will only be an 'au revoir' and that we shall meet again soon. Thanks for everything, all our love to you both.

Elaine

POSTSCRIPT

Elaine Marie Madden, the expatriate Briton who answered her country's call but never found the home she'd been looking for all her life, died in Pont St Esprit in June 2012 in her ninetieth year. It was only after her death that I discovered so much more about her family background, her life during the war and after it. I can see her now, sitting in her airless flat in the unfriendly town she disliked so much, where I interviewed her in 2008. Elegant, alert, cigarette in hand, talking animatedly about her war experiences, the barest hint of French inflection in her rich voice, her testimony punctuated by laughter and tears.

We never met again after that, but we would speak occasionally on the phone. She said she missed English conversation and liked 'English friends' to call her. Her health and breathing deteriorated and the last time we spoke early in 2012 she had a nurse with her. I learned of her death from a fellow former pupil of the British Memorial School. Now that I know more about her life than I did when I interviewed her, there are so many questions I wish she was still here to answer, gaps that remain unfilled, mysteries unresolved.

Without doubt the war was the central energising force in her life. Nothing after it seemed to match up, nor make full use of her talents. Though there were happy times – her visit to Australia was one – the post-war years were marked by tragedy and hardship. The letters written in 1967 to her Australian cousin, which Valda kept all her life, touch on her sorrows, regrets and frustrations.

After their brief *rapprochement* in 1946, Elaine did stay in touch with her father for a while, though they never met again. Larry's brother Jack found him a job on the railways on his return to Australia but this didn't last and his efforts to be re-engaged by the Imperial War Graves Commission were unsuccessful. He lived near to his divorced and childless sister Elaine Gainsford ('Aunty Elaine') in a Sydney suburb until his death at sixty-six in August 1965. Larry had a hard life and a not particularly happy one, with family tragedy, personal troubles and the misfortune to be of an age where he was eligible to serve in both World Wars. His last years close to his sister were probably the most settled: he'd come home. The death notice in the local paper spoke of '*Harold Lawrence Madden, beloved husband of the late Caroline Madden, loved father of Elaine (South Africa)*'. There was at least one positive outcome: Larry's death may well have sparked or reignited the correspondence between Elaine and her Madden relatives that resulted in her visit to Australia two years later.

Another death closer to home was much harder to bear. Shortly after the family's move to Africa, Lawrence, her beautiful blonde-haired boy, developed leukaemia and died in 1949 at the age of three. Elaine and Michel must have been devastated, though by then their marriage was in trouble. The closed expatriate community of bored wives in Leopoldville proved too tempting. Elaine became inured to his infidelity: '*He couldn't have been faithful to any woman. He even slept with his employer's wife.*' They stayed together and moved to Bujumbura, capital of Ruanda-Urundi, by the shores of Lake Tanganyika. In 1952 a daughter, Jennifer, was born in Brussels. When she returned with the month-old baby she found Michel living with another woman. That was the last straw: she moved out of the family home and took refuge with friends. Reconciled to life as a single parent, she found work as an accountant as soon as Jenny was six months old. Eventually they divorced and she reverted to her maiden name.

Elaine was still an attractive woman of thirty-five when in 1958 she met '*the second love of my life*', Willy, a Belgian lawyer. They lived happily together until 1970 when he was offered a professorship in law at the University of Bujumbura. The job came with free married quarters so they planned to marry. While Elaine was away visiting Jenny in Brussels she learned that Willy had been in a car accident. Her fiancé was dead.

Ruanda-Urundi was about to erupt in horrific inter-ethnic violence. Jenny persuaded her mother that there was nothing left for her in Africa and that she should return to Belgium. Leaving the ghosts of past tragedies behind, she quit Bujumbura just before the 1972 massacre of Hutus by the Tutsi-dominated military.

Back in Brussels, she found a satisfying job with a travel company organising game safaris and enjoyed a settled middle age. But she never remarried or found another love.

Money was always tight. To earn a small pension she carried on working until she was almost seventy. She had no war pension, '*nothing from the British*'. She applied for a British passport after the war but they told her she was no longer entitled to one because her father was Australian. She couldn't get an Australian passport either because she'd never lived there. So she settled for a Belgian one. It was a lasting hurt that her country wouldn't acknowledge her as one of its own: '*I've been British all my life but now I'm a foreigner in England as well*.'

Other players in Elaine's story went their separate ways. After their night together in London in 1945 she never spoke to André Wendelen again. He died in 1976 aged sixty-one, still enjoying a successful diplomatic career. Hardy Amies went back to fashion after the war, establishing an internationally successful couture house and a distinguished reputation as dressmaker to Queen Elizabeth II. He died in 2003, aged ninety-three. Elaine did meet 'Monsieur Bernard' again briefly, when he visited Leopoldville as regent in 1947. In 1950 he gave up the regency in favour of the new King Baudouin, Leopold's son. Charles, Prince of Flanders never married – at least officially – and died in 1983. Elaine remained estranged from her Belgian relatives, received nothing from her grandparents' estate and had no contact with Simone after their wartime parting. Soon after that, early in 1942, Simone married, settled in London and went on to have two children. There was one late reconciliation. On the birth of their first grandchild, Elaine and Michel Blaze finally '*became friends*'. He died of cancer in 2004 at the age of eighty-four.

Elaine's hopes of finding roots in Australia weren't realised. The 1967 trip was the only one. She stayed in touch with Valda for a time, but over the years contact seems to have ceased. Nevertheless, a significant collection of family photographs from Elaine's childhood in Ypres and Poperinghe, together with some of baby Lawrence, obviously cherished by Larry, are still held by younger members of the Madden family.

Like many of her generation, Elaine never spoke in detail of her war experiences until the last years of her life and was suspicious of those who did: '*The more people talk, the less true it is in general.*' In 2001, now approaching her eighties and living close to Jenny in Pont St Esprit in southern France, she took the long journey north, back to Ypres, to take part in a reunion of former pupils of the British Memorial School. Here she met her old schoolfriends Rene and Dorothy again and so many others she hadn't seen for sixty years. Here she started talking about the past and answering the questions of the press and television people intrigued by this unique gathering of elderly British folk who happened to grow up among Flanders' fields. The story of Elaine's part in Britain's secret war began to unfold and she later appeared in television documentaries in Belgium and the UK. Some things though were still painful to talk about: she could never speak of her time in the camps without breaking down. She really didn't want to be taken back to that time and those places.

Public recognition in Britain of her wartime mission came only after her death. It wasn't until December 2013 that the Prince of Wales unveiled a memorial on a quiet country lane in Bedfordshire, '*To honour and remember the women who flew out from RAF Tempsford and other airfields and ports to aid resistance movements in occupied Europe 1941–1945*'. Elaine Madden is among the seventy-five names inscribed on the marble column with its mosaic of a dove flying beneath a full moon.

Until the end she was ambivalent about her wartime achievements. On the one hand determinedly modest: '*Why make me out to be something special?*' she wrote to me in 2009. '*Everyone did their bit … I was just young and excited and willing to do anything except join the ATS! Not a heroine.*' But then, on the other, she wasn't embarrassed to express pride: '*Still at my age I'm glad of my life. I can still look in the mirror and feel proud.*' As she told the journalist who came to interview her for *Radio Times* in 2009: '*If I died tomorrow I'd be very happy. I'm lucky because I've done something, haven't been a nonentity behind a desk. I had the courage to do something, and that has helped me a lot. At least I had the war. I didn't wish for one, but I'm happy I had it. It's something to remember.*'

Not a heroine? There are certainly others who displayed more dash and daring, many who suffered more, some who gave their lives. But she risked a great deal in answering her country's call. Of the 182 agents sent by T Section into the field, a third were killed in action or died in captivity. Only weeks before the 1944 Imogen mission, four T Section agents were captured, tortured and beheaded. Elaine was one of only two women to be parachuted into Belgium by SOE and one of very few British women to witness the horror of the concentration camps so soon after their liberation. A strong character with all-too human flaws, she took extraordinary risks during times of great danger for a cause and a country she believed in. That makes her a heroine in my book.

SOURCES

The principal sources are my interview with Elaine conducted in June 2008 and several hours of filmed interview conducted by Testimony Films earlier that year. I also referred to the following written sources:

National Archives files

Special Operations Executive:
HS 6/44 Brabantio mission: André Wendelen
HS 6/112 Imogen mission: Elaine Madden
HS 6/211 Verstrepen Group organisation (mission orders)
HS 6/210 Verstrepen Group organisation (agents)
HS 7/20 Special Allied Airborne Reconnaissance Force: Vicarage
HS 7/21 Special Allied Airborne Reconnaissance Force: Vicarage
HS 9/973/7 Elaine Madden Personnel file
HS 9/1576/5 André Wendelen Personnel file
HS 9/163/9 Michel Ghislain Blaze Personnel file

War diaries
WO 167/1298 62 Coy AMPC War Diary 1939–40
WO 166/16081 375 Coy Pioneers War Diary 1944
WO 166/17654 375 Coy Pioneers War Diary 1945

Books

Amies, Hardy. *Just So Far*. Collins 1954.

Amies, Hardy. *Still Here*. Weidenfeld & Nicholson 1984.

Beardon, James. *The Spellmount Guide to London in the Second World War*. History Press 2013.

Cunningham, Cyril. *Beaulieu: The Finishing School for Secret Agents*. Pen & Sword 2005.

Elliott, Sue & James Fox. *The Children Who Fought Hitler*. John Murray 2009.

Foot, M.R.D. *SOE in the Low Countries*. St Ermin's Press 2001.

Jesse, F. & H.M. Harwood. *London Front 1939–40*. Constable 1940.

Levine, Joshua (ed.). *Forgotten Voices: Dunkirk*. Ebury 2011.

Mackenzie, William. *The Secret History of SOE. The Special Operations Executive 1940–1945*. St Ermin's Press 2000.

Marks, Leo. *Between Silk and Cyanide: A Codemaker's War 1941–45*. History Press 2013.

Pattinson, Juliette. *Behind Enemy Lines: Gender, Passing and the Special Operations Executive in the Second World War*. Manchester University Press 2011.

Perquin, Jean-Louis. *Resistance: The Clandestine Radio Operators*. Histoire & Collections, Paris.

Riols, Noreen. *The Secret Ministry of Ag. & Fish*. Macmillan 2013.

Stafford, David. *The True Story of the Special Operations Executive*. BBC Books 2000.

Storey, Neil & Molly Housego. *Women in the Second World War*. Shire 2012.

Military records

Harold Lawrence Madden. AIF 3880, 1915–22. National Archives of Australia.

Harold Lawrence Madden. Auxiliary Military Pioneer Corps 13013341, 1940–46. Army Personnel Centre, Historical Disclosures.

Other

Seven-page letter from Elaine to Rene Fletcher at the end of June 1940 recounting her escape from Poperinghe through Dunkirk.

Canadian Sailors', Soldiers' and Airmen's Leave Guide for London. Canadian YMCA.

The Carpetbaggers: a History of 801/492nd Bombardment Group (H) USAAF. Carpetbaggers Museum.

Clearing the Dead. Article by Peter E. Hodgkinson. University of Birmingham Centre for First World War Studies, 2007.

London 1939. Ward Lock guide.

St Dunstan-in-the-West: The Church and its History, compiled by Robbie Millen.

Secret Report on the Special Allied Airborne Reconnaissance Force, 10 July 1945.

SOE syllabus of lectures, February 1944.

The Women Agents of the Special Operations Executive F Section: Wartime Realities and Post-war Representations. Elizabeth Kate Vigars. Unpublished PhD thesis. Leeds University, 2011.

The Reconstruction of Ieper: a walk through history. Dominiek Dendooven & Jan Dewilde. In Flanders Fields Museum, Ieper.

The Ypres Times. Journal of the Ypres League 1921–39. Collection held by the Imperial War Museum.

ACKNOWLEDGEMENTS

My biggest debt of gratitude is to Steve Humphries of Testimony Films, who first told me about the amazing woman he'd just interviewed in the south of France. Steve shared hours of untransmitted interview material with me as well as supplying vital encouragement. His assistant producer, Lizi Cosslett, gave unstinting help on photos and much else. Jimmy Fox in Paris organised the British Memorial School reunion in 2001, was my co-author for *The Children Who Fought Hitler* that first featured Elaine and provided the initial background on her that started this long journey.

I am most grateful to Neville Madden and Danny Colgan in Australia and Patricia Anderson in Canada who provided invaluable information about the Maddens in general and Larry Madden in particular, including his First World War military records. Neville also gave me access to numerous family photographs and I am particularly grateful for his permission for their use. On the Duponselle side of the family, Mary Francombe, Elaine's cousin (though they never met) and daughter of her Aunt Josephine, helpfully answered my many queries.

Kennith Schrijvers and Christine Locke willingly and efficiently translated (respectively) Flemish and French documents and other material for me, and my field trip to Brussels would have been far less productive without the on-the-ground help and hospitality of Virginia Lee. She walked the length of Avenue Louise in drenching rain with me without complaint and solved the mystery location of the liberation day tank incident. I am also grateful to the helpful staff of the Archives de l'Etat in Brussels, and to

Dominiek Dendooven of the In Flanders Fields Museum, Ieper, for supplying photos and information about pre-war Ypres.

In the UK Brian Bloice and John Brown, via the Streatham Society, provided information about St Helen's School and Streatham in the early war period. Rebecca Haslam, Administrator of the Guild Church of St Dunstan-in-the West, Fleet Street was most helpful and, needless to say, the wonderful National Archives at Kew kept me engaged for hours poring over their collection of wartime files, some of them only recently released to public view.

I acknowledge with thanks the work of Kate Vigars in her fascinating PhD thesis about the women of F Section, which provided useful information about the selection and training of women agents. At the Carpetbaggers Museum at RAF Harrington, I'd like to thank Roy Tebbutt for unearthing the names of the Liberator crew who flew Elaine out on her SOE mission, and Jedburgh expert Clive Bassett who supplied other useful background on Special Forces. Les Hughes, who seems to know more about the Special Allied Airborne Reconnaissance Force than anyone else, was most helpful, and Norman Brown of the Royal Pioneer Corps Association helped me interpret Larry Madden's Second World War service record.

Andrew Duncan, the journalist who turned up in his sports car to interview Elaine for *Radio Times* in 2009 and who she was so taken with, generously gave me access to his original notes, which provided many insights into her post-war life and state of mind. Jane Lomas, fellow Guardian Masterclass student, was a conscientious and helpful reader and Martin Mortimore provided valuable technological assistance at the beginning and end of this long project. My Brentham friends Rosanna, Nita and Ann lived through every stage of it with me on our early morning walks and were never less than interested and supportive.

Finally I'd like to thank my agent, Jane Turnbull, for suggesting the idea in the first place and for keeping faith in it – and me – on what has been a sometimes bumpy road. And my partner, companion and driver along the way, Bevan Jones.

Sue Elliott

INDEX